Crazy Busy Keto Cookbook #2020

750 Easy and Quick Keto Recipes for Busy People to Lose Weight and Live Health (21-Day Meal Plan Included)

By Emily Walton

Legal & Disclaimer

The information and contents herein are not designed to replace or take the place of any form of medical or professional advice and are not meant to replace the need for independent medical, financial, legal or other professional advice or services, as may be required. The content and information in this book have been provided for educational and entertainment purposes only.

The content and information in this book have been compiled from reliable sources and are accurate to the author's best knowledge, information, and belief. The author cannot guarantee this book's accuracy and validity and cannot be held liable for any errors and/or omissions. Further, changes will be periodically made to this book when needed. It is recommended that you consult with a health professional who is familiar with your personal medical history before using any of the suggested remedies, techniques, or information in this book.

Upon using the contents in this book, you agree to hold harmless the author from and against any damages, costs, and expenses, including any legal fees potentially resulting from the application of the information provided You agree to accept all risks associated with using the information presented inside this book.

Table of Content

Introduction

Several years ago, I decided to start following a keto diet. I had heard so many amazing things about how beneficial a keto diet can be. From helping you lose weight to improving your overall health, there were too many advantages that the diet offered for me to ignore it. I did some research about what the diet entailed, set my start date and then dove right in!

Right away, I was surprised by how much cooking you had to do on a keto diet. To follow the diet properly, you need to make almost every meal from scratch! Not only did that mean more time in the kitchen, but it also meant I needed to find more keto-friendly recipes. Almost every day I was searching online, flipping through cookbooks, and entering nutritional information into my calculator to see if a recipe would meet my keto needs. It was a lot of work!

Right away, I decided that I would start keeping track of my favorite keto recipes, write down exactly how I made each dish and put everything together in a convenient cookbook. Surely, my keto efforts would help other people as well! After all, we are all on this keto journey together- let's make it as easy as possible!

This book is written for anyone who wants to give keto dieting a try. Whether you have been following a keto lifestyle for years or are just beginning, you will find many recipes in these pages that are sure to please. In addition, the book is written for any level of cook. The professional chefs will find new and exciting dishes and the culinary novices will as well! As I said before, the goal is to make keto cooking as easy as possible and include everyone on our keto adventure!

So, if you have been struggling to find exciting keto recipes or just tired of spending all day in the kitchen, this book will solve your problems. You will have an abundance of keto-friendly recipes at your fingertips and also enjoy the fact that they are all easy and fast to make. No need to sift through recipes online or contemplate if they qualify as "low carb", this book will take away all those questions.

Open up this cookbook and get ready to find amazing, creative, unique and delicious recipes that all fit perfectly into the keto guidelines. I know that you will find some recipes that will instantly become your new favorites and I hope you try every single one. Happy cooking!

Chapter 1 The Basics of Keto Diet

What Is a Ketogenic Diet?

Ketogenic (keto for short) diet is a way to rein in rampant carbohydrates (sugars) in blood and food. There is a lot of science behind even the simplest meals, but the problem is how to make it digestible and usable in everyday life. Make matters worse; not all bodies react the same way to the same foods. Rather than being a comprehensive fix-all diet, keto is perhaps best used to test how the body tolerates carbohydrates or lack thereof.

Glucose or blood sugar is a fairly simple carbohydrate, and it can be used as an energy source at the core of many bodily processes. Almost all carbohydrates that enter human digestion get broken down to glucose, which then seeps through the intestinal lining into the bloodstream. The more complex the carb, the longer it takes to create glucose and vice versa, and here is the first problem as modern, processed food is loaded with simple, refined sugars that surge into the bloodstream to wreak havoc on endocrine systems. The body has tightly regulated hormonal cycles, but constant glucose barrage flattens the endocrine response and leads to all sorts of health problems.

Is a Ketogenic Diet Healthy?

Each body will respond differently to the ketogenic diet, but it can never do direct harm. Instead of eating carbohydrates to quickly create an avalanche of glucose, eating proteins and fats, which is what keto diet consists of, will nudge the body towards using other organs in the body, distributing the digestive load. In other words, the body can and does adapt to turning proteins and fats to energy but activates an alternative pathway that uses compounds known as ketones as an intermediary step. An abundance of ketones in the bloodstream is called "ketosis" and can be tested by soaking special keto sticks with urine. People with kidney problems might have additional issues on a keto diet, as excess ketones are mostly eliminated through urine.

The upside of ketosis is that the body starts preparing itself for using other fats, such as those found in fat cells. Because glucose is the type of fuel used immediately, but fats take time to burn, the body starts preemptively burning fats and storing glucose in the liver. Some small amount of glucose is created too, though the process consumes more energy than it produces. Having the body uses its own systems is the only legitimate way to burn fat, no matter what the latest glitzy food supplement says.

Why Should You Try This Diet?

Keto diet is the perfect starting point for a dietary makeover. Everyone can try it – children have been placed on the keto diet, and it helped them subdue epileptic seizures that do not respond to medication. The mechanism behind this is unknown but may be due to brain cells becoming impervious to glucose; ketones use an alternative pathway to enter cells but are still usable by mitochondria, the powerhouse of the cell. However, microscopic invaders that thrive on glucose, such as fungi and bacteria, suddenly find themselves starved and bayed by the immune system.

Glucose is normally oxidized within the mitochondria to produce energy in a process that's akin to burning and may disrupt nearby cells and nerve signals if excessive. By restricting glucose intake, this chain disruption slows down and lets the cells and organs self-regulate. In people with type 2 diabetes, the keto diet helps control glucose levels and keeps insulin cycles from spiking. The only problem with the keto diet is the lack of scientific studies showing just how powerful it is; that's up to the dieter to try and see for themselves.

What To Avoid On Keto Diet?

Ketosis is generally achieved when you consume 20-50g of carbs a day for 2-3 days. This might sound easy, but a single 125g apple has 17g of carbs and a mere 32g slice of rye bread has 15g. Reaching for just one more piece of candy or half a cup of ice cream is enough to stop ketosis and resume the normal glucose digestion cycle. In short, the keto diet asks us to drop anything sweet and plenty of foods that don't even taste so but contain carbohydrates nonetheless.

Sugar: Sugar is the big no-no, cut out all soft drinks, fruit juice, sports drinks and vitamin water. Avoid sweet, cookies, cakes, candy, chocolate, donuts, frozen treats, etc.

Starch: Bread, pasta, potato, sweet potato, porridge, muesli are by far the worst offenders, as they are eaten habitually with all meals in limitless quantities.

Fruits: Fruit is another thing to watch out for because many fruits are rich in sugar and they produce a lot of carbohydrates, which can ruin your plans if you don't pay attention. Such as apple, banana, mango, pear, grape, pineapple, cherry, orange, kiwi, clementine, peach and plum.

Carbonated Drinks: Beer, cola, soda and other beverages also contain a large number of carbs, so you should cut them out from your diet.

Note that the keto diet rarely produces dramatic results and it might take months or even years before there's a noticeable improvement. This is because health problems often progress for years before any action is taken, so improvement can never come overnight.

Who Can Benefit From The Keto Diet Plan?

Anyone willing to try new diets should also try keto and will receive at least some indirect benefits. The most vulnerable patients, such as elderly and children, can go on keto as well because they have families who will cook for them and urge them to stay away from carbohydrates. Those with mystery ailments and skin conditions, especially ones that resist medical treatment, should try keto as well. Note that the most extreme form of keto revolves around eating 0g of carbohydrates, which shouldn't be done if without dire need.

Not only does the food nourish the body, but it also sustains the mind; people under severe stress usually take some form of junk food to relieve the pressure and feel at least some joy in the day. Junk food producers are well aware of this emotional need and thus supply the general public with nauseating quantities of carbohydrates in their products. Going on keto diet reveals internal weaknesses and habits that keep the person locked in the cycle of gorging on carbs and experiencing the hormonal crash once the glucose wave passes; this can be a challenge in its own right.

How To Transition To a Keto Diet, The Right Way

Correct dietary choices are made every minute of every hour of every day, and the same applies to switch over to keto diet. The main obstacle in adopting the keto diet is that the person had already made plenty of wrong choices during childhood and adolescence. Because habits are extremely resilient to change, the switch must be thoroughly prepared. The first step is to examine the environment and identify carbohydrate sources. Candy, potato chips and other sneaky snacks are usually the worst offenders, as they don't satiate but still bring in the calories and carbohydrates. Any food that is eaten without conscious thinking should be mercilessly weighed and judged. The second step is to ditch all the carbs in our vicinity, to throw them in the trash. Once keto diet starts showing results, it's common for the dieter to feel elated and decide to celebrate with junk food, thus ruining the progress.

Keto Diet Tips for Best Results

Prepare keto meals ahead of time and freeze them if possible to help with cravings. Constantly scan the environment for carbohydrate sources and eliminate junk food with extreme prejudice to avoid snacking. Some low-carb fruits, such as avocado, strawberry, raspberry should be eaten after the main dish, preferably one made in accordance with keto principles. Simply eating less bread or pasta takes a massive effort to accomplish and is a monumental achievement. Find a community of people on the keto diet for recipes, tips and emotional support.

Chapter 2 Breakfast Recipes

Decadent Baked Eggs with Bacon

Serves: 4, Preparation: 5 minutes, Cooking: 20 minutes

Ingredients

8 eggs
1 tbsp. fresh parsley, finely chopped
1 tbsp. basil, chopped
1/4 cup of Gruyere cheese, grated
4 slices of bacon, finely chopped
2 tbsps. extra virgin olive oil
A dash of salt
1 large scallion, cut into thin slices
3/4 cup of goat cheese, crumbled
1 cup cherry tomatoes, halved or quartered if large enough

Instructions

1. Preheat the oven to 400⁰F.
2. In a bowl beat eggs with parsley, basil and salt.
3. Heat the olive oil in a skillet on Medium-high. Sauté the scallion and chopped bacon until bacon is crispy and scallions are soft and bright green.
4. Add grated Gruyere cheese and cook further for 2 - 3 minutes or until the cheese has fully melted.
5. Pour in the egg mixture and stir until combined.
6. Transfer the mixture into an 8x10 baking dish. Sprinkle with crumbled goat cheese and cover with cherry tomatoes.
7. Bake for about 15 minutes or until cheese melted. Serve hot.

Nutrition information:

Calories: 341 Carbohydrates: 4.6 g Protein: 16g Fat: 28g Fiber: 2g

Slow Cooker Parmesan Noodles

Serves: 4, Preparation: 15 minutes, Cooking: 4 hours and 30 minutes

Ingredients

4 large zucchinis, spiralized
1/2 cup of olive oil
2 tbsps. minced garlic
1 tbsp. fresh oregano
1 tbsp. fresh thyme
1/2 cup water
1 cup grated Parmesan cheese
Salt and pepper to taste

Instructions

1. Clean zucchini and create noodles with the aid of a spiralizer (if you do not have one, check your grocery store for zucchini already spiralized).
2. Pour the olive oil on the bottom of your crock pot. Add the garlic, zucchini, oregano, thyme and water. Season with the salt and pepper and stir.
3. Cover and cook on Low for 4 hours.
4. Open lid and add grated Parmesan cheese.
5. Cover again and cook on High for 30 minutes. Serve hot.

Nutrition information:

Calories: 376.5 Carbohydrates: 5g Proteins: 12g Fat: 36g Fiber: 1g

Coconut and Avocado Almond Milkshake

Serves: 3, Preparation: 5 minutes

Ingredients

2 1/2 cups coconut milk (canned)
Half an avocado, pitted
1/4 cup coconut flakes (unsweetened)
1 oz. almond slices
2 tbsps. stevia granulated sweetener (optional)
2 cups ice cubes

Instructions

1. Place all ingredients in your high-speed blender; blend until smooth completely.
2. Serve in chilled glasses.

Nutrition information:

Calories: 378 Carbohydrates: 10.4g Protein: 4g Fat: 37g Fiber: 3g

Turkey and Egg White Omelet with Mascarpone

Serves: 4, Preparation: 5 minutes, Cooking: 5 minutes

Ingredients

8 egg whites
4 slices of smoked turkey breast, finely chopped
1 medium tomato, chopped
1/2 cup of plain Greek yogurt
4 tbsps. Mascarpone cheese
2 tbsps. olive oil

Instructions

1. In a bowl beat the egg whites with yogurt, smoked turkey, tomato and cheese.
2. Heat the oil in a nonstick frying pan and pour in the egg white mixture.
3. Cook omelet for 2 minutes on each side, or until the egg whites have set.
4. Serve immediately.

Nutrition information:

Calories: 223 Carbohydrates: 4g Protein: 14g Fat: 15g Fiber: 0.3g

Spinach and Bacon Deviled Eggs

Serves: 6 , Preparation: 15 minutes, Cooking: 10 minutes

Ingredients

6 large hard-boiled eggs
1/2 cup of olive oil
3 slices of bacon, chopped
2 cups fresh spinach, chopped
1/2 cup of mayonnaise
2 tbsps. yellow mustard
2 tbsps. grated Parmesan cheese
Salt and pepper to taste

Instructions

1. Place the eggs in a saucepan, cover completely with cold water.
2. Once the water begins to boil, turn off the heat and let cook for 10 minutes.
3. Transfer eggs into a bowl with cold water.
4. Peel eggs, halve and remove the yolks; reserve yolks.
5. Heat the olive oil in a frying pan over Medium-high heat and sauté the bacon. When mostly crispy, add in spinach.
6. In a meantime, in a large bowl stir the egg yolks, mayonnaise, mustard, Parmesan and salt and pepper.
7. Add spinach with bacon mixture and stir again to combine thoroughly.
8. Fill the egg whites with the mixture and place on a platter.
9. Refrigerate for one hour and serve.

Nutrition information:

Calories: 433 Carbohydrates: 6g Protein: 11g Fat: 39.5g Fiber: 3g

Homemade Almond Spread

Serves: 4, Preparation: 15, Cooking: 25 minutes

Ingredients

3 cups almonds, roasted
1 pinch of salt
1 tsp. cinnamon
1 tsp. vanilla extract
2 tbsps. natural granulated sweetener (Stevia, Truvia, etc.)

Instructions

1. Preheat the oven to 350⁰F.
2. Line one rimmed sheet with parchment paper and spread almonds.
3. Roast for 10 - 12 minutes. Remove almonds from the oven and let them cool for 5 - 10 minutes.
4. Place almonds in a food processor along with all remaining ingredients.
5. Process for 10 minutes or until completely smooth.
6. Store in a glass jar and keep refrigerated.

Nutrition information:

Calories: 248 Carbohydrates: 9g Protein: 9g Fat: 22g Fiber: 4.7g

Waffles with Crispy Bacon

Serves: 4, Preparation: 10 minutes, Cooking: 10 minutes

Ingredients

1/3 cup fresh butter, melted
4 slices bacon
2 eggs
3 cups of almond flour
1 1/2 tsps. baking soda
2 tsps. natural sweetener (Stevia, Truvia, etc.)

Ingredients

1. Microwave the butter about 30 seconds; set aside.
2. Heat the skillet on Medium-high and brown bacon until crispy. Remove bacon and drain on a paper towel. Set aside.
3. In a small bowl, combine flour, baking soda and sweetener.
4. Add eggs and stir thoroughly. Add melted butter and stir.
5. Preheat the waffle iron according to your iron's directions.
6. Spoon the batter close to the edges.
7. Cook waffles to your preference.
8. Serve hot with the bacon on the side.

Nutrition information:

Calories: 390 Carbohydrates: 5g Proteins: 14.5g Fat: 13.8g Fiber: 2.6g

Coconut Waffles

Serves: 4, Preparation: 10 minutes, Cooking: 10 minutes

Ingredients

4 eggs
2 cups almond flour
1 tbsp. coconut flour
1/2 tsp. baking soda
1/2 tsp. sea salt
1/2 tsp. ground cinnamon
1/4 cup coconut milk (canned)
1 cup almond milk (unsweetened)
1/4 cup shredded coconut, unsweetened
2 tbsps. natural sweetener (Stevia, Erythritol, etc.)
1 1/2 tsps. vanilla extract

Instructions

1. Preheat your waffle iron according to its instructions.
2. In a bowl, whisk the eggs yolks.
3. Add the almond flour, coconut flour, baking soda, pinch of salt, cinnamon, almond milk, coconut milk, shredded coconut, and sweetener; stir well.
4. In a separate bowl, beat the egg whites until become froth.
5. Add the egg whites to the egg yolk batter mixture and pour the vanilla extract; stir well.
6. Pour the batter in a waffle iron and cook according to your preference.
7. Serve hot.

Nutrition information:

Calories: 202 Carbohydrates: 7.3g Protein: 7g Fat: 17.2g Fiber: 4g

Spinach with Eggs

Serves: 6, Preparation: 5 minutes, Cooking: 20 minutes

Ingredients

1 1/2 lbs. (about 2 ½ cups) frozen spinach, thawed and drained
2 green onions, finely chopped
1 bunch of fresh dill, chopped
6 large eggs
2 tbsps. olive oil
Salt and pepper to taste

Instructions

1. Heat a non-stick frying pan over High heat with olive oil.
2. Add the spinach, chopped spring onion, and dill.
Stir and cook for about 5 - 6 minutes, or until spinach is wilted and onion is translucent.
4. When the water is completely evaporated add in the eggs, stirring occasionally.
5. Season the salt and pepper to taste.
6. Lower the heat, cover and let it cook for 10 - 12 minutes or until the eggs are done. Serve hot.

Nutrition information:

Calories: 124 Carbohydrates: 2.3g Protein: 7.3g Fat: 9.9g Fiber: 1g

Dill, Zucchini and Feta Muffins

Serves: 4, Preparation: 10 minutes, Cooking: 25 minutes

Ingredients

1 1/2 cups almond flour
2 tbsps. natural sweetener (Stevia, Truvia, etc.)
2 tsps. baking powder
1/2 tsp. salt
1/2 tsp. fresh dill
1/4 cup almond milk (unsweetened)
1 butter stick, softened
2 eggs
2/3 cup feta cheese, crumbled
3/4 cup shredded zucchini

Instructions

1. Preheat oven to 400⁰F. Grease enough muffin tins for 12 muffins; set aside.
2. In a large bowl, combine the almond flour, sweetener, baking powder, salt and dill.
3. In a separate bowl, combine the almond milk, softened butter and eggs.
4. Stir the cheese and shredded zucchini and combined well.
5. Stir the almond milk mixture to the dry ingredients and gently stir.
6. Fill the prepared muffin cups about two-thirds full.
7. Bake for 20 to 25 minutes. Or until the muffins come out clean when checked.
8. Serve warm or cold.

Nutrition information:
Calories: 105 Carbohydrates: 1.6g Protein: 2.2g Fat: 10.6g Fiber: 0.8g

Lemon Zucchini Muffins

Serves: 4, Preparation: 10 minutes, Cooking: 25 minutes

Ingredients

2 cups of almond flour
1/2 cup of natural granulated sweetener (Stevia, Truvia, etc.)
1 tbsp. baking powder
1 tsp. salt
Zest from half a lemon
3/4 cup roasted almonds, finely chopped
2 eggs, beaten
1/2 cup almond milk
1/3 cup olive oil
1 cup zucchini, shredded and drained

Instructions

1. Preheat the oven to 400⁰F.
2. Grease one 12-cup muffin tin with the oil.
3. In a bowl combine the flour, sweetener, baking powder, salt and lemon zest. Add finely chopped almonds and stir again.
4. In a separate bowl, whisk the eggs, almond milk and olive oil.
5. Combine dry ingredients with egg mixture and stir. Add shredded zucchini and stir until just combined.
6. Spoon the batter into prepared muffin tin. Bake for 20-25 minutes.
7. Serve warm or cold.

Nutrition information:
Calories: 145 g Carbohydrates: 3.8g Protein: 3.5g Fat: 14g Fiber: 8g

Greens, Berries and Coconut Smoothie

Serves: 4, Preparation: 5 minutes

Ingredients

1/2 avocado, pitted
1 1/4 cups of fresh raspberries
3/4 cup coconut milk
1/2 cup water
1 cup of fresh baby spinach leaves
1 tsp. pure vanilla extract
Ice cubes (optional)

Instructions

1. Place all ingredients from the list in a high-speed blender; blend until smooth well.
2. Serve.

Nutrition information:
Calories: 53 Carbohydrates: 6g Proteins: .9g Fat: 3.2g Fiber: 3g

Marinated Corned Beef with Eggs

Serves: 8, Preparation: 15 minutes, Cooking: 15 minutes

Ingredients

2 tbsps. butter, softened on room temperature
2 tbsps. olive oil
2 green onions, finely diced
1/2 cup red bell pepper, finely diced
1 lb. corned beef, finely diced
1 tbsp. mustard (Dijon, English, ground stone)
1 tbsp. Worcestershire sauce
1/4 tsp. ground nutmeg
8 eggs
Salt and freshly ground black pepper to taste

Instructions

1. Heat butter in a pan over Medium heat.
2. Sauté the green onions with a pinch of salt until softened.
3. Add bell pepper and cook for 2 - 3 minutes.
4. Transfer the mixture to a mixing bowl and add the corned beef, Worcestershire sauce, mustard, pepper and nutmeg. Place the mixture in a container, cover and refrigerate overnight.
5. Remove corned beef from the fridge for 15 minutes before cooking,
6. Heat some oil in a large frying pan and add the corned beef; cook for 5 minutes.
7. Crack the eggs, one by one, over corned beef and cook for 3 minutes.
8. Serve hot.

Nutrition information:

Calories: 196 Carbohydrates: 2g Proteins: 13g Fat: 15g Fiber: .4g

Omelet with Prosciutto, Cheese and Basil

Serves: 4, Preparation: 10 minutes, Cooking: 5 minutes

Ingredients

8 eggs
7 oz. of prosciutto, finely chopped
8 oz. grated Halloumi cheese (Paneer cheese works too or Tofu)
1/2 cup of yogurt
1 bunch of fresh basil, chopped
Salt and pepper to taste
Enough olive oil for frying

Instructions

1. Heat the oil in a skillet and brown the prosciutto until crispy.
2. Transfer to a plate with kitchen paper towel to drain.
3. In a bowl beat the eggs with yogurt, cheese, basil, and the salt and pepper.
4. Heat the oil in a non-stick frying pan and pour the egg mixture.
5. Cook for 2 - 3 minutes, and then flip and cook for 1 - 2 minutes.
6. Serve immediately.

Nutrition information:

Calories: 478 Carbohydrates: 5.2g Proteins: 27.5g Fat: 39g Fiber: 0g

Baked Broccoli with Eggs and Feta

Serves: 6, Preparation: 15 minutes, Cooking: 25 minutes

Ingredients

1 large head of broccoli
6 eggs
8 oz. feta cheese, crumbled
1/2 cup olive oil
1/2 tbsp. sweet paprika
1 tsp. finely chopped parsley
1/2 tsp. dry thyme
2 pinches of salt and freshly ground pepper

Instructions

1. Preheat oven to 360^{0}F.
2. Boil the broccoli in pot with salted water until softened, for about 6 - 7 minutes.
3. Heat the large baking pan.
4. Transfer cooked broccoli in a baking pan.
5. Crack the eggs over the broccoli one by one.
6. Season the salt, pepper, paprika, parsley and thyme.
7. Add crumbled feta cheese evenly.
8. Drizzle with the oil, place in oven, and bake for about 10 - 15 minutes or until the eggs are done.
9. Serve hot.

Nutrition information:

Calories: 320 Carbohydrates: 8g Proteins: 15g Fat: 27g Fiber: 2.6g

Baked Omelet with Mushrooms & Beet Greens

Serves: 8, Preparation: 10 minutes, Cooking: 25 minutes

Ingredients

2 tbsps. olive oil, divided
2 scallions, finely chopped
1 clove garlic, minced
2 cups beet leaves, chopped
2 cups of mushrooms, sliced
8 eggs
1/2 tsp. ground thyme
1/2 tsp. salt and ground black pepper
1 cup grated Parmesan cheese

Instructions

1. Preheat oven to 400⁰F.
2. Heat the oil in a large frying pan, and sauté chopped scallions and garlic until softened.
3. Add beet leaves and mushrooms; cook, stirring occasionally, until beet leaves are softened or for about 10 minutes.
4. In a large bowl, whisk together eggs, thyme, salt, and pepper.
5. Add egg mixture to the beet leaves mixture.
6. Add the Parmesan cheese and stir until well combined.
7. Pour the batter in one oiled baking dish.
8. Bake 10 - 12 minutes or until cooked thoroughly.
9. Slice and serve warm.

Nutrition information:
Calories: 178 Carbohydrates: 2.5g Protein: 12g Fat: 13g Fiber: 1g

Roly-poly Scrambled Eggs

Serves: 6, Preparation: 10 minutes, Cooking: 5 minutes

Ingredients

12 eggs
Sea salt to taste
1/4 cup of almond milk
1/3 cup of fresh butter
Sweet red paprika, for serving

Instructions

1. Beat the eggs and almond milk with a pinch of salt.
2. Heat butter in a small non-sticking skillet at Medium heat.
3. Pour the egg mixture into the pan and cook in a Low heat, stirring continuously for 2 - 3 minutes.
4. Remove the eggs from heat and place on plates.
5. Sprinkle with red paprika and serve.

Nutrition information:
Calories: 219 Carbohydrates: 1g Proteins: 11g Fat: 19g Fiber: .2g

Slow-Cooker Spicy Scrambled Eggs

Serves: 8, Preparation: 10 minutes, Cooking: 3 hours

Ingredients

1 tbsp. beef tallow
2 green onions, finely sliced
2 cloves garlic, finely chopped
2 pinches of crushed red pepper flakes, or to taste
1 tsp. cumin
8 eggs
Salt and pepper to taste
1 tbsp. fresh chopped dill and parsley, for serving

Instructions

1. Heat the tallow in skillet, and sauté the green onions and garlic until soft, for about 3 - 4 minutes. Season it with the salt, hot pepper and cumin.
2. Transfer the onion to the inner stainless pot in the crock pot.
3. In a bowl, whisk the eggs with a pinch of salt and red pepper flakes.
4. Pour the egg mixture over the green onions in your crock pot.
5. Cover and cook on High for 2 - 3 hours.
6. Sprinkle with chopped parsley or dill and serve hot.

Nutrition information:
Calories: 187 Carbohydrates: 3.7g Proteins: 13.7g Fat: 13.5g Fiber: .7g

Chapter 3 Vegetarian Recipes

Braised Eggplant in a Tomato Sauce

Serves: 4, Preparation: 10 minutes, Cooking: 40 minutes

Instructions

2 scallions, finely chopped
2 tbsps. olive oil
1 cup of button mushrooms
2 eggplants, cut into slices
3 tbsps. minced garlic
2 tbsps. almond flour
2 tbsps. tomato puree
1 1/2 cups of red wine
1 cup of water
1 cup of bone broth
1/4 cup of fresh thyme, finely chopped
Salt and ground pepper to taste
Grated Parmesan cheese, topping (optional)

Instructions

1. Heat the olive oil in a skillet. Sauté scallions and mushrooms for 2 - 3 minutes.
2. Add the eggplant and sauté for 2-3 minutes until golden.
3. Add garlic and stir for 2 - 3 minutes.
4. Sprinkle with the almond flour and stir with a wooden spoon.
5. Add the tomato puree and stir again. Pour wine, water and bone broth and stir well.
6. Cover and cook for 30-35 minutes at Medium-Low temperature.
7. Add chopped thyme, add cheese (if adding in), salt and pepper stir and cook for 5 minutes.
8. Serve hot.

Nutrition information:
Calories: 75 Carbohydrates: 8.5g Proteins: 2.4g Fat: 4.2g Fiber: 4g

Cauliflower Mash in Red Sauce

Serves: 2, Preparation: 10 minutes, Cooking: 15 minutes

Ingredients

2 tbsps. olive oil
1 medium head of cauliflower, cut in florets
1 medium onion, finely chopped
2 garlic cloves, minced
1/2 cup of chopped chives
Chopped parsley to taste
1 tbsp. coconut aminos
2 cups of water
1 pinch of turmeric
1 pinch of black pepper
Salt to taste

Instructions

1. Heat the oil in a large pot at Medium-high heat.
2. Sauté the onion and the garlic until soft.
3. Add the coconut aminos and sauté for 2 minutes at Low heat.
4. Add in water as well as the turmeric, salt and pepper.
5. Cook for 10 - 12 minutes; stir.
6. Transfer the cauliflower mixture in a blender and blend for 30 - 45 seconds.
7. Return it in a pot, drizzle with olive oil, adjust seasonings to taste and serve.

Nutrition information:
Calories: 71 Carbohydrates: 4.7g Protein: 2g Fat: 4.8g Fiber: 1.4g

Roasted Brussels Sprouts with Bacon

Serves: 4, Preparation: 10 minutes, Cooking: 30 minutes

Ingredients

1 ½ lbs. Brussels sprouts
2 tbsps. olive oil
Salt and pepper to taste
6 slices bacon, cut into pieces

Instructions

1. Preheat oven to 400⁰F.
2. Clean and cut the Brussels sprouts into halves.
3. Place Brussels sprouts in a large baking dish and drizzle with olive oil.
4. Season with the salt and pepper.
5. Sprinkle bacon evenly over Brussels sprouts.
6. Bake for 20-30 minutes. Serve hot.

Nutrition information:
Calories: 247 Carbohydrates: 7g Protein: 13.4g Fat: 19.2g Fiber: 3.2g

Boosting Kale, Cucumber and Avocado Smoothie

Serves: 2, Preparation: 10 minutes

Ingredients

1 cup of fresh kale leaves, finely chopped
1 cup of cucumber, chopped
1/3 cup of avocado, cut in cubes
1/2 cup of celery, chopped
2 tbsps. fresh mint leaves
1 cup of water
1 cup of ice cubes, or as needed

Instructions
1. Place all ingredients in your fast-speed blender.
2. Blend until smooth.
3. Serve in chilled glasses and drink.

Nutrition information:
Calories: 14 Carbohydrates: 2.3g Proteins: .6g
Fat: .5g Fiber: .8g

Crispy Cheddar Kale Chips

Serves: 2, Preparation: 15 minutes, Cooking: 10 minutes

Ingredients

1/4 cup of garlic-infused olive oil
Sea salt and ground black pepper to taste
1/2 cup of Cheddar cheese, grated
2 cups of kale, roughly chopped soft stems

Instructions
1. Preheat oven to 400⁰F.
2. Rinse and place the kale on a few sheets of kitchen paper towel to dry.
3. Clean and break kale into small pieces.
4. Pour the olive oil and season with salt and

pepper to taste. Toss to coat.
5. Line a baking dish with parchment paper.
6. Spread kale pieces in a single layer in a baking dish and sprinkle with grated Cheddar cheese.
7. Bake for about 10 minutes, or until the kale pieces become crispy.
8. Serve.

Nutrition information:
Calories: 80 Carbohydrates: 2g Protein: 4.6g Fat: 5.6g Fiber: 1g

Green Bean Soup with Red Pepper Flakes

Serves: 4, Preparation: 5 minutes, Cooking: 45 minutes

Ingredients

2 tbsps. olive oil
1 green onion, diced
2 cloves garlic, minced
2 cups of fresh green beans
1/2 cup of fresh cilantro, chopped
1 carrot, finely sliced
2 cups of water
1 cup of vegetable broth
1 tsp. crushed red pepper flakes
1/4 tsp. chili powder
1 tsp. cumin
Salt and ground pepper to taste

Instructions

1. Heat the oil in a large pot and sauté the onion and garlic with a pinch of salt until soft.
2. Add the green beans and cilantro and stir for further 2 minutes.
3. Add all remaining ingredients and give a good stir.
4. Cover and cook for 30 - 35 minutes or until green beans are soft.
5. Adjust salt and pepper and serve hot.

Nutrition information:
Calories: 54 Carbohydrates: 5g Proteins: 8g Fat: 3.6g Fiber: 2g

Green Keto Puree

Serves: 4, Preparation: 10 minutes, Cooking: 20 minutes

Ingredients

1 scallion, chopped
2 tbsps. extra virgin olive oil
2 cups of fresh spinach leaves
1 cup of Swiss chard, tough stems removed
3 cups of water

1/4 cup of coconut milk
Sea salt and black ground pepper to taste

Instructions
1. Heat the olive oil in a skillet and sauté the scallion for about 2-3 minutes.

12

2. Add the Swish chard and spinach leaves, water and salt and pepper to taste; stir.
3. Bring to the boil and let it simmer for 15 minutes.
4. Transfer spinach mixture in a food processor along with the coconut milk and blend until creamy.
5. Adjust salt and pepper and serve.
Nutrition information:
Calories: 72 Carbohydrates: 2.4g Protein: .9g Fat: 7g Fiber: 2.5g

Hearty Asparagus Salad with Creamy Dressing

Serves: 4, Preparation: 10 minutes
Ingredients
10 ounces frozen cut asparagus, thawed
1/2 avocado, chopped
2 small spring onions, finely chopped
Sea salt to taste
1/2 cup of Greek yogurt
3 tbsps. grated Parmesan cheese
1 tbsp. mustard (Dijon, English, ground stone)
2 tbsps. extra virgin olive oil
Instructions
1. In a salad bowl, combine the asparagus, avocado, and onions; sprinkle with a pinch of the salt, and set aside.
2. In a separate bowl, whisk together Greek yogurt, Parmesan cheese and mustard.
3. Add to the asparagus mixture and toss until well coated.
4. Drizzle with little olive oil and serve immediately or refrigerate until serving.
Nutrition information:
Calories: 243 Carbohydrates: 19.6g Proteins: 26g Fat: 16.2g Fiber: 14.4g

Creamy Spinach Puree

Serves: 4, Preparation: 10 minutes, Cooking: 5 minutes
Ingredients
1 tbsp. beef tallow
2 cups of frozen spinach, drained
2 clove garlic, minced
Salt and fresh-ground black pepper to taste
1/2 cup of water
1 cup of heavy cream
3/4 cup of grated Parmesan cheese
Instructions
1. Thaw (about two hours) and drain the spinach in a colander.
2. Heat the tallow in a large pot and sauté garlic, spinach with a pinch of salt and pepper.
3. Pour water, cover and boil for three minutes or until spinach begins to wilt.
4. Transfer spinach in a blender along with cream and Parmesan cheese; blend for 25 - 35 seconds or until combined well.
5. Taste and adjust salt and ground pepper.
6. Serve.
Nutrition information:
Calories: 325 Carbohydrates: 6.2g Protein: 10.2g Fat: 30.2g Fiber: 2g

Mayo- Mustard Asparagus and Mushrooms Salad

Serves: 4, Preparation: 15 minutes, Cooking: 15 minutes
Ingredients
20 large spears of asparagus
2 cups of mushrooms
1/2 cup of mayonnaise
2 tbsps. yellow mustard
Juice of 1 lemon
Salt and ground pepper to taste
Instructions
1. Cut the woody part of the asparagus, and place in pot with salted water.
2. Boil asparagus for 10 minutes over Medium-high heat. Remove asparagus in colander, allow it to cool, and cut into pieces.
3. Place the asparagus pieces in a large salad bowl.
4. Rinse the mushrooms and cut them into thin slices. Put them in a bowl with asparagus.
5. Season with the salt and pepper to taste, add the mayonnaise and mustard and stir; pour lemon juice to taste, stir and serve.
Nutrition information:
Calories: 151 Carbohydrates: 13.5g Protein: 4g Fat: 10.4g Fiber: 3g

Spiced Cucumber and Fennel Salad

Serves:6 , Preparation: 10 minutes, Cooking: 20 minutes

Ingredients

2 cups cucumber, cut into pieces
2 fennel bulbs, thinly sliced
3 hot peppers
3 cloves garlic (peeled and left whole)
1 tbsp. coriander seeds
1 cinnamon stick (broken into several pieces)
2 cups white vinegar
1/2 tsp. red pepper flakes
1 cup water
3 tbsps. stevia sweetener, granulated
2 tbsps. kosher salt
1 bay leaf

1 tsp. black peppercorns
Olive oil, for serving

Instructions

1. Place all ingredients in a large and deep pot. Cook covered for about 15 - 20 minutes over Medium heat.
2. Transfer mixture in colander to drain.
3. Remove all ingredients from colander in a salad bowl, drizzle with olive oil and serve.

Nutrition information:
Calories: 27 Carbohydrates: 3.2g Proteins: .5g Fat: 1g Fiber: .7g

Steamed "Italiano" Broccoli

Serves: 4, Preparation: 10 minutes, Cooking: 10 minutes

Ingredients

1 1/2 lbs. fresh broccoli florets (or thawed frozen)
1/2 cup Italian salad dressing

Instructions

1. Place broccoli florets in steamer basket above 2-inch boiling water.
2. Cover and steam for about 4 minutes or until broccoli is soft.

3. Remove from the steam, drain and place broccoli in serving plate.
4. Drizzle with Italian salad dressing and toss to coat. Serve.

Nutrition information:
Calories: 100 Carbohydrates: 8.5g Protein: 2.6g Fat: 7g Fiber: 2.4g

Warm Avocado Zucchini Salad

Serves: 4, Preparation: 5 minutes, Cooking: 20 minutes

Ingredients

2 tbsps. olive oil
1 spring onion, finely chopped
2 cloves of garlic
3 medium zucchinis, sliced
1 large avocado
1 tbsp. fresh thyme, finely chopped
Salt and black ground pepper to taste
1 lemon (zest and juice)

Instructions

1. Heat the olive oil in a frying skillet over Medium-high heat.
2. Sauté the onion and garlic with a pinch of salt

until soft, for about 4 - 5 minutes.
3. Add the zucchini and cook for about 2 - 3 minutes.
4. Add the lemon zest, thyme, and season with the salt and pepper; stir well.
5. Add avocado and lemon juice and cook for further 3 - 4 minutes.
6. Remove from the heat; let it cool for 10 minutes and serve.

Nutrition information:
Calories: 158 Carbohydrates: 10g Proteins: 2.5g Fat: 13g Fiber: 5g

Wild Greens, Asparagus with Cheese Sauce

Serves: 6, Preparation: 10 minutes, Cooking: 25 minutes

Ingredients

1 1/4 lbs. mustard greens, cut coarsely
1 bunch of asparagus, cut into about four pieces

For the cheese sauce
1/2 cup of olive oil

1 clove of garlic, cleaned finely minced
1 tbsp. rosemary leaves, finely chopped
1 tsp. hot dried paprika
1 cup cream cheese (full fat)

14

Salt and ground black pepper to taste
Instructions
1. Boil salted water in a saucepan with plenty of salted boiling water.
2. Boil the greens and asparagus for about 7 to 10 minutes.
3. Drain well and put in a salad bowl.
Cheese sauce:
1. In a pan heat the olive oil and garlic over Medium heat.

2. Add the cheese, rosemary leaves, and hot dried paprika, salt and freshly ground pepper; stir well.
3. Stir for 15 - 20 seconds and remove from the heat.
4. Pour hot cheese sauce over the greens and asparagus. Serve.
Nutrition information:
Calories: 303 Carbohydrates: 5.8g Protein: 5.3g Fat: 30.5g Fiber: 2.6g

Creamy Broccoli and Bacon Casserole

Serves: 4, Preparation: 15 minutes, Cooking: 35 minutes
Ingredients
1 tbsp. olive oil
2 cups of broccoli florets, cooked
8 eggs
1/4 cup water
1 cup of cottage cheese
1 tsp. fresh thyme
Salt and ground black pepper to taste
3 ounces of bacon, crumbled
2 tbsps. feta cheese, crumbled
Instructions
1. Preheat the oven to 380⁰F.
2. Coat the casserole dish with olive oil.
3. Place the broccoli florets (cooked) on a bottom of casserole dish; sprinkle with the pinch of salt and pepper.

4. Add the cottage cheese and fresh thyme over the broccoli.
5. In a bowl, whisk the eggs with 1/4 cup of water; season with the salt and pepper.
6. Pour the egg mixture over the broccoli, and sprinkle with crumbled bacon and crumbled feta cheese.
7. Place the casserole in the oven and bake for 35 minutes.
8. Let it rest for 10 minutes before slicing and serving.
Nutrition information:
Calories: 303 Carbohydrates: 5g Proteins: 22g Fat: 22g Fiber: 1.3g

Delicious Spinach and Bacon Casserole

Serves: 5, Preparation: 15 minutes, Cooking: 30 minutes
Ingredients
1 tsp. tallow
8 slices bacon
3/4 cup fresh spinach, chopped
8 eggs
1 cup Parmesan cheese, grated
2 pinch of salt and pepper
Instructions
1. Preheat the oven to 400⁰F.
2. Grease one casserole dish with the tallow.
3. Lay the bacon slices on the bottom of casserole dish.
4. Sprinkle chopped spinach leaves over the bacon,

and sprinkle with little salt.
5. In a bowl, whisk the eggs along with Parmesan cheese and the pinch of salt and pepper.
6. Pour the egg mixture over the spinach evenly.
7. Place in oven and cook for 20 minutes.
8. Turn off the oven but leave the casserole for 10 - 15 minutes inside.
9. Serve hot.
Nutrition information:
Calories: 365 Carbohydrates: 2.3g Proteins: 27g Fat: 27g Fiber: .2g

Steak Strips and Zucchini Omelet Casserole

Serves: 5, Preparation: 10 minutes, Cooking: 30 minutes

Ingredients

1 tbsp. lard
1 lb. bacon, cut into strips
1 spring onion, finely diced
3 large sized zucchinis, grated
1 tsp. sea salt and ground black pepper
6 eggs
1/2 cup of feta cheese, crumbled

Instructions

1. Preheat oven to 350⁰F.
2. Grease one large casserole dish with the lard.
3. Place the bacon strips in a casserole dish, and cover with diced spring onion and zucchinis.
4. Season with the salt and pepper.
5. Beat the eggs in a bowl with a pinch of salt, pepper and crumbled feta cheese.
6. Pour the egg mixture in a casserole dish.
7. Bake for 30 minutes or until the eggs are cooked.
8. Serve hot.

Nutrition information:

Calories: 344 Carbohydrates: 6g Proteins: 22.5g Fat: 25.7g Fiber: 1.3g

Instant Pot Zucchini Noodles with Parmesan

Serves: 4, Preparation: 15 minutes, Cooking: 5 minutes

Ingredients

2 cups zucchini noodles
Salt and fresh cracked pepper to taste
2 tbsps. olive oil
2 cloves garlic, minced
1 tbsp. green pepper, chopped
3 tbsps. fresh basil (chopped)
1 tsp. red pepper flakes
1 cup water
1/4 cup Parmesan cheese

Instructions

1. Pour oil to the inner pot in the Instant Pot.
2. Cut zucchini into thin, noodle-like strips with a mandolin. Season zucchini noodles with the salt and pepper.
3. Place zucchini in Instant Pot, and add minced garlic, green pepper, fresh basil, red pepper flakes and water over zucchini.
4. Lock lid into place and set on the Manual setting for 5 minutes.
5. When the timer beeps, press "Cancel" and carefully flip the Quick-release valve to let the pressure out.
6. Remove zucchini noodles on a serving plate, sprinkle with Parmesan cheese and serve.

Nutrition information:

Calories: 87 Carbohydrates: 4.6g Proteins: 1.9g Fat: 7.7g Fiber: 1.5g

Slow Cooker Brown Cremini Mushroom Gravy

Serves: 3, Preparation: 5 minutes, Cooking: 4 hours

Ingredients

1 lb. Cremini mushrooms (or white mushrooms, shiitake mushrooms)
1 medium onion, finely chopped
1 cup of cream
1 cup of almond milk (unsweetened)
1/4 cup white dry wine
1 tbsp. butter
Salt and red ground pepper to taste

Instructions

1. Place mushrooms along with all ingredients in Slow Cooker; stir gently to combine.
2. Cover and cook on High for 1-2 hours or on Low for 3-4 hours.
3. Open lid, stir well, adjust salt and pepper and allow to cool.
4. Store in glass jar and keep refrigerated.

Nutrition information:

Calories: 53 Carbohydrates: 2.4g Protein: 1g Fat: 3.9g Fiber: 0.1g

Slow Cooker Creamed Portobello Mushrooms

Serves: 4, Preparation: 10 minutes, Cooking: 3 hour and 30 minutes

Ingredients

1 1/2 lbs. Portobello mushrooms, halved
Salt and ground white pepper to taste
1 tbsp. butter
1/2 cup of bone broth
2 tbsps. brandy
1 tbsp. almond flour
3/4 cup of fresh cream
2 tbsps. chopped fresh parsley

Instructions

1. Place mushrooms in your Slow Cooker along with salt and pepper, butter, bone broth, brandy and almond flour.
2. Cover and cook on High for 3 hours.
3. Open lid and stir cream; cover and cook on High for further 25 - 30 minutes.
4. Serve hot with chopped parsley.

Nutrition information:

Calories: 110 Carbohydrates: 2.5g Proteins: 4g Fat: 6.3g Fiber: .3g

Slow Cooker Zucchini Puree

Serves: 4, Preparation: 5 minutes, Cooking: 9 hours

Ingredients

2 tbsps. garlic-infused olive oil
2 cups zucchini, sliced
2 cups green olives, pitted and chopped
1 chopped tomato
2 tsps. capers
1 tbsp. fresh basil, finely chopped
Salt and pepper to taste
2 tbsps. sesame seeds, toasted (For serving)

Instructions

1. Add all ingredients from the list in your Slow Cooker and stir well.
2. Cover and cook on Low for 7 - 9 hours.
3. Transfer the mixture into blender or food processor and blend it until smooth.
4. Taste and adjust salt and pepper to taste.
5. Sprinkle with toasted sesame seeds and serve.

Nutrition information:

Calories: 133 Carbohydrates: 5.2g Protein: 1.2g Fat: 13g Fiber: 1g

Easy Creamy Cauliflower with Sesame

Serves: 4, Preparation: 10 minutes, Cooking: 4 hours

Ingredients

2 cups cauliflower florets
1 tbsp. fresh butter
1 small onion, chopped
1 cup heavy cream
Salt and pepper to taste
1/2 cup toasted sesame seeds
Fresh parsley leaves, for garnish (or cilantro)

Instructions

1. Add the cauliflower florets together with all ingredients in your Slow Cooker.
2. Cover and cook on Low for 6 hours or on High for 4 hours.
3. Taste and adjust salt; stir well.
4. Serve with chopped parsley.

Nutrition information:

Calories: 261 Carbohydrates: 11.5g Proteins: 5.3g Fat: 23g Fiber: 4.2g

Savory Zucchini Cream with Nuts

Serves: 6, Preparation: 10 minutes, Cooking: 3 hours

Ingredients

6 medium zucchinis, sliced
4 tbsps. ground almonds
1 cup almond milk
Seasoned salt and ground white pepper
1/3 cup of garlic-infused olive oil

Instructions

1. Rinse, clean and cut zucchini in slices.
2. Place all ingredients in your Slow Cooker.
3. Cover and cook on High for 3 hours.
4. Transfer zucchini mixture in a blender; blend for 25 - 30 seconds or until smooth.
5. Adjust salt and pepper and blend again.
6. Serve immediately or keep refrigerated.

Nutrition information:
Calories: 224 Carbohydrates: 7.9g Proteins: 3.5g
Fat: 21g Fiber: 3g

Bok Choy Stir-Fry

Serves: 4, Preparation: 10 minutes, Cooking: 15 minutes

Ingredients

20 oz. bok choy, fresh
2 tbsps. garlic-infused olive oil
2 green onions, finely chopped
2 cloves garlic, minced
1 tbsp. oyster sauce (made with stevia sweetener)
Salt to taste
1 tsp. almond flour
4 tbsps. water

Instructions

1. Rinse your bok choy and drain well.
2. Heat the oil in a skillet and sauté the onion and garlic for 3 - 4 minutes.
3. Add bok choy and stir for approximately 2 - 3 minutes.
4. In a bowl, whisk the oyster sauce, salt, almond flour and water.
5. Pour the mixture over bok choy, turn off the heat, stir, and let sit for 5 minutes.
6. Serve hot.

Nutrition information:
Calories: 134 Carbohydrates: 2.5g Proteins: 1g Fat: 14g Fiber: 0.5g

Chapter 4 Side Dish & Salad Recipes

"Mimosa" Deviled Eggs

Serves: 4, Preparation: 10 minutes, Cooking Time: 20 minutes

Ingredients
8 eggs, hard boiled
2 tbsp. vinegar
4 tbsp. mayonnaise
2 tbsp. mustard
Salt and ground pepper to taste
For serving
2 tsp. spring onions, sliced
1 tsp. sweet red paprika
Instructions
Boil eggs and allow them to cool; peel.

Cut the eggs lengthwise.
Remove the yolks, and place in a bowl.
Add vinegar, mayonnaise, mustard, and the salt and pepper; stir well.
Fill the eggs with the mayonnaise mixture.
Serve with fresh chopped onions and paprika.
Nutrition information:
Calories: 232 Carbohydrates: 6.7g Proteins: 14.3g Fat: 16.2g Fiber: 1g

Aromatic Almond Kale and Zucchini Mash

Serves: 6, Preparation: 5 minutes, Cooking Time: 20 minutes

Ingredients
1/2 cup of ground almonds
1 1/2 cups of water
1 tsp. ground cumin
1 tsp. turmeric powder
Salt and ground black pepper
1 tbsp. fresh grated ginger
4 oz. chopped kale
2 tbsp. olive oil
2 large zucchinis
Juice from 1 lemon
1 scallion, chopped
For serving
Chopped fresh spearmint
Chili powder
Instructions
1. In a pot, add water, ground almonds, cumin,

turmeric, ginger and the salt and pepper; bring to boil and cook for 10 minutes at Low temperature.
2. Add kale in a pot and stir with a wooden spoon.
3. Heat the olive oil in a pan at medium temperature.
4. Cut the zucchini into slices and Sauté for 2-3 minutes until golden brown and soft.
5. Place zucchini in a pot and sprinkle with lemon juice; stir to combine well.
6. Finally, add chopped scallion in a pot and stir.
7. Serve into warm plates.
8. Sprinkle with chopped spearmint and chili powder to taste.
Nutrition information: Calories: 101
Carbohydrates: 4g Proteins: 2.3g Fat: 9g Fiber: 1.7g

Baked Savory Shrimp Cupcakes

Serves: 12, Preparation: 25 minutes, Cooking Time: 20 minutes

Ingredients
1/2 cup of olive oil
1 cup of almond flour
1 tbsp. stevia granulated sweetener
2 tsp. baking powder
1 tsp. baking soda
1 tsp. onion powder
1 tsp. sweet ground paprika
1 tsp. cumin
1 pinch of cayenne pepper
1 tsp. garlic powder

3 medium eggs
3/4 cup of water
2 tsp.tomato puree
For the glaze
1/2 cup of stevia granulated sweetener
2 tbsp. Cognac
For shrimps
1 tbsp.olive oil
12 medium shrimp
Salt and black ground pepper

1 tbsp. chives
Instructions
1. Preheat the oven to 360^0 F.
2. Grease 12 cup cakes and set aside.
3. Heat the olive oil in a frying skillet. Add almond flour and salt.
4. Add the flour and stir with a wire just for one minute to get a golden-brown color.
5. Remove the mixture from the saucepan and transfer to the food processor.
6. Add the sweetener, baking powder, soda, onion, paprika, cumin, cayenne pepper, garlic, and blend at medium speed for 1-2 minutes until all ingredients to combine well.
7. Add the eggs, water and tomato paste. Beat to combine well.
8. Pour batter in each muffin cup about 3/4 of the way full.

9. Bake for 20 minutes or until the cupcakes are golden.
10. Remove from the oven and allow it to cool.
For the glaze
1. Combine the sweetener with cognac until get a smooth glaze.
2. Spread little bit of glaze over each cup cake.
For shrimps
1. Heat the olive oil in a frying pan on High temperature.
2. Season shrimp with the salt and pepper.
3. Sauté shrimp for two minutes in total.
4. Place one shrimp in each cup cake.
5. Sprinkle with chives and serve.
Nutrition information: Calories: 167
Carbohydrates: 2.3g Proteins: 13.9g Fat: 11.4g
Fiber: 0.7g

Braised Mushrooms with Thyme and Lemon

Serves: 4 , Preparation: 5 minutes, Cooking Time: 15 minutes
Ingredients
2 tbsp. olive oil
1 tsp. butter
2 cups of fresh mushrooms, halved or quartered
1 clove of garlic, minced
1 lemon juice
1 tsp. lemon zest
1 tbsp.fresh thyme leaves
Salt and ground pepper to taste
Instructions
1. Heat the olive oil and the butter in a large frying pan.
2. Add the mushrooms and cook, without stirring

for 3 minutes.
3. Stir mushrooms and continue to cook for further 5 - 6 minutes.
4. Add garlic and lemon zest and cook for 1 minute.
5. Season mushrooms with thyme and with the salt and pepper.
6. Drizzle mushrooms with the lemon juice, stir and serve.
Nutrition information: Calories: 121
Carbohydrates: 6.3g Proteins: 6.1g Fat: 8g Fiber: 2g

Fried Artichokes with Parmesan Cheese

Serves: 12, Preparation: 15 minutes, Cooking Time: 10 minutes
Ingredients
6 artichokes, cleaned
1/2 cup of almond flour
Salt and ground black pepper to taste
4 tbsp. grated cheese (Romano or Parmesan)
2 eggs
Olive oil for frying
Enough water
Instructions
1. Rinse and thoroughly clean; slice artichokes and place in a water with lemon.
2. In a bowl, combine the almond flour, salt,

pepper and grated cheese.
3. Beat the eggs and pour it into the flour mixture; stir well.
4. If the butter is too thick, add some water.
5. Heat the oil on a large frying skillet.
6. Roll the artichokes in the batter and fry them for 3-4 minutes turning once.
7. Serve warm.
Nutrition information:
Calories: 80 Carbohydrates: 8.8g Proteins: 5.8g
Fat:3g Fiber: 4.5g

Garlic Marinated Mushrooms

Serves: 8, Preparation: 5 minutes, Cooking Time: 60 minutes

Ingredients

2 1/2 cups fresh white mushrooms
2 cups vinegar, distilled
6 cloves garlic
1/2 tsp. salt

Instructions

1. Soak mushrooms in distilled vinegar, chopped garlic and salt for about 1 hour.

2. Remove mushrooms from the pot and place in colander to drain.

3. Keep refrigerated.

Nutrition information:

Calories: 41 Carbohydrates: 2g Proteins: .8g Fat: 0.1g Fiber: .3g

Green Beans and Tuna Salad

Serves: 8, Preparation: 10 minutes, Cooking Time: 20 minutes

Ingredients

3/4 cup of green beans, boiled
1 cucumber
1 small green hot pepper
1 avocado
1 large zucchini
Juice and zest of 2 limes
3 tbsp. olive oil
Salt and ground black pepper
2 can (11 oz.) tuna fish
3 tbsp. sesame seeds
2 tbsp. fresh mint, finely chopped

Instructions

1. Place green beans in a large salad bowl.

2. Cut the cucumber in half, and then in slices.
3. Clean and slice the pepper, avocado, zucchini and put in a salad bowl; gently stir to combine.
4. Season the salad with the salt and pepper, and pour the lime juice, lime zest and olive oil; toss to combine.
5. Finally, add tuna fish over salad.
6. Sprinkle with sesame and fresh mint and refrigerate for 20 minutes.
7. Serve.

Nutrition information:

Calories: 414 Carbohydrates: 6.5g Proteins: 57g Fat: 17.5g Fiber: 3g

Ground Turkey Cocktail Bites

Serves: 6, Preparation: 10 minutes, Cooking Time: 5 minutes

Ingredients

2 cups ground turkey breast
3 tbsp. mayonnaise
2 tbsp. grated onion
1/2 tsp. celery salt
2 tbsp. fresh parsley, finely chopped
1 tsp. garlic powder
1/2 tsp. Tabasco sauce
3 tbsp. ground almonds
Lemon wedges for serving

Instructions

1. In a large bowl, combine all ingredients in

compact mixture.
2. Refrigerate for 2 hours.
3. Shape the turkey mixture into small bite-size pieces.
4. Heat one nonstick frying pan and cook turkey balls for 5 minutes or until crisp.
5. Serve hot with lemon wedges.

Nutrition information:

Calories: 209 Carbohydrates: 3g Proteins: 38.2 Fat: 5.3g Fiber: .5g

Paneer Cheese Wrapped with Prosciutto

Serves: 6, Preparation: 5 minutes, Cooking Time: 5 minutes

Ingredients

1/2 lbs. Paneer cheese (or use tofu as a substitute)
6 thin slices of prosciutto
1 tbsp. fresh chopped oregano
3 tbsp. extra-virgin olive oil

Lemon wedges for serving

Instructions

1. Cut cheese in 6 sticks.
2. Sprinkle chopped oregano over cheese sticks.

3. Wrap each cheese stick with a strip of prosciutto, and then drizzle with olive oil.
4. Heat one nonstick skillet and fry cheese sticks with prosciutto for about one minute on each side.

5. Serve hot with lemon wedges.
Nutrition information:
Calories: 242 Carbohydrates: 4g Proteins: 25g Fat: 14.5g Fiber: .3g

Herbed Cheese Spread

Serves: 10, Preparation: 5 minutes, Cooking Time:10 minutes
Ingredients
8 oz. cream cheese, full fat
6 oz.goat cheese
1/4 cup Greek yogurt
1 clove garlic, finely sliced
1/2 tsp. dried thyme
1 tbsp. chopped chives
1 pinch of cayenne pepper (optional)
Salt and ground black pepper to taste
Instructions

1. In a bowl, stir all ingredients and stir until thoroughly combined.
2. Place the mixture into a glass bowl and refrigerate for at least 2 hours.
3. Serve cold.
Nutrition information:
Calories: 120 Carbohydrates: 2.4g Proteins: 6.4g Fat: 9.6g Fiber: 0g

Oven Baked Parmesan Shrimp

Serves: 6 , Preparation: 15 minutes , Cooking Time: 12 minutes
Ingredients
2 lbs. shrimp, peeled
Salt and ground pepper
Zest and juice from 1 lemon
1/3 cup of olive oil
2 tbsp. fresh oregano
1/4 cup of ground almonds
2 cloves of garlic
1/2 cup of grated parmesan
Pinch of chili flakes
1 bunch of fresh parsley, chopped
1 tbsp. fresh basil
Lemon wedges for serving
Instructions
1. Preheat the oven to 400⁰F.
2. In a bowl, combine shrimp, lemon zest and

juice, olive oil, and the salt and pepper; stir with the spoon.
3. Add fresh chopped oregano, stir and set aside.
4. Place the garlic, ground almonds, parmesan, chili flakes, fresh oregano, lemon zest in high-fast blender.
5. Blend until the mixture combined well.
6. Add the mixture to the bowl with the shrimps; gentle stir.
7. Lay shrimp in an oven proof baking dish and bake for 10 - 12 minutes.
8. Serve with lemon wedges.
Nutrition information:
Calories: 295 Carbohydrates: 5.7g Proteins: 26g Fat: 19g Fiber: 2.5g

Spicy Cheese Dip

Serves: 6, Preparation: 10 minutes
Ingredients
1 clove garlic, finely sliced
3 tbsp. extra-virgin olive oil
1 chili pepper, finely sliced
1 tsp. ground hot pepper
3/4 cup of feta cheese
1 cup of Greek yogurt
Instructions

1. Add all ingredients in a blender.
2. Blend only for 20 - 30 seconds.
3. Store the cheese dip in a glass bowl.
4. Keep refrigerated until serving.
Nutrition information:
Calories: 156 Carbohydrates: 3g Proteins: 9g Fat: 12g Fiber: 2.5g

Roasted Cocktail Mussels

Serves: 6, Preparation: 20 minutes, Cooking Time: 20 minutes

Ingredients

2 lbs. mussels
3/4 cup of water
Coarse salt for baking dish
3/4 cup of ground almond
1/3 cup of olive oil
4 tbsp. grated parmesan
2 cloves of garlic, chopped
1 bunch of parsley, finely chopped
1 tsp. fresh oregano
2 pinches of salt

Instructions

1. Preheat the oven to 450⁰F.
2. Rinse and clean mussels under cold water.
3. Heat the water in a large pot, add mussels, cover and boil for 5 -6 minutes.
4. Transfer mussels with pierced ladle to a bowl; reserve cooking liquid.
5. Clean mussels, keeping them in a half shell.
6. Sprinkle thick salt in a baking pan, lay the mussels and pour in some of the cooking liquid.
7. In a bowl, stir ground almonds, olive oil, parmesan, garlic, parsley, oregano and the salt. Divide the mixture evenly over mussels.
8. Bake for 15 minutes and serve hot.

Nutrition information:
Calories: 355 Carbohydrates: 8g Proteins: 23g Fat: 25g Fiber: 2g

Smoked Pink Trout Dip

Serves: 6, Preparation: 15 minutes

Ingredients

1 1/2 cups of cream cheese, softened
2 tbsp. sour cream
1 tbsp. lemon juice
1 tsp. grated lemon zest
1 spring onion, finely chopped
2 tsp. finely chopped dill
5 ounces of smoked pink trout, chopped
Salt and ground black pepper to taste

Instructions

1. In a bowl, add cream cheese and sour cream, and beat with an electric mixer until fluffy.
2. Add lemon juice and lemon zest; beat until all ingredients combined well.
3. Season the salt the pepper and add chopped fresh onion and dill; stir.
4. Finally, add chopped smoked trout and gently stir with the spoon.
5. Taste and adjust salt to taste.
6. Transfer cream cheese fish dip in a glass container and cover with plastic wrap.
7. Keep refrigerated until serving.

Nutrition information:
Calories: 247 Carbohydrates: 2g Proteins: 10g Fat: 22g Fiber: 0.2g

Savory and Sour Chicken Salad

Serves: 4, Preparation: 20 minutes, Cooking Time: 35 minutes

Ingredients

4 small chicken breasts
1 bay leaf
6 black peppercorns
1 onion, quartered
2 garlic cloves, halved
1 ¼ cups of white wine
2 ½ cups of water
½ cup of apple cider vinegar
½ cup of white vinegar
2 cups of extra virgin olive oil
Pinch of salt
2 rosemary sprigs
2 thyme sprigs

For the salad:
½ cup of extra virgin olive oil
2 tbsp. wine vinegar
Salt and black pepper
2 cups of mixed salad leaves
2 avocados, chopped
2 boiled eggs, chopped

Instructions

1. Place the chicken breasts in a pan with the bay leaf, peppercorns, onion, garlic, wine, water and vinegar.
2. Pour the olive oil over the chicken, season with the salt, and add the herbs.

3. Cover and let the chicken simmer gently for 30-35 minutes.
4. When cooked, let it cool and keep it in the fridge overnight.
Salad
1. Combine the olive oil, vinegar, salt and pepper in a bowl and blend it using a hand mixer.
2. Place the mixed salad leaves in a large bowl.
3. Drain the chicken and cut it into strips.

4. Put the chicken strips on top of the salad leaves.
5. Add sliced avocado and garnish with the boiled egg.
6. Finally, pour the vinaigrette over the salad and serve immediately.
Nutrition information:
Calories: 347 Carbohydrates: 12 g Proteins: 32g Fat: 19g Fiber: 7g

Green Beans Salad with Creamy Cracked Pepper

Serves: 6, Preparation: 15 minutes, Cooking Time: 3 minutes
Ingredients
2 cups green beans, fresh
2 green onion (white and green parts), chopped
1/2 tsp. salt and ground black pepper to taste
1 cup water
1/2 cup cream cheese (full fat)
1/2 cup sour cream
Ground black pepper to taste
1/4 cup Parmesan cheese, grated
Instructions
1. Clean and rinse green beans in cool water.
2. Use a sharp knife cut off the ends.
3. Place the green beans in your Instant Pot and finely chopped green onions and water. Season

salt and pepper to taste.
4. Lock lid into place and set on the Manual setting for 3 minutes.
5. Use Quick-Release and turn the valve from Sealing to Venting to release the pressure.
6. Transfer green bans mixture to serving bowl.
7. In a bowl, stir cream cheese, sour cream and cracked black pepper; pour over green beans.
8. Sprinkle creamy green beans with grated parmesan cheese and serve.
Nutrition information:
Calories: 134 Carbohydrates: 4g Proteins: 7g Fat: 10g Fiber: 2g

Herbed Brussels Sprouts Salad

Serves: 6, Preparation: 10 minutes, Cooking Time: 3 minutes
Ingredients
2 lbs. Brussels sprouts
1 tbsp. fresh parsley, finely chopped
1 tsp. fresh dill, finely chopped
1 tsp. fresh chives, chopped
Salt and pepper to taste
1 cup water
Salt and ground black pepper to taste
2 tbsp. olive oil for serving
Lemon juice for serving, freshly squeezed
Instructions
1. Place Brussels sprouts into your Instant Pot.
2. Add fresh herbs, salt and pepper to taste and pour water.

3. Lock lid into place and set on the Manual setting for 3 minutes.
4. When the timer beeps, press "Cancel" and carefully flip the Quick-Release valve to let the pressure out.
5. Open the lid and transfer Brussels sprouts in a salad bowl.
6. Drizzle with olive oil and lemon juice and serve.
Nutrition information:
Calories: 119 Carbohydrates: 9g Proteins: 5g Fat: 7g Fiber: 6g

Instant Pot Warm Bok Choi Salad with Mustard Dressing

Serves: 6, Preparation: 5 minutes, Cooking Time: 15 minutes
Ingredients
1 1/2 lbs. bokchoy, trimmed
1 cup or more water
Seasoned salt to taste

1 cup olive oil
1 1/2 tbsp. lime juice
2 tbsp. yellow mustard

Instructions

1. Rinse and clean bokchoy from any dirt.
2. Pour bokchoy in your Instant Pot, sprinkle with a pinch of seasoned salt and pour water.
3. Lock lid into place and set on the Manual setting for 15 minutes.
4. Use Quick Release and turn the valve from Sealing to Venting to release the pressure.
5. Open lid, and with tongue transfer bokchoy in a large salad bowl.
6. In a bowl, whisk olive oil, mustard, seasoned salt and lime juice.
7. Pour dressing over bokchoy salad, toss and serve.

Nutrition information:
Calories: 343 Carbohydrates: 1.5g Proteins: 1g Fat: 37g Fiber: 0.6g

Parmesan Broccoli Salad

Serves: 4, Preparation: 15 minutes, Cooking Time: 3 hours

Ingredients

2 cups broccoli florets, cut into small pieces
1 cup of water
1/4 cup olive oil
1/2 lemon zest
1 1/2 tsp. lemon juice, freshly squeezed
Salt and pepper to taste
½ cup Parmesan cheese

Instructions

1. Wash the broccoli thoroughly and clean from any dirt.
2. Cut the broccoli in florets, and then cut them in small pieces.
3. Place broccoli in your oiled crock pot.
4. Pour water, oil, lemon zest and lemon juice into crock pot.
5. Season salt and black pepper, stir and cover.
6. Cook on Low for 2-3 hours.
7. Open lid, and sprinkle grated Parmesan cheese in your crock pot.
8. Cover again and cook on High for 15 minutes. Serve hot.

Nutrition information:
Calories: 385 Carbohydrates: 7g Proteins: 15g Fat: 33g Fiber: 0.1g

Parmesan Mushrooms

Serves: 4, Preparation: 5 minutes, Cooking Time: 10 minutes

Ingredients

3 tbsp. butter (grass fed), softened
1 1/2 lbs. fresh mushrooms, whole
4 tbsp. Parmesan cheese, grated
1/8 tsp. black pepper, freshly ground

Instructions

1. Heat butter in a large frying skillet over medium heat.
2. Add mushrooms and cook over Medium-high heat until golden.
3. Sprinkle with grated cheese and pepper and cook for further 1 minute.
4. Serve hot.

Nutrition information:
Calories: 149 Carbohydrates: 5g Proteins: 7.5g Fat: 11g Fiber: 7.3g

Almond Lemon Spinach Salad

Serves: 6 , Preparation: 10 minutes

Ingredients

1 1/2 lbs. torn spinach leaves
1/4 cup finely chopped green onions
1/2 green bell pepper, sliced or diced
2 tsp. grated fresh ginger
2 tbsp. fresh lemon juice or to taste
1/3 cup olive oil
1/4 tsp. salt
1/8 tsp. red pepper flakes
2/3 cup chopped almonds, toasted

Instructions

1. Rinse and clean spinach from any dirt and add in a large salad bowl.
2. In a bowl, whisk lemon juice, olive oil, ginger, salt and red pepper flakes.
3. Toss spinach with dressing mixture and sprinkle toasted sliced almonds on top.
4. Serve.

Nutrition information:
Calories: 243 Carbohydrates: 7.5g Proteins: 7g Fat: 20.6g Fiber: 4.5g

Savory and Sour Chicken Salad

Serves: 4, Preparation: 20 minutes, Cooking Time: 35 minutes

Ingredients

4 small chicken breasts
1 bay leaf
6 black peppercorns
1 onion, quartered
2 garlic cloves, halved
1 ¼ cups of white wine
2 ½ cups of water
½ cup of apple cider vinegar
½ cup of white vinegar
2 cups of extra virgin olive oil
Pinch of salt
2 rosemary sprigs
2 thyme sprigs

For the salad:

½ cup of extra virgin olive oil
2 tbsp. wine vinegar
Salt and black pepper
2 cups of mixed salad leaves
2 avocados, chopped
2 boiled eggs, chopped

Instructions

1. Place the chicken breasts in a pan with the bay leaf, peppercorns, onion, garlic, wine, water and vinegar.
2. Pour the olive oil over the chicken, season with the salt, and add the herbs.
3. Cover and let the chicken simmer gently for 30-35 minutes.
4. When cooked, let it cool and keep it in the fridge overnight.

For the Salad

1. Combine the olive oil, vinegar, salt and pepper in a bowl and blend it using a hand mixer.
2. Place the mixed salad leaves in a large bowl.
3. Drain the chicken and cut it into strips.
4. Put the chicken strips on top of the salad leaves.
5. Add sliced avocado and garnish with the boiled egg.
6. Finally, pour the vinaigrette over the salad and serve immediately.

Nutrition information:

Calories: 347 Carbohydrates: 12 g Proteins: 32g Fat: 19g Fiber: 7g

Green Beans Salad with Creamy Cracked Pepper

Serves: 6, Preparation: 15 minutes, Cooking Time: 3 minutes

Ingredients

1 lb. green beans, fresh
2 green onion (white and green parts), chopped
1/2 tsp. salt and ground black pepper to taste
1 cup water
1/2 cup cream cheese (full-fat)
1/2 cup sour cream
Ground black pepper to taste
1/4 cup Parmesan cheese, grated

Instructions

1. Clean and rinse green beans in cool water.
2. Use a sharp knife cut off the ends.
3. Place the green beans in your Instant Pot and finely chopped green onions and water. Season salt and pepper to taste.
4. Lock lid into place and set on the Manual setting for 3 minutes.
5. Use Quick-Release and turn the valve from Sealing to Venting to release the pressure.
6. Transfer green bans mixture to serving bowl.
7. In a bowl, stir cream cheese, sour cream and cracked black pepper; pour over green beans.
8. Sprinkle creamy green beans with grated Parmesan cheese and serve.

Nutrition information:

Calories: 134 Carbohydrates: 4g Proteins: 7g Fat: 10g Fiber: 2g

Warm Spinach, Basil and Parmesan Salad

Serves: 6, Preparation: 10 minutes, Cooking Time: 6 minutes

Ingredients

2 tbsp. olive oil
1 1/2 lbs. spinach chopped
1 green onion, diced
2 cloves garlic, sliced
1/2 cup basil, fresh
Pinch of ground nutmeg
1/4 cup water
Salt and pepper to taste

3/4 cup Parmesan cheese, grated
1 lemon wedges for serving
Instructions
1. Grease the bottom and sides of crock pot with olive oil.
2. Add all ingredients in crock pot and give a good stir.

3. Cover and cook on Low for 4 - 6 hours.
4. Transfer creamy vegetables on a serving plate.
5. Serve hot with lemon wedges.
Nutrition information:
Calories: 142 Carbohydrates: 4g Proteins: 9g Fat: 10g Fiber: 3g

Herbed Brussels Sprouts Salad

Serves: 6, Preparation: 10 minutes, Cooking Time: 3 minutes
Ingredients
2 lbs. Brussels sprouts
1 tbsp. fresh parsley, finely chopped
1 tsp. fresh dill, finely chopped
1 tsp. fresh chives, chopped
Salt and pepper to taste
1 cup water
Salt and ground black pepper to taste
2 tbsp. olive oil for serving
Lemon juice for serving (freshly squeezed)
Instructions
1. Place Brussels sprouts into your Instant Pot.
2. Add fresh herbs, salt and pepper to taste and pour water.

3. Lock lid into place and set on the Manual setting for 3 minutes.
4. When the timer beeps, press "Cancel" and carefully flip the Quick-Release valve to let the pressure out.
5. Open the lid and transfer Brussels sprouts in a salad bowl.
6. Drizzle with olive oil and lemon juice, and serve.
Nutrition information:
Calories: 119 Carbohydrates: 9g Proteins: 5g Fat: 7g Fiber: 6g

Warm Bok Choi Salad with Mustard Dressing

Serves: 6, Preparation: 5 minutes, Cooking Time: 15 minutes
Ingredients
1 1/2 lbs.bokchoy, trimmed
1 cup or more water
Seasoned salt to taste
1 cup olive oil
1 1/2 tbsp. lime juice
2 tbsp. yellow mustard
Instructions
1. Rinse and clean bokchoy from any dirt.
2. Pour bokchoy in your Instant Pot, sprinkle with a pinch of seasoned salt and pour water.
3. Lock lid into place and set on the Manual setting for 15 minutes.

4. Use Quick-Release and turn the valve from Sealing to Venting to release the pressure.
5. Open lid, and with tongue transfer bokchoy in a large salad bowl.
6. In a bowl, whisk olive oil, mustard, seasoned salt and lime juice.
7. Pour dressing over bokchoy salad, toss and serve.
Nutrition information:
Calories: 343 Carbohydrates: 1.5g Proteins: 1g Fat: 37g Fiber: 0.6g

Broccoli Salad with Melted Cheese

Serves: 4, Preparation: 15 minutes, Cooking Time: 3 minutes
Ingredients
1 1/2 lbs. broccoli florets, cut into small pieces
1 cup of water
1/4 cup olive oil
1/2 lemon zest
1 1/2 tsp. lemon juice, freshly squeezed
Salt and pepper to taste

1 can ground Parmesan cheese
Instructions
1. Wash the broccoli thoroughly and clean from any dirt.
2. Cut the broccoli in florets, and then cut them in small pieces.

3. Place broccoli in your oiled crock pot.

4. Pour water, oil, lemon zest and lemon juice into crock pot.

5. Season salt and black pepper, stir and cover.

6. Cook on Low for 2-3 hours.

7. Open lid, and sprinkle grated parmesan cheese in your crock pot.

8. Cover again, and cook on High for 15 minutes. Serve hot.

Nutrition information:

Calories: 385 Carbohydrates: 7g Proteins: 15g Fat: 33g Fiber: 0.1g

Warm Spinach - Basil and Parmesan Salad

Serves: 6, Preparation: 10 minutes, Cooking Time: 6 minutes

Ingredients

2 tbsp. olive oil

1 1/2 lbs. spinach, chopped

1 green onion, diced

2 cloves garlic, sliced

1/2 cup basil, fresh

Pinch of ground nutmeg

1/4 cup water

Salt and pepper to taste

3/4 cup Parmesan cheese, grated

1 lemon wedges for serving

Instructions

1. Grease the bottom and sides of crock pot with olive oil.

2. Add all ingredients in crock pot and give a good stir.

3. Cover and cook on Low for 4 - 6 hours.

4. Transfer creamy vegetables on a serving plate.

5. Serve hot with lemon wedges.

Nutrition information:

Calories: 142 Carbohydrates: 4g Proteins: 9g Fat: 10g Fiber: 3g

Turnip Greens and Almond Salad

Serves: 4, Preparation: 10 minutes, Cooking Time: 30 minutes

Ingredients

1 tbsp. tallow

3 cups turnip greens

1/2 cup slivered almonds, lightly toasted

1/4 tsp. salt and black pepper, freshly ground

1 tbsp. apple vinegar (optional)

Instructions

1. Rinse and clean the turnip greens from any dirt.

2. Heat tallow in a skillet over medium heat.

3. Add turnip greens; season with the pinch of the salt and pepper and sauté for 20 minutes.

4. Add finely chopped almonds, stir and cook for further 10 minutes; stir.

5. Stir in apple cider vinegar.

6. Taste and adjust salt and pepper.

7. Transfer to the salad bowl and allow it to cool before serving.

Nutrition information:

Calories: 141 Carbohydrates: 7.4g Proteins: 6.7g Fat: 9.4g Fiber: 5g

Lobster Egg Salad

Serves: 4, Preparation: 10 minutes

Ingredients

2 can (11 oz.) lobster meat

1 cup mayonnaise

2 boiled eggs, finely chopped

3 tbsp. scallions, green parts only, chopped

1 tbsp. mustard (Dijon, English, or whole grain)

Salt and ground pepper to taste

1 tbsp. capers

1 lettuce heart

Instructions

1. Place the lobster meat, mayonnaise, eggs, green scallions, mustard in a salad bowl.

2. Stir to combine well.

3. Season the salt and pepper to taste.

4. Sprinkle with a capers and garnish with lettuce hearts.

5. Serve and enjoy!

Nutrition information:

Calories: 350 Carbohydrates: 9g Proteins: 21g Fat: 25.5g Fiber: 1.3g

Hearty Artichokes, Green Beans and Egg Salad

Serves: 6, Preparation: 15 minutes, Cooking Time: 35 minutes

Ingredients

4 artichokes, cooked
2 cups green beans, cooked
4 boiled eggs, hard
2 scallions, finely chopped
2 tbsp. fresh mint, finely chopped
2 tbsp. fresh dill, finely chopped
3 tbsp. capers
10 olives, pitted, finely chopped (optional)

Dressing

1/2 cup olive oil
2 tbsp. lemon juice
Sea salt and freshly ground black pepper

Instructions

1. Bring to boil pot with the salted water.
2. Add artichokes and boil for 2 - 3 minutes.
3. Reduce heat; simmer, covered, for about 20-30 minutes.
4. Cut artichokes in quarters and place in a salad bowl.
5. Add green beans, eggs quartered, scallions, dill, mint, caper and olives.

For the Dressing:

1. In a bowl, combine olive oil, salt, pepper, lemon juice and stir well.
2. Pour dressing over the artichokes salad and toss to combine well.
3. Serve immediately.

Nutrition information:

Calories: 348 Carbohydrates: 12g Proteins: 21g Fat: 24g Fiber: 2.4g

Tuna - Avocado Salad with Mayo-Mustard Dressing

Serves: 4, Preparation: 15 minutes

Ingredients

1 avocado, sliced
6 oz. of tuna fish in water
1 tomato, coarsely chopped
1 green onion, chopped
3 tbs. fresh basil, finely chopped
1 tsp. chives, chopped, for garnish

For the sauce

1 tbsp. stone-ground mustard
2 tbs. mayonnaise
1 tsp. apple cider vinegar
Sea salt and ground black pepper to taste

Instructions

1. Place the tuna fish, tomato, onion, avocado, basil in a shallow bowl and stir well.

For the Dressing:

1. In a small bowl stir the mayonnaise, mustard and apple cider vinegar and salt and pepper.
2. Pour the sauce over the salad.
3. Taste and adjust salt and pepper to taste.
4. Sprinkle with chopped chives and serve.

Nutrition information:

Calories: 292 Carbohydrates: 9g Proteins: 33g Fat: 14g Fiber: 5.4g

Chicken Salad with Dandelion Greens

Serves: 6, Preparation: 10 minutes

Ingredients

10 oz. dandelion greens, trimmed and thinly sliced
1/4 cup extra-virgin olive oil
3 tbsp. fresh lemon juice (about 2 small lemons)
Sea salt and freshly ground black pepper, to taste
1 cooked chicken breast, sliced

Instructions

1. Clean and rinse from any dirt dandelion greens and add in a large salad bowl.
2. Add sliced chicken breast in a salad bowl; toss. Season the chicken with the salt.
3. Whisk the olive oil and lemon juice and pour over the salad; toss to combine well.
4. Serve immediately.

Nutrition information:

Calories: 122 Carbohydrates: 5 g Proteins: 4g Fat: 9.5g Fiber: 1.7g

Delicious Avocado Puree

Serves: 8, Preparation: 15 minutes

Ingredients

4 large avocados
Juice of 1 lemon
1 medium onion, finely chopped
1 large tomato, finely chopped
Salt to taste
1 cup of fresh parsley, finely chopped

Instructions

1. Peel and cut avocado in the middle.
2. Remove the pit with a teaspoon, remove the flesh and place into a bowl.
3. Add the onion and tomato and drizzle with lemon juice.
4. Place the mixture in a blender and blend until softened.
5. Season with the salt and blend for an additional 20 seconds.
6. Transfer the avocado pour into glass bowl and sprinkle with chopped parsley.
7. Refrigerate until serving.

Nutrition information:

Calories: 170 Carbohydrates: 8.8g Proteins: 2.4g Fat: 14g Fiber: 7g

Festive Red Cabbage Salad

Serves: 6, Preparation: 15 minutes

Ingredients

1 lb. red cabbage, finely chopped or shredded
2 garlic cloves, finely sliced
4 slices crispy bacon, crumbled
1/2 cup olive oil
2 tbsp. fresh lemon juice
1/2 tsp. mustard seeds
1/2 tsp. tarragon

Instructions

1. Rinse cabbage and clean from any dirt or yellow outer leaves.
2. Place the cabbage in a food processor and finely chopped or shred.
3. Place shredded cabbage in a large salad bowl.
4. Sprinkle with the salt and pepper; add crumbled bacon and sliced garlic. Toss to combine well.
5. In a small bowl, whisk the olive oil, lemon juice, mustard seeds and tarragon.
6. Pour dressing over cabbage salad and toss to combine well.
7. Serve.

Nutrition information:

Calories: 200 Carbohydrates: 8.5g Proteins: 6.3g Fat: 15.5g Fiber: 4.3g

Garlic Sauce for Poultry

Serves: 6, Preparation: 5 minutes

Ingredients

1 cup olive oil
1/2 cup fresh lemon juice
6 large garlic cloves, finely chopped
Salt and freshly ground black pepper to taste
1 peel from one lemon
1/4 tsp. dried sage
1/4 tsp. dried marjoram
1/4 tsp. nutmeg

Instructions

1. Add all ingredients in a high-speed blender; blend for 15 - 20 seconds or until all ingredients combined well.
2. Pour in a glass container, cover and refrigerate before serving.
3. Serve with any kind of poultry.

Nutrition information:

Calories: 338 Carbohydrates: 1g Proteins: 2.6g Fat: 36g Fiber: 0.3g

Tuna and Green Salad a la Italian

Serves: 8, Preparation: 10 minutes

Ingredients

10 oz. salad greens of your choice
1 can (11 oz.) artichoke hearts, drained and quartered

1 can (11 oz.) tuna in water or oil, drained, flaked
1/2 lbs. green beans, cooked, drained
1 pinch salt to taste

1 cup Italian dressing
Instructions
1. Place all ingredients from the list above in a large salad bowl.
2. Pour Italian dressing, and gently stir to combine evenly.

3. Taste and adjust salt if needed.
4. Serve immediately.
Nutrition information:
Calories: 167 Carbohydrates: 7.6g Proteins: 12 g Fat: 9.8g Fiber: 2.8g

Hearty Autumn Salad

Serves: 4, Preparation: 10 minutes
Ingredients
For the salad:
2 cups of lettuce of your choice
1 avocado
1 carrot
1/2 cup of almonds, finely chopped
For the vinaigrette:
4 tbsp. olive oil
2 tbsp. lemon juice, freshly squeezed
1 - 2 tbsp. mayonnaise
Salt and black pepper to taste

Instructions
1. Rinse and chop lettuce, peel avocado and carrot, and place all together in a large salad bowl.
2. In a bowl, whisk all ingredients for dressing.
3. Sprinkle almonds over salad.
4. Pour dressing and toss to combine well.
5. Serve immediately.
Nutrition information:
Calories: 223 Carbohydrates: 8.7g Proteins: 3.8g Fat: 19.5g Fiber: 6g

Homemade Spicy Harissa Paste

Serves: 6, Preparation: 15 minutes, Cooking Time: 10 minutes
Ingredients
5 red chili peppers
2 tbsp. extra-virgin olive oil
4 cloves of garlic, sliced
2 tsp. cumin seeds
2 tsp. coriander seeds
2 tbsp. white wine
3 tbsp. chopped fresh parsley
Salt to taste
Instructions
1. Heat the oil in a nonstick skillet and fry the chili peppers for 2-3 minutes.
2. Put peppers in a bowl, cover with aluminum foil and allow it to cool.
3. In a skillet roast the cumin and coriander seeds

for 2 minutes.
4. When the peppers cooled down completely, remove the peel with gloves and cut them in the middle to remove the seeds.
5. Place cleaned peppers in mortar along with garlic, cumin and coriander seeds; beat until you get a smooth mixture.
6. Stir in the wine, add a little bit of oil and beat until you get a smooth paste.
7. Add chopped parsley and season the salt.
8. Serve or keep refrigerated.
Nutrition information:
Calories: 27 Carbohydrates: 4g Proteins: 1.1g Fat: 1g Fiber: 1g

Keto Canary Island Red Sauce

Serves: 6, Preparation: 10 minutes, Cooking Time:10 minutes
Ingredients
2 large red bell peppers, cut into chunks
1 bunch fresh cilantro
3 cloves garlic
1 tbsp. ground sweet paprika
1/4 cup olive oil
1 chili pepper
2 tbsp. ground almonds
Instructions

1. Combine all ingredients in a blender; blend until finely smooth.
2. Place in a glass jar and refrigerate for 1 hour.
3. Serve.
Nutrition information:
Calories: 101 Carbohydrates: 4.2g Proteins: 0.8g Fat: 9.2g Fiber: 1.4g

Keto Hollandaise Sauce

Serves: 4, Preparation: 5 minutes, Cooking Time: 10 minutes

Ingredients

3 egg yolks
1/4 cup water
2 tbsp. lemon juice, freshly squeezed
1/2 cup cold butter, cut into 8 pieces
1/8 tsp. cayenne pepper
1/8 tsp. paprika
Salt to taste

Instructions

1. Separate the eggs. Heat the egg yolks, water and lemon juice in a small saucepan over low heat.

2. Cook, stirring constantly, until the mixture begins to bubble.

3. Add the butter and stir until melted and sauce is thickened.

4. Add the paprika and cayenne pepper, and season with the salt to taste.

5. Remove from heat and allow it to cool.

6. Serve. Keep refrigerated.

Nutrition information:

Calories: 246 Carbohydrates: 1g Proteins: 2.3g Fat: 26.4g Fiber: 0.1g

Nutty Sauce for a Roast

Serves: 6, Preparation: 5 minutes, Cooking Time: 2 hours

Ingredients

1 cup bone broth (if preferred, can use homemade)
1 cup water
1 cup red wine
1 tbsp. fresh parsley, finely chopped
1 tbsp. fresh basil, finely chopped
1/3 cup ground almonds
1 tbsp. fresh butter
Lemon juice, to taste
Salt and freshly ground white pepper to taste

Instructions

1. Add all ingredients to the inner pot in the crock pot.

2. Cover and cook on Low setting for 1 - 2 hours.

3. Serve warm or cold.

4. Keep refrigerated.

Nutrition information:

Calories: 84 Carbohydrates: 1.5g Proteins: 1.5g Fat: 8g Fiber: 1g

Keto Mock Hollandaise Sauce

Serves: 6, Preparation: 5 minutes, Cooking Time: 10 minutes

Ingredients

2 egg whites
1 cup mayonnaise
2 tbsp. lemon juice, freshly squeezed
1/2 tsp. dry mustard
Salt to taste

Instructions

1. Separate the eggs.

2. In a saucepan, beat slightly the egg whites.

3. Add mayonnaise, lemon juice, dry mustard, and salt; beat until combined well.

4. Place the saucepan over medium-low heat and stirring constantly, cook the sauce until thick, but do not boil.

5. Remove the saucepan from the heat and let it cool.

6. Serve or keep refrigerated.

Nutrition information:

Calories: 34 Carbohydrates: 3.2g Proteins: 1.3g Fat: 1g Fiber: 0.1g

Marinated Olives

Serves: 4, Preparation: 5 minutes, Cooking Time:

Ingredients
24 large olives, black and green
2 tbsp. extra-virgin olive oil
2 tbsp. red wine
2 cloves garlic, thinly sliced
2 tsp. coriander seeds, crushed
1/2 tsp. crushed red pepper
1 tsp. dried thyme
1 tsp. dried rosemary, crushed

Instructions
1. Place olives and all remaining ingredients in a large container or bag and shake to combine well.
2. Cover and refrigerate to marinate overnight.
3. Serve.

Nutrition information:
Calories: 102 Carbohydrates: 2.7g Proteins: 0.5g Fat: 10g Fiber: 1.5g

Béchamel Sauce for Seafood

Serves: 4, Preparation: 5 minutes, Cooking Time: 10 minutes

Ingredients
3 egg yolks
1 cup Béchamel sauce
1/4 cup whipping cream
1 tsp. lemon juice, freshly squeezed
1/4 cup grated Parmesan cheese

For Béchamel Sauce
2 tablespoons butter
2 tablespoons coconut flour
1 1/4 cups almond milk, heated
Salt and freshly ground pepper to taste

Instructions
1. In a small saucepan, heat almond milk.
2. Meanwhile, make the Béchamel sauce. In a medium saucepan, melt butter, then add flour while whisking until it is combined into a paste. Add heated almond milk, stirring until it thickens. Bring to a boil, then lower heat and continue to cook for 2-3 minutes longer. Then remove from heat and set aside.
3. In another saucepan, whisk eggs yolks with the whipping cream.
4. Add the Béchamel sauce and simmer over low heat; stir to avoid the sauce burning.
5. Remove from heat and stir in grated cheese. Serve.

Nutrition information:
Calories: 252 Carbohydrates: 1.6g Protein: 6.3g Fat: 24.8g Fiber: 0g

Mushrooms and Wine Steak Sauce

Serves: 8, Preparation: 5 minutes, Cooking Time: 15 minutes

Ingredients
3 tbsp. fresh butter
4 oz. fresh button mushrooms, rinsed
1/4 cup onion, finely chopped
1 clove garlic, minced
1 cup bone broth (if preferred use homemade)
1 1/2 tbsp. grated tomato
1/8 tsp. ground black pepper, freshly ground
2 tsp. almond flour
1 tbsp. water
2 tbsp. dry red wine

Instructions
1. Heat butter in a saucepan over medium heat. Add mushrooms, onion and garlic; sauté for about 3 - 4 minutes.
2. Stir in bone broth, tomato paste and black pepper. Bring to the boil; reduce heat to low and simmer, covered, for 5 minutes.
3. Blend the almond flour with water. Add some of the hot mushroom sauce into almond mixture and return to saucepan.
4. Pour wine and stir sauce until thickened.
5. Serve hot or cold.
6. Keep refrigerated.

Nutrition information:
Calories: 75 Carbohydrates: 1.4g Proteins: 5g Fat: 5.5g Fiber: 0.4g

Black Olive Paste

Serves: 4 , Preparation: 5 minutes, Cooking Time: 15 minutes

Ingredients
1/2 lbs. black olives, pitted
4 tbsp. capers
2 cloves garlic, finely chopped
2 tbsp. mustard
1/2 cup of olive oil
Freshly ground black pepper
Fresh thyme (optional)

Instructions

1. Place all ingredients in a high-speed blender and blend until smooth.
2. Place in a glass jar or container and refrigerate for 2 hours.
3. Serve.

Nutrition information:
Calories: 125 Carbohydrates: 6.2g Proteins: 1.5g Fat: 11g Fiber: 4g

Roasted Radicchio Salad

Serves: 4, Preparation: 10 minutes, Cooking Time: 20 minutes

Ingredients
1 lb. radicchio,cut in wedges
1/4 cup olive oil
1 tbsp. fresh thyme, chopped
2 tbsp. lemon juice, freshly squeezed
Salt and pepper to taste

Instructions
1. Preheat oven to 450⁰F.
2. Cut radicchio into wedges and rinse in cold water; gently shake off excess water.
3. Place radicchio in large bowl; drizzle with olive oil, sprinkle with thyme, salt, and pepper and toss to coat.
4. Arrange radicchio wedges on rimmed baking sheet.
5. Roast for about 10 - 13 minutes.
6. Stir and bake for further 6 - 7 minutes.
7. Arrange radicchio on platter, sprinkle with a pinch of salt and pepper, drizzle generously with lemon juice and serve.

Nutrition information:
Calories: 164 Carbohydrates: 5.4g Proteins: 2g Fat: 15g Fiber: 1.2g

Romaine Lettuce with Roquefort Dressing

Serves: 8, Preparation: 15 minutes, Cooking Time: 10 minutes

Ingredients
1 lb. Romaine lettuce
3 cherry tomatoes, chopped
1 green onion, sliced thin rings
1/2 cup white mushrooms, well cleaned, and thinly sliced
1/4 cup of extra-virgin olive oil
1/2 cup cream cheese (full fat)
1/3 cup Roquefort cheese
Freshly-ground black pepper, to taste

Instructions
1. Rinse and clean the lettuce and place in a salad bowl.
2. Add cherry tomatoes, green onion and mushrooms; toss to combine.
3. In a bowl, whisk the olive oil, cream cheese, ground pepper and Roquefort cheese. Pour the dressing over salad and toss to combine well.
4. Serve.

Nutrition information:
Calories: 101 Carbohydrates: 5.11g Proteins: 7g Fat: 6.5g Fiber: 2.5g

Savory and Sweet Rhubarb Puree

Serves: 4 , Preparation: 15 minutes, Cooking Time: 15 minutes

Ingredients

1 lb.rhubarb, cut into slices
2 tbsp. olive oil
2 tbsp. water
1 piece of fresh ginger, peeled, finely shredded
1/4 cup stevia sweetener, granulated
1 cinnamon stick
2 tbsp. mustard (Dijon, English, ground stone)

Instructions

1. Clean and cut rhubarb into slices.
2. Place the rhubarb into a saucepan with water, ginger, stevia sweetener and the cinnamon stick.
3. Simmer over low heat about 10 - 12 minutes or until the rhubarb is tender.
4. Remove the cinnamon stick and ginger and transfer the rhubarb mixture in a blender or food processor.
5. Blend on high to create a smooth puree.
6. Add mustard and stir for 20 - 30 seconds.
7. Serve.

Nutrition information:

Calories: 76 Carbohydrates: 6.2g Proteins: 1.5g Fat: 5g Fiber: 4.5g

Tangy Lemon and Dill Vinaigrette

Serves: 4, Preparation: 10 minutes, Cooking Time: 15 minutes

Ingredients

4 tbsp. white wine vinegar
4 tbsp. Dijon mustard
4 tbsp. fresh dill, chopped
2 tsp. finely chopped garlic
2 fresh lemon juice, or to taste
1/3 cup extra-virgin olive oil
Salt and freshly ground black pepper to taste

Instructions

1. Stir vinegar and mustard together in a small bowl until smooth.
2. Stir the dill, chopped garlic, and lemon juice into vinegar mixture.
3. Slowly, pour the olive oil into the mixture while whisking continuously until the dressing is creamy and smooth.
4. Season with the salt and ground black pepper.
5. Ready!

Nutrition information:

Calories: 189 Carbohydrates: 3.7g Proteins: 1g Fat: 19g Fiber: 0.5g

Chapter 5 Snack Food Recipes

"Crocked" Button Mushrooms

Serves: 6, Preparation: 5 minutes, Cooking Time: 10 minutes

Ingredients

1 1/2 lbs. fresh button mushrooms, rinsed
1 cup white wine
2 tbsp. vinegar
1/2 cup olive oil
1/2 tsp. garlic powder
Salt and freshly ground pepper to taste
1 dash hot pepper powder
1 pinch parsley flakes
1 pinch of dry basil

Instructions

1. In a large pot, place all ingredients and cook for 3 - 4 minutes on Medium-high heat.
2. Remove from the heat and allow to cool completely.
3. Place mushrooms in colander to drain.
4. Serve or keep refrigerated.

Nutrition information:

Calories: 200 Carbohydrates: 4.5g Proteins: 4g Fat: 18.5g Fiber: 1.2g

Baked Almond Crusted Zucchini Slices

Serves: 6, Preparation: 15 minutes, Cooking Time: 15 minutes

Ingredients

2 large zucchinis, sliced
1 cup almond flour
1 egg
Sea salt and ground black pepper to taste
1 tsp. garlic powder
1 tsp. onion powder
1 tsp. fresh thyme, chopped fine

Instructions

1. Preheat oven to 450⁰F.
2. Line a baking sheet with parchment paper and set aside.
3. In a bowl, beat the egg.
4. In a separate bowl, combine almond flour, salt and black pepper, garlic and onion powder, thyme.
5. Dip zucchini slices in the egg and let excess drip off, drop in the almond flour mixture to coat.
6. Place coated zucchini slices onto prepared baking sheet.
7. Bake for 13 - 15 minutes flipping once.
8. Serve warm.

Nutrition information:

Calories: 173 Carbohydrates: 6g Proteins: 8g Fat: 13g Fiber: 3.4g

Mini Bacon-Chicken Skewers

Serves: 6, Preparation: 15 minutes, Cooking Time: 35 minutes

Ingredients

2 chicken breast fillets, cut into cubes
Salt and ground pepper to taste
10 slices of bacon
1 cup of cream cheese
1 cup of yogurt
2 tbsp. mayonnaise
2 tbsp. mustard

Instructions

1. Cut the chicken into small pieces; season the salt and pepper.
2. In a bowl, combine mayonnaise, yogurt, mustard, and the salt and pepper.
3. Add the chicken pieces and stir.
4. Cover and refrigerate for 2 - 3 hours.
5. Preheat the oven to 360⁰F.
6. Cut bacon into bits.
7. Thread chicken and bacon on skewers one after another.
8. Place the chicken-bacon skewers in a baking dish.
9. Bake for 15 minutes, and then, turn and bake for further 10 minutes.
10. Serve hot.

Nutrition information:

Calories: 542 Carbohydrates: 3g Proteins: 29g Fat: 46g Fiber: 0.2g

Grilled Goat Skewers with Yogurt Marinade

Serves: 4, Preparation: 20 minutes, Cooking Time: 10 minutes

Ingredients

1 lb. boneless goat loin, cut into 1/2 cubes
Marinade
1 tbsp. lemon juice
1 cup yogurt
1/4 tsp. ground ginger
1/2 tsp. turmeric
1/2 tsp. ground cumin
1 tbsp. ground coriander
1/2 tsp. salt

Instructions

1. Cut boneless goat loin, cut into 1/2 cubes.
2. In a bowl, whisk together all ingredients for marinade. Add the goat to the bowl and stir to coat with the marinade evenly. Cover and refrigerate overnight.
3. Remove the bowl with marinated goat 15 - 20 minutes before grilling.
4. Preheat your grill to High according to manufacturer instructions.
5. Remove the meat from the marinade, and dry on kitchen paper towel. Thread goat meat on skewers.
6. Grill for about 4 - 5 minutes on each side.
7. Serve hot.

Nutrition information:

Calories: 131 Carbohydrates: 1.4g Proteins: 24g Fat: 3g Fiber: 1g

Pancetta Muffins

Serves: 12, Preparation: 15 minutes, Cooking Time:15minutes

Ingredients

6 slices pancetta cut in small cubes
2 cups of almond flour
2 tsp. baking soda
1/4 tsp. salt
2 tbsp. spring onion chopped (only white parts)
1 1/2 cups grated Parmesan cheese
1 1/2 tsp. ground allspice
2 eggs
3/4 cup almond milk (unsweetened)
1/2 cup olive oil
1 cup water

Instructions

1. Lightly grease a muffin cups; set aside.
2. In a bowl, stir the almond flour, baking soda, salt, allspice powder, spring onion, parmesan cheese and pancetta.
3. In a second bowl, whisk almond milk, eggs, olive oil, and salt.
Combine the almond flour mixture with eggs mixture and stir well.
4. Pour the batter in muffins cups (3/4 of each muffins cup).
5. Pour water to the inner stainless-steel pot in the crock pot, and place the trivet inside (steam rack or a steamer basket).
6. Place the muffins cups on trivet, cover and cook on High for 2 - 3 hours.
7. Serve warm or cold.

Nutrition information:

Calories: 233 Carbohydrates: 1.5g Proteins: 8g Fat: 22g Fiber: 0.1g

Almond Ginger Stir-Fry

Serves: 4, Preparation: 5 minutes, Cooking Time: 20 minutes

Ingredients

2 tbsp. olive oil
1 cup whole almonds
2 cloves garlic, halved
1 lb. button mushrooms
2-3 tsp. minced fresh ginger
1/3 cup water
3 tbsp. coconut aminos
2 tbsp. almond flour
Salt to and d black pepper to taste

Instructions

1. Heat the olive oil in large skillet over medium heat.
2. Add almonds and cook and stir for about 8 minutes until lightly browned.
3. Remove almonds with slotted spoon on a plate and set aside.
4. In a same skillet add little oil, and sauté garlic with a pinch of salt for 2 - 3 minutes.

5. Add mushrooms and ginger, and. stir-fry about 5 minutes.
6. In small bowl combine water, coconut aminos and almond flour and mix thoroughly.
7. Add the mixture to skillet; cook and toss about 2 minutes.
8. Taste and adjust the salt and pepper.
9. Serve hot.

Nutrition information:
Calories: 343 Carbohydrates: 8g Proteins: 17g Fat: 27g Fiber: 5g

Chili Almond Coated Turkey Bites

Serves: 6, Preparation: 15 minutes, Cooking Time: 20 minutes

Ingredients
1 lb. ground turkey
3 tbsp. mayonnaise
2 tbsp. onion grated
2 tbsp. parsley minced
Salt to taste
3 drops of hot pepper sauce as Tabasco (optional)
4 tbsp. ground almonds

Instructions

1. In a bowl, stir all ingredients except almonds until well combined.
2. Shape the mixture into small bite-size pieces and roll in ground nuts.
3. Cover and refrigerate until serving.

Nutrition information:
Calories: 190 Carbohydrates: 4g Proteins: 16.5g Fat: 12g Fiber: 0.8g

Cold Cheese Dip

Serves: 6, Preparation: 15 minutes, Cooking Time: 5 minutes

Ingredients
4 bacon slices, cooked and crumbled
2 tbs. chopped green onions
1 cup shredded Swiss or Beaufort (or gruyere) cheese
3/4 cup cream cheese, softened
1/2 cup mayonnaise
1/2 tsp. yellow mustard
1/8 tsp. freshly ground black pepper

Instructions
1. In a skillet fry the bacon until crispy; remove

from heat and let cool on kitchen paper towel.
2. Chop green onion in thin slices.
3. Combine all ingredients in a large bowl, along with crumbled bacon, and stir with a spoon.
4. Cover ball with plastic membrane and refrigerate for 2 hours.
5. Serve.

Nutrition information:
Calories: 347 Carbohydrates: 3g Proteins: 9.5g Fat: 33g Fiber: 0.1g

Creamy Chicken Topped Cucumbers

Serves: 18, Preparation: 15 minutes, Cooking Time: 5 minutes

Ingredients
8 oz. chicken breast, finely chopped
4 tbsp. mayonnaise
2 tbsp. yellow mustard
2 tbsp. green onions, finely chopped
1/8 tsp. garlic powder
Ground black pepper to taste
3 cucumbers, cut into thin slices

Instructions
1. Line a shallow dish with the parchment paper.
2. Slice cucumbers into thin slices and place on a

dish.
3. In a bowl, combine chicken, mayonnaise, mustard, green onion, garlic powder and ground black pepper.
4. Top each cucumber slice with 1 or 1 1/2 tablespoon chicken mixture.
5. Refrigerate for 2 hours or more and serve.

Nutrition information:
Calories: 28 Carbohydrates: 2g Proteins: 1.5g Fat: 2g Fiber: 0.5g

Baby Bella Mushrooms Stuffed with Olives

Serves: 10, Preparation: 15 minutes, Cooking Time: 10 minutes

Ingredients

20 Baby bella mushrooms
2 cups cream cheese, at room temperature
20 olives green or black
1/4 cup fresh parsley, finely chopped
1/2 tsp.salt and ground black pepper

Instructions

1. In a bowl, stir well cream cheese.
2. Shape balls from cream cheese and put one olive in a center.

3.Place mushrooms on a serving plate and place the cream cheese balls on each mushroom.
4. Generously sprinkle with chopped parsley.
5. Refrigerate for 4 - 6 hours.
6. Serve cold.

Nutrition information:

Calories: 183 Carbohydrates: 3,5g Proteins: 4g Fat: 17g Fiber: 0,7g

Curry Seasoned Almonds

Serves: 12, Preparation: 15 minutes, Cooking Time: 5 minutes

Ingredients

1 tbsp. curry powder
1 tbsp. chili powder
1 1/2 tbsp. celery salt
1 tbsp. stevia sweetener, granulated
2 tbsp. olive oil
1 lb. whole almonds

Instructions

1. In a bowl, combine curry and chili powder, celery salt and stevia; set aside.
2. Heat the olive oil in a large frying skillet and

fry almonds for 2 - 3 minutes (stir frequently).
3. Sprinkle almonds curry mixture and stir until well coated.
4. Transfer almonds on a baking pan and let cool for 15 minutes.
5. Serve.

Nutrition information:

Calories: 236 Carbohydrates: 7g Proteins: 7.2g Fat: 20g Fiber: 4g

Dark Avocado Bars

Serves: 8, Preparation: 15 minutes, Cooking Time: 5 minutes

Ingredients

1/2 cup coconut oil, melted
3 tbsp. coconut butter
2 medium avocados
1/3 cup dark cacao nibs (60% - 69% cacao solid)
1/4 cup stevia sweetener, granulated
1 tsp. pure vanilla extract

Instructions

1. Melt coconut oil, coconut butter, avocados, cacao, stevia and vanilla in microwave oven for 10 - 13 seconds.

2. Line with parchment paper a large shallow dish and pour the coconut mixture.
3. Freeze for 4 hours or overnight.
4. Remove dish from freezer and cut into pieces. Serve.
5. Store in a container and keep in freezer.

Nutrition information:

Calories: 228 Carbohydrates: 5.5g Proteins: 2g Fat: 22g Fiber: 3.7g

Fried Kale Fritters

Serves: 4, Preparation: 10 minutes, Cooking Time: 10 minutes

Ingredients

1 cup almond flour
1/4 cup water
1 green chili, chopped finely
1/4 tsp. red chili powder
1/4 tsp. turmeric powder
1 tsp. cumin seed powder

Ground black pepper
1 tsp. cooking soda
1 bunch of kale, finely chopped
1/2 cup olive oil for frying

Instructions

1. In a large bowl, combine the almond flour,

water, chili pepper, soda and the spices and stir well.
2. Add kale to the almond flour mixture and toss to coat well.
3. Heat the oil in a large frying pan on high-medium heat.
4. Scoop a tablespoon of the mixture and place in a pan.

5. Fry kale until golden color and crisp from both sides.
6. Remove kale fritters with slotted spoon and place on plate lined with absorbent paper.
7. Serve hot.
Nutrition information:
Calories: 187 Carbohydrates: 9g Proteins: 4g Fat: 15g Fiber: 2.6g

Frozen Coconut Mocha Smoothie

Serves: 2, Preparation: 10 minutes, Cooking Time: 10 minutes

Ingredients
2 cups unsweetened coconut milk, canned
2 tsp. instant coffee granules
1 tsp. cocoa powder
2 - 3 tbsp. natural sweetener (such Stevia, Truvia)
1/2 tsp. vanilla extract
1 cup ice cubes, crushed (optional)
Instructions
1. Add all ingredients in a blender and blend until combined well.

2. Pour the mixture in a freezer-safe container and freeze for about 4 hours.
3. Remove from the fridge 15 minutes before serving.
4. Give a good stir and serve.
Nutrition information:
Calories: 489 Carbohydrates: 8g Proteins: 5g Fat: 48.5g Fiber: 1g

Goat Cheese Spread

Serves: 6, Preparation: 10 minutes, Cooking Time: 10 minutes

Ingredients
1 cup goat cheese, crumbled
1 cup of cream cheese
1/4 cup plain yogurt
1 clove of garlic, sliced
1 tbsp. chopped chives
1/2 tsp. dried thyme
Salt and freshly ground black pepper to taste
Instructions

1. In a bowl, combine all ingredients until thoroughly combined.
2. Refrigerate the mixture for 3 - 4 hours.
3. Serve cold.
Nutrition information:
Calories: 143 Carbohydrates: 3.5g Proteins: 13g Fat: 8.5g Fiber: 3g

Hot Bacon Bombs

Serves: 8, Preparation: 15 minutes, Cooking Time: 10 minutes

Ingredients
3 slices bacon crumbled
3 slices pancetta, cut in small cubes
1 cup cream cheese
1 chili pepper
Hot smoked paprika
1/2 tsp. dried basil
1/4 tsp. onion powder
1/4 tsp. garlic powder
Salt and pepper to taste
Instructions

1. In a bowl, stir all ingredients until combined well.
2. Shape mixture into balls and place on a baking sheet lined with parchment paper.
3. Refrigerate for at least 4 hours.
4. Serve cold.
5. Keep refrigerated.
Nutrition information:
Calories: 221 Carbohydrates: 6.5g Proteins: 6g Fat: 19g Fiber: 1g

Keto Buffalo Cauliflower

Serves: 6, Preparation: 10 minutes, Cooking Time: 35 minutes

Ingredients
1 tbsp. fresh butter, softened
2 tbsp. olive oil
1 cup water
1 cup coconut aminos (soy sauce substitute)
1 cup almond flour
1 tsp. garlic powder
1/2 tsp. onion powder
1 tsp. salt and ground black pepper to taste
1 large head of cauliflower, cut into florets

Instructions
1. Preheat oven to 400⁰F.

2. Add all ingredients except cauliflower in a blender; blend until smooth.
3. Place the cauliflower florets in oiled large rimmed baking sheet and pour the sauce to over them.
4. Bake in the oven for 30 - 35 minutes.
5. Serve hot or cold.

Nutrition information:
Calories: 87 Carbohydrates: 3g Proteins: 3g Fat: 7g Fiber: 1g

Keto Choco Mousse

Serves: 3, Preparation: 15 minutes, Cooking Time: 35 minutes

Ingredients
4 tbsp. cocoa powder, unsweetened
1 1/2 cups coconut oil, melted
1/4 cup of heavy cream
3 tbsp. stevia granulated sweetener (or to taste)
1 tbsp. pure vanilla extract
Shredded coconut, unsweetened

Ingredients
1. Melt the coconut oil in a microwave oven.
2. In a mixing bowl, beat the coconut oil and

heavy cream with an electric mixer about 3 - 4 minutes or until soft and creamy.
3. Add the remaining ingredients and mix on Low speed for 2-3 minutes until the mixture is thick.
4. Serve with unsweetened shredded coconut.

Nutrition information:
Calories: 234 Carbohydrates: 6g Proteins: 2g Fat: 23g Fiber: 2g

Peanut Cinnamon Bombs

Serves: 12, Preparation: 10 minutes, Cooking Time:

Ingredients
3/4 cup coconut oil, melted
3/4 cup peanut butter
3/4 cup butter, salted and melted
3/4 cup of natural sweetener (such as Stevia, Truvia)
1/2 tsp. cinnamon
4 tbsp. cocoa powder
1/4 cup peanut, ground

Instructions
1. Melt the coconut butter in a microwave oven for 20 -25 seconds.

2. Place all ingredients in your fast-speed blender except ground peanuts; and blend to combine well.
3. Make small balls and roll each ball in a ground peanut.
4. Place on a baking sheet lined with parchment paper. Freeze for 3 hours.
5. Serve and enjoy!

Nutrition information:
Calories: 281 Carbohydrates: 4.5g Proteins: 5g Fat: 27g Fiber: 2g

Roasted Cheesy Snacks

Serves: 6, Preparation: 15 minutes, Cooking Time: 15 minutes

Ingredients

1 tbsp. almond butter, unsweetened
1/2 cups of almond flour
1 1/2 cups of Parmesan cheese
1/4 tsp. fresh oregano, finely chopped
1/4 tsp. rosemary, finely chopped
1/4 tsp. fresh basil, finely chopped
1 large egg

Instructions

1. Preheat the oven to 350⁰F.
2. In a bowl, combine the almond flour, almond butter and grated Parmesan cheese.
3. Add fresh herbs and stir well.
4. Add the egg and stir again.
5. Scoop a tablespoon of mixture and place on a baking sheet lined with parchment paper.
6. Bake for 12 - 15 minutes.
7. Remove from the oven and allow to cool.
8. Serve.

Nutrition information:

Calories: 119 Carbohydrates: 1.3g Proteins: 10g Fat: 8g Fiber: 0.3g

Roasted Kale Chips with Lemon Zest

Serves: 4, Preparation: 10 minutes, Cooking Time: 15 minutes

Ingredients

3/4 lbs. kale
2 tbsp. olive oil
2 tsp. lemon juice, freshly squeezed
2 tbsp. lemon zest from about 2 large lemons
Kosher salt

Instructions

1. Preheat the oven to 350⁰F.
2. Place the kale leaves on a baking sheet and pour the olive oil and lemon juice. Season with the salt and sprinkle the lemon zest.
3. Bake for 10 - 15 minutes, turning 2 - 3 times, do not burn.
4. Serve warm or cold.

Nutrition information:

Calories: 132 Carbohydrates: 6g Proteins: 9g Fat: 8g Fiber: 2g

Roasted Smoky Spiced Almonds

Serves: 6, Preparation: 10 minutes, Cooking Time: 1 hour

Ingredients

1 cup stevia granulate sweetener (or to taste)
2 tbsp. water
1/2 tsp. smoked paprika
1/4 tsp. cayenne pepper
3/4 tsp. seasoned salt
2 cups whole natural almonds

Instructions

1. Preheat oven to 350⁰F.
2. In a bowl, combine stevia sweetener, water, smoked and cayenne pepper and salt and spices in bowl.
3. Add almonds in a spice mixture, toss until combined well.
4. Spread coated almonds in a baking sheet to dry for about 1 hour.
5. Serve.

Nutrition information:

Calories: 292 Carbohydrates: 9g Proteins: 10g Fat: 24g Fiber: 5g

Savory Spinach and Mushrooms Frittata

Serves: 6, Preparation: 15 minutes, Cooking Time: 25 minutes

Ingredients

8 large eggs
1 cup almond milk, unsweetened
1 cup Parmesan cheese
Salt and pepper to taste
3 cloves garlic, minced
2 tbsp. green onions, finely sliced
1 cup spinach, frozen and drained
4 oz. mushrooms, sliced

Instructions

1. Preheat oven to 375⁰F.

2. In a large mixing bowl, combine all ingredients and whisk with the help of an electric mixer.

3. Pour the mixture into oiled baking pan and bake for 20-25 minutes, let cool on a wire rack for 15 minutes, and then cut and serve.

4. Keep refrigerated in container.

Nutrition information:

Calories: 118 Carbohydrates: 0.5g Proteins: 11g Fat: 8g Fiber: 0.5g

Spicy Spinach Squares

Serves: 14, Preparation: 15 minutes, Cooking Time: 35 minutes

Ingredients

1 cup almond flour
1/2 tsp. salt and ground black pepper
1 tsp. baking soda
1 tbsp. cayenne pepper
1 cup almond milk
2 eggs
3/4 cup fresh butter, melted and cooled
1 green oniononly white parts, finely chopped
1 lb. frozen chopped spinach, defrosted
3/4 cup grated Parmesan or cheddar cheese

Instructions

1. Preheat the oven to 350⁰F.

2. Line a baking dish with parchment paper.

3. In a bowl, combine the almond flour, salt and pepper, baking soda, and cayenne pepper until combine well.

4. Beat the almond milk, eggs, and butter with the help of electric mixer.

5. Combine almond mixture with almond milk mixture and beat again until combined well.

6. Fold in the cheese, onion and spinach and stir well with spatula.

7. Pour the mixture in a prepared baking dish, place in oven and bake for 35 minutes.

8. Let it cool and slice into squares. Keep refrigerated.

Nutrition information:

Calories: 87 Carbohydrates: 3g Proteins: 3g Fat: 7g Fiber: 1.5g

Chapter 6 Sauces, Dressing& Dip

American Jack Daniel's Sauce (Keto version)

Serves: 4, Preparation: 10 minutes, Cooking: 25 minutes

Ingredients

1 cup water
2 tsps of garlic, minced
1 1/2 cups of natural granulated sweetener, such stevia
2 tbsps of hot sauce
2 tbsps of coconut aminos (soy sauce substitute)
1 cup of lemon juice
1/4 cup of Jack Daniels Whiskey
2 tbsps of unsalted butter
1/4 tsp of cayenne pepper

Instructions

1. In a small saucepan, pour the water, garlic, stevia sweetener, hot sauce and coconut aminos.
2. Cook and stir over Moderate heat for about 15 -20 minutes until sweetener dissolve, and the sauce thickens.
3. Remove from heat and add the lemon juice, whiskey, butter and cayenne pepper; stir well until sauce is smooth and shine.
4. Let it cool and keep refrigerated in a glass container up to 3 hours.

Nutrition information:

Calories: 60 Carbohydrates: 5g Proteins: 1g Fat: 4g Fiber: 0.2g

Fresh Mushroom Sauce

Serves: 4, Preparation: 10 minutes, Cooking: 15 minutes

Ingredients

1/4 cup of garlic-infused olive oil
1 tsp of garlic, minced
1 lb. fresh white mushrooms, sliced
1 cup of cherry tomatoes, cut into halves
1/2 cup green onions (scallions), finely chopped
1/2 tsp salt and ground black pepper to taste

Instructions

1. Heat the olive oil in a frying skillet.
2. Add minced garlic along with mushrooms, and cook, stirring frequently, until mushroom liquid starts to evaporate, about 5 - 6 minutes.
3. Add cherry tomatoes, green onions, and season with the salt and black pepper.
4. Bring to boil, reduce heat, cover and cook for about 5 minutes or until the sauce is done.
5. Remove from heat and serve hot or cold.
6. Keep refrigerated in a covered glass bowl.

Nutrition information:

Calories: 118g Carbohydrates: 4g Proteins: 3g Fat: 10g Fiber: 1.3g

Spicy Citrus BBQ Sauce

Serves: 4, Preparation: 10 minutes, Cooking: 15 minutes

Ingredients

2 tbsps of olive oil
1 large onion, finely chopped
1/2 tsp of ground red pepper (cayenne)
1 chili pepper, seeded and finely chopped
1 1/2 cups lime juice (freshly squeezed)
2 tbsps of stevia granulate sweetener (or to taste)
1 tbsp of fresh cilantro, finely chopped
1/4 tsp of salt or to taste

Instructions

1. Heat the olive oil in a saucepan, and cook the onion, ground red pepper, and chili pepper, stirring frequently, until onion is tender, about 5 minutes. At this point, add all remaining ingredients.
2. Bring to boil and reduce heat to Low; cook for further 10 minutes, stirring occasionally.
3. Remove the sauce from heat and allow it to cool.
4. Serve immediately or keep refrigerated.

Nutrition information:

Calories: 65g Carbohydrates: 6g Proteins: 1g Fat: 5g Fiber: 0.7g

Italian Pesto Dip with Ground Almonds

Serves: 4, Preparation: 10 minutes

Ingredients
2 cups of fresh basil
2 cloves of garlic, minced
3 tbsps of ground almonds, salted
3/4 cup extra virgin olive oil
1 tbsp of lemon juice
Salt and ground black pepper
4 tbsps of ground Parmesan cheese

Instructions
1. Place all ingredients (except Parmesan) in a food processor and pulse until well combined.
2. Add the Parmesan cheese and pulse for 30 - 45 seconds.
3. Taste and adjust salt and pepper to taste.
4. Keep refrigerated.

Nutrition information:
Calories: 433g Carbohydrates: 3g Proteins: 4g Fat: 45g Fiber: 1g

Keto "Chimichurri" Sauce

Serves: 6, Preparation: 10 minutes

Ingredients
1/2 cup of fresh oregano leaves, finely chopped
1/2 cup of fresh parsley, finely chopped
1/2 cup fresh cilantro, finely chopped
3 fresh bay leaves
2 jalapenos peppers, chopped
3 cloves of garlic
1 tbsp of salt
1 tbsp of chili powder
1/2 cup apple cider vinegar
1/2 cup of olive oil

Instructions
1. Add ingredients from the list above in your food processor or blender.
2. Blend or process until smooth and all ingredients are united well.
3. Serve immediately or keep refrigerated.

Nutrition information:
Calories: 207g Carbohydrates: 8g Proteins: 1.2g Fat: 19g Fiber: 4g

Keto Bearnaise Sauce

Serves: 6, Preparation: 15 minutes, Cooking: 20 minutes

Ingredients
1 onion, finely chopped
1/2 cup fresh tarragon, finely chopped
2 tsps of crushed black pepper grains
1/2 cup of dry white wine
1/3 cup of vinegar
6 egg yolks
2 sticks of fresh butter
2 tsps of fresh parsley, finely chopped
Salt and ground black pepper to taste

Instructions
1. In a saucepan, combine the onions, half of tarragon, pepper grains, wine and vinegar.
2. Bring to boil and cook stirring until 1/3 of the liquid evaporates.
3. Transfer the mixture in a metal bowl. Place the bowl over heated bath (Bain-marie).
4. Add the egg yolks one by one stirring continuously until the sauce begins to thicken.
5. Add the butter cut in small pieces, stirring all the time, until the sauce becomes shiny and smooth.
6. Remove the bowl from the Bain-marie and add the remaining tarragon and chopped parsley; stir well.
7. Season the salt and pepper to taste and allow the sauce to cool. Keep refrigerated.

Nutrition information:
Calories: 356g Carbohydrates: 4g Proteins: 4g Fat: 36g Fiber: 1.2g

Mustard Sauce with Rosemary

Serves: 4, Preparation: 10 minutes, Cooking: 10 minutes

Ingredients

2/3 cup of stone ground mustard (or yellow)
2/3 cup of garlic-infused olive oil
2 tbsps of fresh rosemary
2 tsps of fresh thyme
1 tbsp of coconut aminos (soy sauce substitute)
Salt and ground black pepper to taste

Instructions

1. Pour all ingredients in a food processor or in a blender and pulse or blend for 30 - 45 seconds or until the sauce is shiny and smooth.
2. Keep refrigerated in a glass container.

Nutrition information:

Calories: 371g Carbohydrates: 3g Proteins: 2g Fat: 39g Fiber: 4g

Olive and Almond Dip

Serves: 6, Preparation: 15 minutes

Ingredients

2 cups of black olives, pitted
1/4 cup of olive oil
1/2 cup of mayonnaise
1/4 cup of ground almonds (without salt)
1 tbsp of fresh lemon juice
Pinch of salt

Instructions

1. Rinse the olives and remove pits.
2. Place olives in your fast-speed blender along with all ingredients: blend until shiny and smooth.
3. Serve immediately or keep refrigerated in a covered glass bowl.

Nutrition information:

Calories: 162g Carbohydrates: 7g Proteins: 2g Fat: 14g Fiber: 2g

Perfect Basting Sauce (for grilling chicken)

Serves: 6, Preparation: 10 minutes, Cooking: 15 minutes

Ingredients

4 cups of apple cider vinegar
1/2 cup of coconut aminos (soy sauce substitute)
1 tsp of garlic powder
1 tsp of poultry seasoning
6 bay leaves
1 tsp of crushed red pepper
1 tsp of fresh thyme (chopped fine)
1 tsp of fresh rosemary (chopped)
1 tsp of lemon pepper

Instructions

1. Combine all ingredients in a saucepan and bring to boil; stir well. Remove the saucepan from the heat, cover and let it cool completely.
2. Remove bay leaves and keep refrigerated in a glass container up to 2 hours.

Nutrition information:

Calories: 52g Carbohydrates: 1.5g Proteins: 0.2g Fat: 5g Fiber: 0.2g

Smoky Peppercorn Basting Sauce for Poultry

Serves: 4, Preparation: 10 minutes

Ingredients

1/2 cup coconut aminos or teriyaki sauce
1/4 cup mustard (Dijon, English, ground stone)
1/4 cup chicken fat, melted
1/2 tsp of coarsely ground black pepper
1/2 tsp of liquid smoke
1/8 tsp of salt and crushed red pepper flakes

Instructions

1. Combine all ingredients in a bowl, and whisk with a fork or spoon until all ingredients are well combined.
2. Keep refrigerated in a glass container or a bowl.

Nutrition information:

Calories: 153g Carbohydrates: 7g Proteins: 2g Fat: 13g Fiber: 0.2g

Yogurt Sauce with Feta and Green Onions

Serves: 4, Preparation: 5 minutes

Ingredients

2 cups of unsweetened almond milk
1 cup of chopped fresh onion
3/4 lb. crumbled feta cheese
1 cup of Greek yogurt
Juice of 2 limes
Zest from the 2 limes
1 tbsp of fresh mint leaves, finely chopped
Salt and freshly ground black pepper

Instructions

1. Heat the milk in a saucepan over Medium heat.
2. Add grated feta cheese, fresh onions, and lime juice; stir briefly to dissolve the cheese and the sauce to thicken.
3. Remove from the heat and let it cool for a while.
4. Finally, add the yogurt, mint, lemon zest and stir well.
5. Sprinkle with the salt and the freshly ground pepper and let it cool completely before serving.
6. Keep refrigerated.

Nutrition information:

Calories: 203g Carbohydrates: 4.5g Proteins: 17g Fat: 13g Fiber: 0.6g

Spicy Creamy Horseradish Dip

Serves: 4, Preparation: 10 minutes

Ingredients

1 cup whipping cream
1/2 cup freshly ground horseradish
1/2 cup mayonnaise
2 tbsps of ground stone mustard or yellow
Dash of cayenne pepper

Instructions

1. Whip cream with a hand mixer in a bowl until it forms stiff peaks.
2. Fold all remaining ingredients and mix for another 30 - 45 seconds.
3. Serve or keep refrigerated.

Nutrition information:

Calories: 230g Carbohydrates: 6g Proteins: 2g Fat: 22g Fiber: 0.01g

Spicy Citrus Sauce

Serves: 6, Preparation: 10 minutes, Cooking: 10 minutes

Ingredients

1 onion, finely chopped
1 tsp of red chili pepper (chopped)
1/4 tsp of ground red pepper
1 tbsp of olive oil
1/2 cup grapefruit juice (freshly squeezed)
1/2 cup lemon juice (freshly squeezed)
1/2 cup lime juice
5 - 6 drops of honey, liquid stevia or agave
1 tbsp of fresh cilantro

Instructions

1. Place all ingredients in a saucepan over Moderate heat.
2. Stir for 8 - 10 minutes and remove from the heat.
3. Let the sauce cool, and keep it refrigerated in a glass bowl or container.

Nutrition information:

Calories: 55g Carbohydrates: 6g Proteins: 1g Fat: 3g Fiber: 0.7g

Slow Cooker Delicious Meat Sauce

Serves: 4, Preparation: 10 minutes, Cooking: 80 minutes

Ingredients

1 tbsp of beef tallow (or beef fat reserved from cooking)
1 lb. ground beef
Salt and ground black pepper to taste
2 scallions, finely chopped
1 small hot red pepper, chopped
2 cloves of garlic (minced)
1 grated tomato
1/2 cup canned mushrooms
2 tbsps of coconut aminos (soy sauce substitute)
1 bay leaf
1 tbsp of fresh oregano (minced)

Instructions

1. Grease the inner pot of your Crock Pot with tallow.
2. Add ground beef and generously sprinkle with salt and ground pepper to taste.
3. Add all remaining ingredients and give a good stir.
4. Cover and cook on Low for 80 minutes.
5. Taste and adjust salt and pepper.
6. Serve hot.

Nutrition information:
Calories: 247g Carbohydrates: 4g Proteins: 15g Fat: 19g Fiber: 1.5g

Spicy MustardAvocado Dip

Serves: 4, Preparation: 15 minutes

Ingredients

2 large avocados
1 onion (large, finely chopped)
1/2 cup fresh cilantro, coarsely chopped
3 tbsps of fresh lemon juice
1/4 tsp of crushed red pepper flakes
Kosher salt to taste
3 tbsps of mustard (Dijon, English, ground stone)
2 tbsps of mayonnaise (optional)

Instructions

1. Slice avocado and remove the skin and a pit.
2. Place all ingredients in your high-speed blender and blend until smooth.
3. Keep refrigerated in a covered glass bowl or container.

Nutrition information:
Calories: 148g Carbohydrates: 8g Proteins: 2g Fat: 12g Fiber: 5g

Zesty and Sweet Basting Sauce

Serves: 4, Preparation: 5 minutes, Cooking: 10 minutes

Ingredients

1/4 cup onion, finely diced
1 cup chili sauce (sugar free)
10 drops of liquid stevia sweetener
1 tbsp of ground stone mustard
1 tbsp of Worcestershire sauce
1/4 cup dry red wine

Instructions

1. Combine all ingredients from the list above in saucepan; bring to boil and stir periodically.
2. Reduce heat to Low and cook for further 5 minutes.
3. You can use this sauce for basting or as a dipping sauce.

Nutrition information:
Calories: 45g Carbohydrates: 8g Proteins: 1g Fat: 1g Fiber: 0.3g

Chapter 7 Soup & Stew Recipes

Antioxidant Cabbage Soup

Serves: 6, Preparation: 10 minutes, Cooking: 45 minutes

Ingredients

2 tbsps of olive oil
1 small onion, cut in slices
2 cloves of garlic
1 red bell pepper
3 sticks of celery
1 tbsp of tomato paste
1 lb of cabbage, roughly chopped
1 tbsp of coconut aminos (soy sauce substitute)
1 tsp of fresh oregano
1 cup of bone broth
3 cups of water
Salt and ground black pepper
Juice from 1 lemon

Instructions

1. Heat the olive oil in a deep pot at Medium temperature.
2. Sauté the onion, garlic, bell pepper and celery for 3 minutes.
3. Add the tomato paste and sauté for 1 - 3 minutes.
4. Add chopped cabbage and add all remaining ingredients; give a good stir to combine well.
5. Cover and cook at Medium-low temperature for 30 - 40 minutes.
6. Taste and adjust seasonings to taste. Serve warm.

Nutrition information:
Calories: 115g Carbohydrates: 10.2g Proteins: 3g Fat: 7.3g Fiber: 3.5g

Winter Cabbage and Celery Soup

Serves: 4, Preparation: 5 minutes, Cooking: 30 minutes

Ingredients

2 tbsps of olive oil
2 cloves of garlic, minced
1/2 head cabbage, shredded
2 stalks celery, chopped
1 large tomato, diced
3 cups bone broth
3 cups water
1/2 tsp ground black pepper

Instructions

1. Heat the oil in a large pot over Medium heat.
2. Sauté the garlic, celery and cabbage, stirring, for about 8 minutes.
3. Add tomato and continue to cook for further 2 - 3 minutes.
4. Pour the broth and water. Bring to a boil, lower heat to Low, cover and simmer for 20 minutes or until cabbage softened.
5. Sprinkle with ground black pepper, stir and serve.

Nutrition information:
Calories: 393g Carbohydrates: 5.3g Proteins: 5.7g Fat: 4.8g Fiber: 2g

Creamy Cauliflower Soup

Serves: 6, Preparation: 15 minutes, Cooking: 25 minutes

Ingredients

1 green onion, sliced
3 sticks of celery, chopped
2 cloves of garlic
1/4 cup of olive oil
1 head of cauliflower florets
1 tbsp of fresh ginger, finely chopped
1 tsp of ground turmeric
1 tsp of cumin
3 cups of water
1 cup of bone broth
Salt and ground pepper to taste
1 cup of canned coconut milk
1 bunch of parsley, finely chopped

Instructions

1. Heat the olive oil in a pot at Medium-high temperature, and sauté the onion, garlic and cauliflower florets for 2-3 minutes.
2. Add ginger, turmeric and cumin; stir and sauté for one minute.
3. Pour water, broth, and the salt and pepper to

taste.
4. Cover and cook for 20 minutes or until vegetables softened.
5. Transfer the mixture into your food processor or blender, and blend to make a puree.
6. Pour coconut milk and blend for further 30 - 45

seconds.
7. Taste and adjust seasonings to taste. Serve with chopped parsley.
Nutrition information:
Calories: 210g Carbohydrates: 7.8g Proteins: 4g Fat: 18g Fiber: 2.6g

Slow Cooker Beurre Blanc Sauce

Serves: 4, Preparation: 15 minutes, Cooking: 1 hour
Ingredients
4 spring onions, only white parts
1/2 cup white wine
4 tbsps of white wine vinegar
3/4 cup fresh butter, softened
1/3 cup heavy cream
1 tsp of garlic powder
Salt and ground white pepper
Instructions
1. Clean, rinse and chop spring onions (use only white parts).
2. In a saucepan, boil spring onions along with

wine and vinegar.
3. Reduce heat to Low and simmer until only one tablespoon of liquid remains.
4. Place onion along with remaining ingredients in your Slow Cooker.
5. Cover and cook on Low for 1 hour.
6. Open lid and give a good stir. Transfer in a glass jar and refrigerate until consuming.
Nutrition information:
Calories: 199g Carbohydrates: 1.5g Proteins: 1g Fat: 21g Fiber: 0.2g

Brazilian Corned Beef Stew - Keto Gourmet Dish

Serves: 4, Preparation: 10 minutes, Cooking: 20 minutes
Ingredients
1 lb of corned beef, cut into strips
12 oz of bacon, cut into cubes
2 tbsps of lard
2 small green onions, sliced
1 tbsp of chopped coriander
1 tbsp of chopped parsley
1/2 tbsp of chopped fresh chives (optional)
1/2 cup of almond flour
1/4 cup of water
Instructions
1. Soak meat in water overnight.

2. Heat the lard in a frying skillet, and fry bacon and green onions.
3. Add meat and cook for 10 minutes or until soft.
4. Make a slurry of the almond flour with water and pour over meat.
5. Sprinkle with seasonings, give a good stir, cover and cook for 7 - 8 minutes at Low heat.
6. Serve hot.
Nutrition information:
Calories: 476g Carbohydrates: 1.5g Proteins: 32g Fat: 38.6g Fiber: 0.3g

Chilly Avocado Soup

Serves: 4, Preparation: 2 hours
Ingredients
1 medium avocado, peeled and cut small cubes
1 yellow pepper, finely chopped
1 spring onion, finely chopped
4 leaves of fresh mint
1 cup coconut milk
1 tbsp of olive oil
2 tsps of cardamom
Salt to taste (optional)
Instructions

1. Wash and clean your avocado, yellow pepper and mint. Cut avocado in half, remove skin and pit.
2. Place all ingredients in a high-speed blender. Blend until completely smooth and creamy.
3. Refrigerate for 2 hours and serve cold.
Nutrition information:
Calories: 282g Carbohydrates: 13g Proteins:3.5 Fat: 24.7g Fiber: 6g

Instant Pot Chicken and Bacon Stew

Serves: 6, Preparation: 10 minutes, Cooking: 20 minutes

Ingredients

2 tbsps of olive oil

1 1/2 lbs. chicken breast, skinned boneless

4 slices bacon

1 green onion, chopped (or scallion)

2 green bell pepper, chopped

2 celery sprigs, diced

1/2 tsp of dried thyme

2 cloves of garlic, minced

2 cups of bone broth (if preferred, can use homemade)

3 tbsps of almond flour

Salt and ground black pepper to taste

Instructions

1. Press Saute button on your Instant Pot. When the word "hot" appears on the display, add the oil and sauté the chicken for about 5 minutes.

2. Add the green onions, bell pepper, celery, garlic and thyme and stir for 2 minutes.

3. Add the flour, and cook, stirring frequently two-three minutes.

4. Stir the bone broth and almond flour and pour into Instant Pot.

5. Season with the salt and ground pepper, stir and turn off the Saute button.

6. Lock lid into place and set on the Soup/Stew setting to High heat for 8 minutes.

7. When the timer beeps, press "Cancel" and carefully flip the Quick Release valve to let the pressure out.

Nutrition information:

Calories: 414g Carbohydrates: 5g Proteins: 49.5g Fat: 22g Fiber: 1,5g

Chilly Lobster Soup

Serves: 4, Preparation: 5 minutes, Cooking: 7 minutes

Ingredients

2 cans (15 oz) of lobster meat

2 tbsps of extra virgin olive oil

1 tbsp of fresh chives, chopped

1 large tomato, diced

Salt and ground pepper to taste

1/4 cup of ground almonds

2 tsps of cardamom seeds

1 cup of red wine

1 cup of water

Instructions

1. Add the lobster meat in a large pot; drizzle with extra virgin olive oil and season with the salt and pepper, cardamom and chopped chives.

2. Add grated tomato, red wine and water; cook for 6 - 7 minutes at Medium heat.

3. Add the ground almonds and stir well.

4. Adjust seasoning to taste.

5. Serve immediately.

Nutrition information:

Calories: 407g Carbohydrates: 6.4g Proteins: 80g Fat: 7.3g Fiber: 0.8g

Spicy Cabbage Soup

Serves: 6, Preparation: 5 minutes, Cooking: 15 minutes

Ingredients

1 tbsp of beef tallow

1 medium onion, chopped

2 cloves garlic, minced

1/2 medium head sliced cabbage

1 medium tomato, chopped

1 tbsp of coconut aminos (soy sauce substitute)

1/4 cup ground almonds

Salt to taste

4 cups of water

Spicy ground paprika to taste

Instructions

1. In a nonstick pan heat the tallow.

2. Sauté the onion and garlic until soft and golden brown.

3. Add grated tomato and coconut aminos; stir well.

4. Add cabbage, water, seasonings and ground almonds; cover and simmer at Medium heat for 10 minutes.

5. Add spicy ground paprika to taste and cook for further 2 - 3 minutes.

6. Adjust salt and serve hot.

Nutrition information:

Calories: 79 Carbohydrates: 8.7g Proteins: 2.3g Fat: 4.3g Fiber: 3g

Slow Cooker Thick Chicken Soup with Herbs

Serves: 6, Preparation: 10 minutes, Cooking: 5 hours 20 minutes

Ingredients

1 green onion, finely sliced
1 lb of chicken breast, boneless
1 small tomato
1 tsp of dry coriander
1 tsp of red ground paprika
1 tsp of fresh ginger, grated
Salt and ground pepper to taste
1/2 tsp of turmeric
1/4 tsp of ground cinnamon
1/2 tsp of garlic powder
1 cup water
3 tbsps of almond flour
1 1/2 tbsps of cold water

Instructions

1. Season chicken breast with the salt and pepper and place in your Crock Pot.
2. In a medium-sized bowl, combine tomatoes, coriander, paprika, ginger, turmeric, cinnamon and garlic powder; add water, stir and pour in Crock Pot.
3. Cover and cook on Low for 8 hours or at High for 4-5 hours.
4. In a small bowl, dilute the almond flour in water and pour the mixture into Crock Pot.
5. Cover again and cook on High for further 15-20 minutes or until thickened.
6. Adjust salt, stir and serve hot.

Nutrition information:
Calories: 273g Carbohydrates: 8.2g Proteins: 22.4g Fat: 17.4g Fiber: 4g

Slow Cooker Green Beans Power Soup

Serves: 4, Preparation: 5 minutes, Cooking: 8 hours

Ingredients

2 lbs. green beans - trimmed and cut diagonally in half
1 small onion, diced
1 clove garlic, minced
1 carrot, sliced
1 small zucchini (optional)
1 tbsp of grated Parmesan cheese (topping, optional)
2 tbsps of fresh cilantro, chopped
2 cups vegetable stock (or beef, chicken, bone broth)
2 cups water
1 tsp of chili powder
1 tsp of cumin
Salt and ground pepper to taste

Instructions

1. Place all ingredients in the Slow Cooker and stir well.
2. Cover and cook on Low for 6-8 hours.
3. Taste and adjust seasonings.
4. Serve hot.

Nutrition information:
Calories: 65g Carbohydrates: 9.3g Proteins: 5.6g Fat: 1g Fiber: 3.6g

Slow Cooker Keto Kimchi Soup

Serves: 6, Preparation: 10 minutes, Cooking: 3 hours

Ingredients

1/2 lb of fresh pork belly
Sea salt and black pepper or to taste
3/4 lb of Napa cabbage, chopped
1/2 cup of spring onions, finely chopped
1/4 cup of fresh button mushrooms
1 tsp of stevia sweetener
1 tsp of ground paprika
2 tbsps of coconut aminos (soy sauce substitute)
3 tbsps of sesame oil
4 cups of water

Instructions

1. Cut pork belly into pieces and season with the salt and pepper.
2. Place meat in Slow Cooker and add chopped Napa cabbage, spring onions and mushrooms.
3. In a small bowl, stir water, sesame oil, stevia, ground paprika and coconut aminos.
4. Pour mixture in your Slow Cooker over meat and vegetables.
5. Cover and cook on High for 3 hours.
6. Taste and adjust seasonings.
7. Serve.

Nutrition information:
Calories: 225g Carbohydrates: 1g Proteins: 17.7g Fat: 17g Fiber: 0.3g

Weight-Loss Cream of Broccoli Soup

Serves: 4, Preparation: 10 minutes, Cooking: 20 minutes

Ingredients

1 lb. broccoli
2 green onions, finely chopped
2 stalks of celery, chopped
1 cup cauliflower floret
3 tbsps of olive oil
½ cup heavy cream
2 cups water
1/2 tsp of garlic powder
Salt and pepper to taste

Instructions

1. In a stock pot, heat the oil and sauté the green onion and chopped celery.
2. Add in the broccoli and cauliflower.
3. Season the salt and pepper to taste and add the garlic powder.
4. Pour water into pot, stir and cook for 15 - 20 minutes.
5. When ready, pour the soup into blender and blend until the soup is smooth.
6. Serve.

Nutrition information:

Calories: 138g Carbohydrates: 7.4g Proteins: 2.9g Fat: 11g Fiber: 3g

Wild Mushroom Soup with Eggs

Serves: 4, Preparation: 5 minutes, Cooking: 20 minutes

Ingredients

2 tbsps of extra-virgin olive oil
1 lb. wild mushrooms (chanterelles or porcini)
1 scallion, finely chopped
2 garlic cloves, minced
2 cups bone broth
2 cups water
2 egg yolks
2 tbsps of lemon juice
Salt and freshly ground pepper to taste

Instructions

1. Heat the oil in a pot over Medium-high heat.
2. Add mushrooms and stir for 3 minutes; season the salt and pepper.
3. Reduce the heat to Medium, add the scallion and garlic, and cook for 3 minutes.
4. Pour the bone broth and water, stir, cover and cook for 10 - 12 minutes.
5. In a bowl, whisk egg yolks with a pinch of salt and lemon juice.
6. Pour the egg mixture in a pot, turn off heat, and stir for further 2 - 3 minutes.
7. Taste and adjust the salt and pepper to taste. Serve hot.

Nutrition information:

Calories: 145g Carbohydrates: 5g Proteins: 9.6g Fat: 9.7g Fiber: 1.3g

Spinach Soup with Shiitake mushrooms

Serves: 4, Preparation: 10 minutes, Cooking: 15 minutes

Ingredients

2 tbsps of olive oil
1 medium onion, chopped
2 cloves of garlic, minced
2 cups of water
1/2 bunch of spinach
2 cups of shiitake mushrooms, chopped
2 tbsps of almond flour
1 tbsp of coconut aminos
1 tsp coriander dry
1/2 tsp of ground mustard
Salt and ground black pepper to taste

Instructions

1. Heat the olive oil and sauté the garlic and onion until golden brown.
2. Add the coconut aminos and the mushrooms and stir for a few minutes.
3. Pour water, chopped spinach and all remaining ingredients.
4. Cover and cook for 5 - 6 minutes or until spinach is tender.
5. Taste and adjust salt and the pepper.
6. Stir for further 5 minutes and remove for the heat.
7. Serve hot.

Nutrition information:

Calories: 204g Carbohydrates: 12g Proteins: 21g Fat: 8g Fiber: 4.3g

Vegan Artichoke Soup

Serves: 4, Preparation: 15 minutes, Cooking: 1 hour 5 minutes

Ingredients

1 tbsp of butter
6 artichoke hearts, halved
2 cloves of garlic, minced
1 small onion, chopped
1 cup bone broth
2 cups of water
2 tbsps of almond flour
Salt and ground black pepper to taste
2 tbsps of olive oil
Fresh chopped parsley to taste
Fresh chopped fresh basil to taste

Instructions

1. Heat the butter in a large pot, and add artichoke hearts, garlic and chopped onion.
2. Stir and cook until artichoke hearts tender.
3. Add bone broth, water and almond flout; season with the salt and pepper.
4. Bring soup to boil and cook for 2 minutes.
5. Add little olive oil, parsley and basil, stir and cook uncovered for 1 hour.
6. When ready, push the soup through sieve.
7. Taste and adjust salt and pepper.
8. Serve.

Nutrition information:

Calories: 160g Carbohydrates: 6g Proteins: 7g Fat: 12g Fiber: 0.5%

Seafood Soup

Serves: 6, Preparation: 10 minutes, Cooking: 25 minutes

Ingredients

1/2 cup of olive oil
1 spring onion, cut in cubes
2 tbsps of fresh celery, chopped
2 cloves of garlic, minced
1 large tomato, diced
2 bay leaves
1 tsp of anise
6 large, raw shrimps
1 sea bass and 1 seabream fillets, cut in pieces; about 1 1/2 lbs.
12 mussels, rinsed in plenty of cold water
Salt and ground black pepper
3 tbsps of chopped parsley, for serving
6 cups of water

Instructions

1. Heat the olive oil in a large pot and sauté in the onion, garlic and celery for 4 -5 minutes over Medium heat.
2. Add bay leaves, anise and grated tomato; stir and cook for further 5 minutes.
3. Add shrimp and fish and pour 6 cups of water; season with little salt and pepper.
4. Cover and cook for 10 - 12 minutes on Low heat. Serve hot with chopped parsley.

Nutrition information:

Calories: 264g Carbohydrates: 2g Proteins: 19g Fat: 20g Fiber: 0.5g

Beef Stew

Serves: 4, Preparation: 5 minutes, Cooking: 1 hour 35 minutes

Ingredients

1 1/2 lbs. beef fillet, cut in cubes
1 green onion (white and green parts), chopped
2 cloves of garlic, minced
1 small carrot
1 grated tomato
1 tsp of fresh basil (chopped)
1 tsp of fresh oregano chopped
3 cups bone broth (or water)
1/2 cup white vinegar
1 tsp of salt
1 tbsp of lard

Instructions

1. Heat the lard in a large skillet and sauté beef meat with a pinch of salt.
2. Add the onion and garlic and cook until soft.
3. Add grated tomato and the carrot and stir for further 2 minutes.
4. Add all the other ingredients cover and cook on Low heat for about 1 1/2 to 1 3/4 hours until the beef is tender.
5. Serve hot.

Nutrition information:

Calories: 574g Carbohydrates: 3g Proteins: 46g Fat: 42g Fiber: 1g

Chicken and Greens Soup

Serves: 4, Preparation: 12 minutes, Cooking: 1 hour 40 minutes

Ingredients

1/4 cup of olive oil
1 1/2 lbs. chicken breast; boneless, cut into cube
1 spring onion, cut into cubes
1 clove of garlic, finely chopped
1 1/2 lettuces of choice, chopped
1 cup of fresh spinach, finely chopped
1 bunch of dill finely chopped, without the thick stalks
1/2 tbsp of sweet chill powder
1 tsp of fresh mint, chopped
1 tsp of fresh thyme, chopped
Salt and freshly ground pepper
5 cups of water

Instructions

1. In a deep pot, heat the olive oil to a High heat and sauté the chicken for about 5 - 6 minutes.
2. Add the onion and sauté for about 3 minutes until softened.
3. Add the garlic, the lettuce, spinach, dill, mint, thyme and sauté for about 3-4 minutes, stirring with a wooden spoon.
4. Sprinkle with chili, salt, freshly ground pepper and pour 5 cups of water.
5. Bring to boil and cook for 1 1/2 hours on Low heat.
6. Serve hot.

Nutrition information:

Calories: 188g Carbohydrates: 4.5g Proteins: 20g Fat: 10g Fiber: 3g

Fragrant Greens Soup

Serves: 6, Preparation: 10 minutes, Cooking: 15 minutes

Ingredients

1/3 cup olive oil
1 leek, the white and some of tender green part, sliced
2 fresh onions, white and tender green part, finely chopped
1 lb of various greens of choice, coarsely chopped
Salt and ground pepper to taste
1/4 tsp of nutmeg
6 cups of water
1/2 cup of fresh dill, finely chopped

Instructions

1. Pour the oil in a pot, and sauté the leek, fresh onions and greens for 5 minutes; stir.
2. Season with the salt and pepper, grated nutmeg and pour water; bring to boil.
3. Cover and cook for 8 - 10 minutes over Medium-low heat.
4. When the vegetables softened, transfer them in a blender; blend until soft.
5. Serve in a bowl, and sprinkle each serving with fresh dill and freshly ground pepper.

Nutrition information:

Calories: 157g Carbohydrates: 6g Proteins: 4g Fat: 13g Fiber: 1g

Delicious Pork Stew

Serves: 4, Preparation: 10 minutes, Cooking: 34 minutes

Ingredients

2 tbsps of lard
2 spring onions, finely chopped
1 1/2 lbs. pork boneless, cut into cubes
Sea salt and black ground pepper to taste
1 red bell pepper (cut into thin strips)
1/2 cup of water
1/2 tsp of cumin
1/2 tsp of caraway seeds

Instructions

1. Heat the lard in a large skillet over Medium-high heat.
2. Sauté the spring onions for 3 - 4 minutes; stir.
3. Add the pork and simmer for about 5 minutes.
4. Add all remaining ingredients and stir well.
5. Lower heat, cover and cook for 25 minutes over Low heat.
6. Taste and adjust salt and pepper to taste.
7. Serve hot.

Nutrition information:

Calories: 375g Carbohydrates: 3g Proteins: 30g Fat: 27g Fiber: 1g

Chicken and Shredded Cabbage Stew

Serves: 4, Preparation: 10 minutes, Cooking: 40 minutes

Ingredients

2 tbsps of chicken fat
1/2 cup of green onions, chopped
2 cloves of garlic, sliced
2 chicken breast fillets, cut in pieces
1/2 tsp of nutmeg
2 tbsps of yellow mustard
1 3/4 cups of water
1 cup of white wine
1/4 cup of apple cider vinegar
6 whole cloves
1 carrot; peeled, sliced
1/2 tsp of salt
1/4 tsp of pepper
1 cup shredded cabbage

Instructions

1. Heat chicken fat in a large Dutch oven over Medium-high temperature.
2. Add green onions, garlic chicken and cook about 5 - 6 minutes.
3. Spread mustard over chicken pieces; stir nutmeg, salt and pepper, water, wine, vinegar, cloves and carrot; bring to a boil.
4. Cover, reduce heat to Low and cook 20 minutes.
5. Add shredded cabbage, stir, cover and cook for about 10 - 12 minutes.
6. Taste and adjust salt and pepper to taste.
7. Serve hot in a bowls.

Nutrition information:

Calories: 173g Carbohydrates: 6g Proteins: 26g Fat: 5g Fiber: 2g

Cold Cauliflower and Cilantro Soup

Serves: 4, Preparation: 3 hours, Cooking: 25 minutes

Ingredients

1 1/2 lbs. cauliflower
1 cup unsweetened almond milk
1/2 tsp of fresh ginger, grated
3 bunches fresh cilantro
3 tbsps of garlic-infused olive oil
2 pinches of salt

Instructions

1. Heat water in a large pot until boiling. Place the steamer in a pot and put in the cauliflower.
2. Cover and steam cauliflower for 6 - 7 minutes.
3. Remove the cauliflower along with all ingredients from the list above in a high-speed blender.
4. Blend until smooth or until desired texture is achieved.
5. Pour the soup in a glass container, cover and refrigerate for 2 - 3 hours.
6. Serve cold.

Nutrition information:

Calories: 141g Carbohydrates: 7.5g Proteins: 3.5g Fat: 11g Fiber: 3.5g

Creamy Broccoli Soup with Nutmeg

Serves: 4, Preparation: 15 minutes, Cooking: 10 minutes

Ingredients

2 tbsps of olive oil
2 green onions, finely chopped
1 lb. broccoli floret, frozen or fresh
6 cups of bone broth (cold)
1 cup of cream
Salt and ground pepper to taste
1 tbsp of nutmeg

Instructions

1. Heat the olive oil in a pot over Medium-high heat.
2. Add the onion in and sauté it until becomes translucent.
3. Add the broccoli, season with the salt and pepper, and bring to boil.
4. Cover the pot and cook for 6 - 8 minutes.
5. Transfer the broccoli mixture into blender, and blend until smooth.
6. Pour the cream, and blend for further 30 seconds.
7. Return the soup in a pot and reheat it.
8. Adjust salt and pepper and serve hot with grated nutmeg.

Nutrition information:

Calories: 322g Carbohydrates: 5g Proteins: 35g Fat: 18g Fiber: 0.4g

Creamy Mushroom Soup with Crumbled Bacon

Serves: 6, Preparation: 15 minutes, Cooking: 50 minutes

Ingredients

1 tbsp of lard
2 lbs of white mushrooms
1/2 cup of water
3 1/2 cups of almond milk
2 green onions, finely sliced
3 sprigs of fresh rosemary
2 cloves garlic, finely chopped
6 slices of bacon, fried and crumbled
Salt and ground black pepper

Instructions

1. Heat the lard in a large skillet and sauté green onions and garlic over Medium-high heat.
2. Season with the salt and pepper, and rosemary; pour water and cook for 5 minutes.
3. Add the mushrooms and sauté for 1-2 minutes.
4. Pour the almond milk, stir, cover and simmer for 40 minutes over Low heat.
5. Remove the rosemary and transfer the soup in your blender; blend until creamy and soft.
6. Season with salt and pepper to taste, and if necessary, add some warm water.
7. Chop the bacon and fry in a hot pan until it becomes crispy.
8. Serve your soup in bowls and sprinkle with chopped bacon.

Nutrition information:

Calories: 108g Carbohydrates: 5.5g Proteins: 8g
Fat: 6g Fiber: 2g

Hungarian Turkey Stew (Keto adapted)

Serves: 6, Preparation: 15 minutes, Cooking: 1 hour 55 minutes

Ingredients

1/3 cup almond flour
1 tsp of salt and ground pepper
2 1/2 lbs. turkey thighs; skinned & boned, cut into 1-inch cubes
2 tbsps of olive oil
1 cup green onions, finely chopped
1/2 cup mushrooms, sliced
1 grated tomato
1 cup dry white wine
1 tbsp of ground paprika
1/2 tsp of marjoram
1 cup water or bone broth
1/2 cup of heavy cream
3 slices of turkey bacon, cooked and crumbled (optional)

Instructions

1. In Ziploc bag, combine almond flour, salt and pepper. Add the turkey meat in batches, and coat well with almond flour mixture.
2. Heat the oil in a large frying pan and sauté turkey cubes for 4 - 5 minutes over Medium heat; stir.
3. In Dutch oven, sauté green onions with a pinch of salt until translucent.
4. Add mushrooms, carrot, grated tomato and wine. Bring mixture to boil, reduce heat to Low and simmer for 10 -12 minutes. Stir in paprika, marjoram, water or bone broth and turkey; bring mixture to boil.
6. Reduce heat, cover and simmer 1 1/2 hours or until turkey are totally tender.
7. Serve in a bowls with fresh cream and crumbled bacon.

Nutrition information:

Calories: 277g Carbohydrates: 6g Proteins: 34g
Fat: 13g Fiber: 2g

Light Grouper Soup with Celery

Serves: 6, Preparation: 15 minutes, Cooking: 1 hour 55 minutes

Ingredients

5 celery stalks, cut into three pieces each
1 tbsp of dried oregano
7 -8 saffron fibers
1 carrot preferably organic, sliced
8 cups of water
2 small grouper fish, about 3 1/2 - 4 lbs., washed and cleaned
3/4 cup of olive oil
2 tbsps of lemon juice
Salt and ground black pepper

Instructions

1. Add celery and carrot in a large and wide pot, and sprinkle with oregano and saffron.
2. Place the fish pieces and pour the olive oil.
3. Pour water and bring to boil over Medium-high heat; cover and simmer for 15 minutes.
4. Season with the salt and pepper.
5. Remove the fish from the pot, and place on a large plate.
6. Strain the broth, return to pot, and cook for further 10 minutes.
7. Remove soup from heat and pour the lemon juice.
8. Taste and adjust salt to taste.
9. Clean carefully the fish and serve immediately with hot soup.

Nutrition information:

Calories: 291g Carbohydrates: 3g Proteins: 27g Fat: 19g Fiber: 1g

Perfect Pork Stew

Serves: 4, Preparation: 15 minutes, Cooking: 1 hour 45 minutes

Ingredients

1/2 cup of olive oil
2 lbs of pork, cut into cubes
1 cup of red wine
1 small carrot, cut into slices
1 cup of white mushrooms, sliced
1 green onion, finely chopped
1 small diced tomato
1 cup of bone broth or water
1/2 tsp of oregano
1 bay leaf
Salt and ground black pepper to taste

Instructions

1. In a large pan, pour the oil and sauté the pork for 2 - 3 minutes.
2. Add the onion and sauté for 2 - 3 minutes; season with the salt and pepper.
3. Pour wine and stir for two minutes.
4. Add carrots, mushrooms, green onion, tomato, broth or water, oregano and bay leaf.
5. Bring to boil, lower heat, cover and cook for 1 1/2 hours on Low heat.
6. Taste and adjust salt and pepper to taste.
7. Serve hot.

Nutrition information:

Calories: 741g Carbohydrates: 3g Proteins: 18g Fat: 73g Fiber: 1g

Spicy Ground Bison Meat Stew

Serves: 4, Preparation: 10 minutes, Cooking: 35 minutes

Ingredients

2 tbsps of lard
1 1/2 lbs. grass-fed bison, ground (or an equivalent substitute)
2 spring onions, finely chopped
2 cloves of garlic, minced
1 grated tomato
2 tbsps of mustard (Dijon, English, ground stone)
1 tbsp of chili powder
2 bay leaves
2 tsps of cumin
1 tsp of cinnamon
2 tsps of salt and ground black pepper
1 cup bone broth
Fresh cilantro and lime wedges to garnish

Instructions

1. Heat the lard in a large skillet over Medium-high heat.
2. Add ground bison meat and sauté for 3 - 4 minutes; stir.
3. Add sliced onions and garlic and sauté until translucent.
4. Add grated tomato and tomato paste and cook for 5 minutes.
5. Add all remaining ingredients and bring to boil.
6. Cover, lower heat to Low, and cook for 20 minutes.
7. Adjust seasonings and serve hot with fresh cilantro and a squeeze of lime.

Nutrition information:

Calories: 312g Carbohydrates: 4g Proteins: 38g Fat: 16g Fiber: 2g

Swiss chard Soup with Fresh Herbs

Serves: 4, Preparation: 10 minutes, Cooking: 25 minutes

Ingredients

1/4 cup extra virgin olive oil
2 spring onions (only green parts finely chopped)
1 clove of garlic, minced
2 lbs. Swiss chard, tender stems and leaves; cut into pieces
3 cups bone broth (or water)
1 tbsp of fresh dill, parsley and thyme; chopped
Salt and black ground pepper to taste

Instructions

1. Heat the oil in a large pot over Medium-high heat.
2. Sauté the green parts of spring onions and garlic with a pinch of salt for 3 - 4 minutes.
3. Add chopped Swiss chard and bone broth; bring to the boil and let it simmer for 10 minutes. Add chopped dill and parsley and cook for further 5 minutes.
4. Transfer your soup in a food processor. Blend into a very smooth soup.
5. Adjust seasonings and serve hot.

Nutrition information:

Calories: 75g Carbohydrates: 6g Proteins: 6g Fat: 3g Fiber: 3g

Chapter 8 Poultry Recipes

Chicken Breast Stuffed with Asparagus

Serves: 4, Preparation: 15 minutes, Cooking: 30 minutes

Ingredients

2 large skinless and boneless chicken breast halves

8 asparagus spears, trimmed

1/2 cup shredded Parmesan cheese

1/4 cup ground almonds

Salt and black pepper to taste

Instructions

1. Preheat oven to 375⁰F. Grease the baking dish; set aside.

2. Place each chicken breast between two sheets freezer bags on a solid surface.

3. Sprinkle each side with salt and pepper.

4. Place 4 spears of asparagus down the center of a chicken breast and spread about 1/4 cup of Parmesan cheese over the asparagus.

5. Repeat with the other chicken breast and roll the chicken around the asparagus and cheese to make a compact roll.

6. Place the rolls seam sides down in the prepared baking dish, and sprinkle each with about 2 tablespoons of ground almonds.

7. Bake for about 25 - 30 minutes.

8. Allow to cool for 10 minutes.

9. Serve warm.

Nutrition information:

Calories: 236 Carbohydrates: 3.8g Proteins: Fat: 32g Fiber: 2g

Roasted Chicken with Swiss

Serves: 6, Preparation: 10 minutes, Cooking: 50 minutes

Ingredients

1/4 lb. mushrooms

2 lbs. boneless, skinless chicken breasts

6 oz. Swiss cheese

1 cup bone broth

1/2 cup dry white wine

1 cup of almond flour or finely ground almonds

1/2 cup of melted butter

Instructions

1. Preheat oven to 350⁰F.

2. Slice cheese and mushrooms.

3. Place chicken in a greased 9x13 baking dish.

4. Top each piece with a slice of Swiss cheese and arrange mushrooms over the chicken and cheese.

5. Combine the bone broth with wine and pour over chicken. Sprinkle with ground almonds.

6. Drizzle melted butter over the top of ground almonds.

7. Bake 45-50 minutes or until chicken is cooked thoroughly.

Nutrition information:

Calories: 175 Carbohydrates: 2.6g Proteins: 19g Fat: 11g Fiber: 0.2g

White Mushroom and Chicken Stew

Serves: 4, Preparation: 5 minutes, Cooking: 20 minutes

Ingredients

1 tbsp. olive oil

1 lb. chicken breasts, skinless and boneless

1 lb. fresh white mushrooms

2 green onions

1 cup diced celery

1 tsp. minced garlic

1 small tomato, chopped

1/2 tsp. salt

2 cups fresh green beans, trimmed and halved

Instructions

1. Heat the oil in a large frying skillet until hot.

2. Add chicken; cook until brown, 3-4 minutes a side; remove from skillet.

3. Add mushrooms, green onion, celery and garlic; cook, stirring frequently, for about 6-8 minutes or until tender.

4. Add the tomato, salt and chicken; top with green beans.

5. Cover and simmer until chicken is cooked thoroughly, for about 5-6 minutes.

6. Serve hot.

Nutrition information:

Calories: 102 Carbohydrates: 8.4g Proteins: 8.5g Fat: 4.5g Fiber: 3g

Oven Roasted Creamy Spiced Chicken

Serves: 4, Preparation: 10 minutes, Cooking: 50 minutes

Ingredients

2 tsps. chicken fat
1 fresh whole chicken, cut up
1/2 cup ground almonds
1/4 tsp. cayenne pepper
1/2 tsp. onion powder
1/8 tsp. ground ginger
1/2 tsp. garlic powder
1/3 cup plain yogurt

Instructions

1. Preheat oven to 360^0F.
2. Grease large baking tray with the chicken fat; set aside.
3. Cut the chicken in large parts.
4. Rinse chicken pieces and pat dry.
5. In a large bowl, combine ground almonds, onion powder, garlic powder, cayenne pepper and ginger.
6. Dip chicken pieces in yogurt, and then roll in a ground almond mixture.
7. Place breaded chicken in prepared baking dish.
8. Bake, uncovered, for 45-50 minutes or until chicken is tender.

Nutrition information:

Calories: 420 Carbohydrates: 2.8g Proteins: 31g Fat: 321g Fiber: 1g

Cold Shredded Chicken and Cabbage Salad

Serves: 4, Preparation: 15 minutes, Cooking: 30 minutes

Ingredients

1 lb. red cabbage, shredded
2 cloves garlic, finely chopped
1 lb. cooked chicken, shredded
4 tbsps. olive oil
3 tbsps. lemon juice (freshly squeezed)
Salt to taste
3 tbsps. mustard (Dijon, English, or whole grain)

Instructions

1. Shred the cabbage and place in a large salad bowl; season with the salt and toss.
2. Add garlic over the cabbage.
3. Add shredded chicken and pour with olive oil; toss.
4. Add the mustard and gently stir with wooden spoon.
5. Refrigerate for 30 minutes, sprinkle with the fresh lemon juice and serve.

Nutrition information:

Calories: 209 Carbohydrates: 7.3g Proteins: 23.5g Fat: 9.5g Fiber: 3.3g

Crunchy Chicken Nuggets with Coconut Aminos

Serves: 5, Preparation: 15 minutes, Cooking: 3 minutes

Ingredients

2 egg whites
Salt and ground black pepper to taste
2 1/2 cups ground almonds
2 lbs. skinless, boneless chicken breasts, cut into 20 pieces
1/4 cup garlic-infused olive oil
3 tbsps. coconut aminos (soy sauce substitute)
1/4 cup water

Instructions

1. Whisk the egg whites, salt and pepper in a bowl.
2. Add the ground almonds into a separate bowl.
3. Dip the chicken pieces in egg mixture.
4. Roll the chicken pieces into almonds until coated.
5. Heat the olive oil in a skillet at Medium-high heat; cook for about 5 - 6 chicken or until golden brown.
6. Whisk the coconut aminos and water and pour over the chicken.
7. Cook for 2 - 3 minutes and remove from the heat.
8. Serve hot.

Nutrition information:

Calories: 564 Carbohydrates: 6.4g Proteins: 54g Fat: 46g Fiber: 6g

Roasted Frozen Parmesan Chicken Wings

Serves: 4, Preparation: 5 minutes, Cooking: 1 hour

Ingredients

2 tbsps. olive oil
20 frozen chicken wings
1 cup grated Parmesan cheese
1 tsp. chives, chopped
2 tsps. dried oregano
Salt and ground pepper to taste
Lemon wedges, for serving

Instructions

1. Preheat oven to 440^{0}F. Grease a roasting pan with the olive oil.

2. Place frozen chicken wings on a baking pan. Sprinkle with chives, oregano, salt and pepper.
3. Bake for 40 minutes.
4. Remove from the oven and sprinkle with the Parmesan cheese.
5. Bake for further 20 minutes.
6. Serve hot with lemon wedges.

Nutrition information:

Calories: 646 Carbohydrates: 1.5g Proteins: 55g Fat: 53g Fiber: 0.4g

Roasted Turkey Breast with Garlic-Parsley Sauce

Serves: 6, Preparation: 10 minutes, Cooking: 1 ½ hours

Ingredients

1/3 cup fresh parsley, finely chopped
3 garlic cloves, minced
1/2 cup lemon juice
1/2 cup garlic-infused olive oil
1 tsp. hot ground paprika (optional)
1 tsp. cumin
2 turkey breasts (4-5 pounds)
Salt and pepper to taste

Instructions

1. Preheat oven to 350^{0}F.
2. Stir the chopped parsley, garlic, lemon juice, olive oil, ground paprika and cumin in a bowl.

3. Season turkey breast with the salt and pepper, and generously brush with prepared mixture.
4. Place turkey breasts in a greased roasting dish and cook for 1 hour.
5. Baste turkey breast with remaining mixture, and roast for further 30 minutes or until the internal temperature reaches 165^{0}F.
6. Remove from the oven and let turkey breast rest for 10 minutes before slicing and serving.

Nutrition information:

Calories: 481 Carbohydrates: 7.3g Proteins: 52g Fat: 23g Fiber: 2g

Slow Cooked Chicken Salad with Spinach

Serves: 4, Preparation: 10 minutes, Cooking: 5 hours

Ingredients

2 tbsps. garlic-infused olive oil
1 1/2 lbs. chicken breast fillet
1 lb. fresh spinach
1 red bell pepper, cut into thin strips
1 red hot chili peppers (optional)
2 tbsps. mustard
1 tbsp. resh basil, finely chopped
1 tbsp. fresh mint, finely chopped
1 tsp. coriander
Sea salt to taste
3 tbsps. lemon juice (freshly squeezed)

Instructions

1. Pour the olive oil to the inner stainless-steel pot of Slow Cooker; place the spinach on the bottom.

2. Cut the chicken fillets into small cubes and place over spinach.
3. Add the bell pepper and red hot chili pepper (if used).
4. Combine all remaining ingredients in a bowl and pour over chicken; gently stir with wooden spoon.
5. Cover and cook on Low for 4-5 hours.
6. Adjust salt to taste and serve hot with lemon juice.

Nutrition information:

Calories: 281 Carbohydrates: 4.7g Proteins: 37.5g Fat: 12g Fiber: 2g

Almond Breaded Chicken Patties

Serves: 4, Preparation: 15 minutes, Cooking: 10 minutes

Ingredients
2 lbs. ground chicken
4 eggs
1 cup of Parmesan cheese
1 cup fresh parsley, finely chopped
3 slices of bacon, fried and crumbled
2 cloves of garlic, finely sliced
Salt and black pepper, freshly ground
Olive oil, for frying

For breading
Almond flour
2 large eggs, beaten
Ground almonds

Instructions
1. In a non-stick pan, fry bacon slices until crispy; allow to cool, crumble, and set aside.
2. Combine ground chicken, cheese, eggs, parsley, bacon, garlic, salt and freshly ground pepper.
3. Use your hands knead the mixture until combined well.
4. Shape from the mixture small patties.
5. Heat the olive oil in a large frying pan at Medium-high heat.
6. Coat chicken patties with almond flour, dip in beaten eggs and cover with ground almonds.
7. Fry the chicken patties in hot oil for about 5 minutes or until golden brown.
8. Place on a serving plate lined with absorbent paper.
9. Serve hot.

Nutrition information:
Calories: 279 Carbohydrates: 4.6g Proteins: 16g
Fat: 23g Fiber: 1.7g

Roasted Stone-Ground Mustard Chicken in Foil

Serves: 4, Preparation: 10 minutes, Cooking: 30 minutes

Ingredients
4 chicken breasts, boneless and skinless
4 garlic cloves, minced
3 tbsps. stone-ground mustard
1 tbsp. olive oil
1 tbsp. Italian seasoning
Sea salt and ground black pepper to taste

Instructions
1. Preheat oven to 450°F.
2. Line one baking dish with aluminum foil and sprinkle little oil.
3. Heat the oil in a frying pan at Medium heat and sauté garlic until soft.
4. Stir in stone-ground mustard, Italian seasoning to your preference.
5. Place chicken breasts on prepared baking dish, season the salt and pepper and cover with aluminum foil.
6. Bake uncovered for 25-30 minutes.
7. Allow to cool, slice and serve.

Nutrition information:
Calories: 315 Carbohydrates: 1.9g Proteins: 51g
Fat: 10.5g Fiber: 1g

Asian Style Ginger Chicken

Serves: 2, Preparation: 15 minutes, Cooking: 30 minutes

Ingredients
1/2 whole chicken, roughly chopped
Salt to taste
1/4 cup ginger, grated
1 tbsp. coconut aminos (soy sauce substitute)
2 tbsps. red wine
1/2 cup of sesame oil
2 tbsps. chopped spring onion

Instructions
1. Rub the chicken with the salt.
2. Place the chicken in a pot fitted with the steamer basket over water. Steam chicken over Medium-high heat for about 30 minutes, or until chicken cooked thoroughly.
3. Drain chicken; reserve 1/2 cup of chicken.
4. In a frying skillet, heat up sesame oil, add ginger, coconut aminos, wine, and reserved chicken; stir for 2 minutes.
5. Remove the chicken on platter, pour sauce and garnish with spring onions; serve.

Nutrition information:
Calories: 468 Carbohydrates: 1g Proteins: 49g Fat: 28g Fiber: 0.2g

Broiled Coconut Aminos - Glazed Chicken Drumsticks

Serves: 4, Preparation: 1 hour 10 minutes, Cooking: 20 minutes

Ingredients

8 chicken drumsticks, skin-on or skinless
2 tbsps. peanut butter
1/4 cup of coconut aminos (from coconut sap)
1/2 tsp. ground ginger
1/2 tsp. salt and freshly ground black pepper

Instructions

1. Preheat the oven's broiler, and line a broiler pan with aluminum foil.
2. In a large bowl, stir together peanut butter, coconut aminos, ginger, salt and pepper.
3. Add the chicken drumsticks and toss to coat. Refrigerate and marinate for one hour.
4. Remove the drumsticks from the fridge and place them in a prepared broiler pan.
5. Broil 13-15 minutes, turn the drumsticks and broil for additional 5 minutes.
6. Serve hot.

Nutrition information:
Calories: 351 Carbohydrates: 2g Proteins: 55g Fat: 13g Fiber: 0.6g

Chicken Breast with Vinegar Sauce

Serves: 4, Preparation: 5 minutes, Cooking: 35 minutes

Ingredients

2 tbsps. olive oil
2 lbs. chicken breasts; boneless, cut into bite-size pieces
1 garlic clove, crushed
1/4 tsp. ginger
3/4 tsp. crushed red pepper flakes
1/4 cup white wine
2 tbsps. stevia granulated sweetener
1/3 cup coconut aminos (from coconut sap)
1 tbsp. apple cider vinegar (preferably non-pasteurized)
1/2 cup water

Instructions

1. Heat the olive oil in a large frying skillet.
2. Add the chicken pieces and cook until lightly browned.
3. Remove chicken, and place on a plate; set aside.
4. Add all remaining ingredients in a skillet and stir for 3 - 4 minutes over Medium heat.
5. Add chicken, stir well, cover and simmer for 20 minutes over Low heat.
6. Serve hot.

Nutrition information:
Calories: 347 Carbohydrates: 2g Proteins: 50g Fat: 13g Fiber: 0.3g

Oven Baked Buffalo Turkey Wings

Serves: 4, Preparation: 10 minutes, Cooking: 1 hour

Ingredients

3 1/2 lbs. turkey wings, cut in half
3/4 cup almond flour
1/2 tsp. salt to taste
1 tsp. cayenne pepper
Olive oil, for frying
1/4 cup almond butter, melted
2 tbsps. white vinegar
2 tbsps. hot red pepper sauce
2 tbsps. fresh celery, chopped

Instructions

1. Preheat the oven on 375⁰F.
2. Combine the almond flour, salt and cayenne pepper on a plate. Dust wings in almond flour mixture, shaking off excess.
3. Heat olive oil in a large heavy skillet over Medium heat. Fry chicken for 10 minutes, turning once. Remove from heat and drain on kitchen paper towels.
4. Combine the almond butter, vinegar and hot pepper sauce in a small bowl. Place wings in a large baking pan; drizzle sauce over wings.
5. Bake wings for 1 hour, turning once halfway through.
6. Serve hot with fresh chopped celery.

Nutrition information:
Calories: 549 Carbohydrates: 2.5g Proteins: 63g Fat: 31g Fiber: 1.2g

Oven Baked Creamy Chicken Thighs

Serves: 4, Preparation: 10 minutes, Cooking: 40 minutes

Ingredients

3/4 cup mayonnaise
1/4 cup yellow mustard
1/2 cup Parmesan cheese, freshly grated
1 tsp. Italian seasoning
1/4 tsp. coriander
1/4 tsp. marjoram
2 lbs. chicken thighs (boneless and skinless)
1/2 tsp. salt and ground black pepper, Cooking oil

Instructions

1. Preheat oven to 400°F.
2. Grease one 8-inch square baking dish with cooking oil.
3. In a bowl combine the mayonnaise, mustard, Parmesan cheese, coriander, marjoram and Italian seasoning.
4. Season generously chicken thigh with salt and pepper and place in a prepared baking dish.
5. Spread with mayo-mustard sauce and bake for 35 - 40 minutes. Serve warm.

Nutrition information:

Calories: 335 Carbohydrates: 7g Proteins: 34g Fat: 18g Fiber: 0.3g

Roasted Turkey Mushroom Loaf

Serves: 6, Preparation: 15 minutes, Cooking: 1 hour

Ingredients

1/2 cup ground almonds
1 tbsp. dried parsley
1/4 tsp. ground allspice
1/2 tsp. dried thyme leaves
1/2 tsp. salt and pepper to taste
1 1/2 lbs. ground turkey
8 oz. turkey, cut into 1/4-inch cubes
1/2 lb. mushrooms, coarsely chopped
1/2 cup spring onion, chopped
2 cloves garlic, minced
1 large egg, beaten
Olive oil

Instructions

1. Preheat the oven to 350°F.
2. In large bowl combine ground almonds, parsley, allspice, thyme, salt and pepper.
3. Add ground turkey, turkey, mushrooms, spring onions, garlic and beaten egg; knead with your hands to get a compact mixture.
4. Grease one 9-inch pie plate with olive oil, shape turkey mixture into round loaf.
5. Bake for 50-60 minutes or until inserted thermometer reaches 160°F.
6. Serve hot.

Nutrition information:

Calories: 310 Carbohydrates: 5.5g Proteins: 34g Fat: 18g Fiber: 2g

Chicken Liver and Pancetta Casserole

Serves: 4, Preparation: 5 minutes, Cooking: 45 minutes

Ingredients

1/4 cup of olive oil
1 onion, finely chopped
2 cloves of garlic
1 1/2 lbs. chicken liver
1/2 tsp. smoked red ground pepper
7 oz. pancetta (cut into strips)
1 tsp. dried thyme
1/2 cup of red wine
1 bunch of parsley, finely chopped
Salt and freshly ground black pepper

Instructions

1. Preheat oven to 350°F.
2. Grease a casserole with olive oil; set aside.
3. Heat the olive oil in a skillet over Medium-high heat.
4. Sauté the onion and the garlic for 3 - 4 minutes.
5. Add pancetta and stir for 1 - 2 minutes.
6. Add chicken liver, smoked pepper, thyme, salt and pepper and cook for 3-4 minutes.
7. Pour the red wine and add chopped parsley; stir.
8. Transfer the mixture in a prepared casserole dish.
9. Bake for 35 - 45 minutes. Serve hot.

Nutrition information:

Calories: 340 Carbohydrates: 4g Proteins: 29g Fat: 22g Fiber: 1g

Chicken Casserole

Serves: 4, Preparation: 15 minutes, Cooking: 35 minutes

Ingredients

1 tbsp. chicken fat
2 lbs. chicken, cubed
Salt and ground pepper to taste
12 oz. frozen or fresh spinach
1/4 cup bacon, crumbled
1 cup of cream cheese, softened
1/2 cup of mayonnaise
1 tsp. garlic powder
1 cup grated Parmesan cheese

Instructions

1. Preheat oven to 350⁰F.
2. Grease one 9 x13 baking dish with chicken fat.
3. Season the chicken generously with the salt and pepper, and place into baking dish.
4. Add the spinach over chicken, and sprinkle with crumbled bacon.
5. In a bowl, combine together the cream cheese, mayo, garlic, and grated Parmesan cheese.
6. Pour the mixture in a casserole.
7. Place in oven and bake for 30 - 35 minutes.
8. Serve hot.

Nutrition information:

Calories: 374 Carbohydrates: 8.5g Proteins: 15g Fat: 32g Fiber: 2g

Chicken with Curry and Coriander Casserole

Serves: 4, Preparation: 10 minutes, Cooking: 25 minutes

Ingredients

1 lbs. chicken breast, cut in cubes
1 tbsp. chicken fat
1 onion, finely sliced
1 carrot
2 tsps. curry powder
1 pinch of saffron
1/2 cup of wine
1/2 cup of bone broth
1 tbsp. fresh coriander leaves
Salt to taste

Instructions

1. Cut the chicken breasts into large cubes.
2. Heat the chicken fat in a casserole and sauté the onion.
3. Add the chicken cubes and brown them on all sides; stir for 2 - 3 minutes.
4. Sprinkle with curry and saffron, stir in the carrot and stir well.
5. Pour the wine and bone broth and stir.
6. Season with the salt, cover and let simmer for 20 minutes.
7. Sprinkle with fresh chopped coriander leaves and serve.

Nutrition information:

Calories: 186 Carbohydrates: 6g Proteins: 26g Fat: 8g Fiber: 2g

Instant Pot Asiago Chicken Wings

Serves: 6, Preparation: 10 minutes, Cooking: 20 minutes

Ingredients

2 tbsps. olive oil
20 frozen chicken wings
1 tsp. salt
1/2 tbsp. garlic powder
2 tsps. dried oregano
1 cup of grated Asiago cheese (or Parmesan)
1/2 can water

Instructions

1. Pour the oil to the inner stainless-steel pot in the Instant Pot.
2. Season frozen chicken wings with salt, garlic powder and oregano.
3. Place the seasoned chicken wings in your Instant Pot and pour water.
4. Lock lid into place and set on the Poultry setting for 20 minutes.
5. Use Quick-release, turn the valve from Sealing to Venting to release the pressure.
6. Transfer chicken wings to serving platter and generously sprinkle with grated cheese.
7. Let rest for 10 minutes and serve.

Nutrition information:

Calories: 438 Carbohydrates: 2g Proteins: 37g Fat: 35g Fiber: 0.5g

Instant Pot Chicken Cilantro Wraps

Serves: 2, Preparation: 10 minutes, Cooking: 12 minutes

Ingredients

2 chicken breasts, boneless and skinless
1 cup bone broth (or water)
Juice of 1 lemon, freshly squeezed
1 green onion, finely chopped
1 cup cilantro, chopped
1 tsp. chili powder
1 tsp. cumin
1 tsp. garlic powder
Sea salt and pepper to taste
12 lettuce leaves, of your choice but should be large enough to use as a wrap.

Instructions

1. Season chicken breasts with the salt and pepper and place in your Instant Pot.
2. Add all remaining ingredients except lettuce leaves; lock lid into place and set on the Poultry setting for 12 minutes.
3. When the timer beeps, press "Cancel" and carefully flip the Quick-release valve to let the pressure out.
4. Open lid and transfer chicken in a bowl; Shred chicken with two forks.
5. Combine shredded chicken with juices from Instant Pot.
6. Add one spoon of shredded chicken in each lettuce leaf and wrap. Serve immediately.

Nutrition information:

Calories: 7163 Carbohydrates: 4g Proteins: 34g
Fat: 5g Fiber: 1g

Instant Pot Perfect Braised Turkey Breast

Serves: 4, Preparation: 10 minutes, Cooking: 30 minutes

Ingredients

2 tbsps. butter, softened on room temperature
4 lbs. turkey breast, boneless
1 cup water
1/2 cup coconut aminos (from coconut sap)
1/2 tsp. fresh rosemary, finely chopped
1/2 tsp. fresh sage, finely chopped
1 tsp. salt and ground red pepper to taste

Instructions

1. Season turkey breasts with salt and pepper.
2. Press Sauté button on your Instant Pot. When the word "Hot" appears on the display, add butter and sear turkey breasts for 3 minutes.
3. Pour water and coconut aminos and stir for 2 minutes.
4. Sprinkle with herbs, and the salt and pepper and stir again. Turn off the Sauté button.
5. Lock lid into place and set on the Manual setting on High Pressure for 28 - 30 minutes (turkey meat is ready when meat thermometer shows 161^0F).
6. When the timer beeps, press "Cancel" and carefully flip the Natural-release for 15 minutes.
7. Remove turkey breast on a plate and allow it to cool for 10 minutes.
8. Slice and serve.

Nutrition information:

Calories: 357 Carbohydrates: 1.5g Proteins: 62g
Fat: 10g Fiber: 0.5g

Delicious Chicken Breast with Turmeric

Serves: 4, Preparation: 15 minutes, Cooking: 4 hours

Ingredients

1/2 cup chicken fat
4 chicken breasts, boneless and skinless
Salt and ground white pepper to taste
4 cloves garlic, finely sliced
1 tbsp. ground turmeric
1 cup of bone broth

Instructions

1. Season the chicken breast with salt and pepper and cut into pieces.
2. Add chicken fat in inner pot of your Slow Cooker and place the chicken breasts.
3. Add the turmeric, garlic and bone broth.
4. Cover and cook on Low for 3 - 4 hours.
5. Transfer the chicken breasts on a serving plate.
6. Serve hot.

Nutrition information:

Calories: 488 Carbohydrates: 2.5g Proteins: 52g
Fat: 32g Fiber: 0.5g

Instant Pot Roasted Whole Chicken

Serves: 4, Preparation: 10 minutes, Cooking: 35 minutes

Ingredients

2 cups water
4 lbs. whole chicken
1/4 cup olive oil
Seasoned salt and black ground pepper to taste
1/4 tsp. dry thyme
1/4 tsp. dry rosemary
1/4 tsp. dry marjoram
1/4 tsp. dry sage

Instructions

1. Pour water to the inner stainless-steel pot in the Instant Pot and place the trivet inside (steam rack or a steamer basket).

2. Rinse well the chicken and pat dry. Rub with olive oil and season to taste with salt and pepper, thyme, rosemary, marjoram and sage.
3. Put the turkey on the trivet into Instant Pot.
4. Press Manual mode and set time for 35 minutes.
5. Use Natural-release, it takes 15 - 20 minutes to depressurize naturally.
6. Remove the chicken on a serving plate and allow it cool for 15 minutes before serving.

Nutrition information:

Calories: 589 Carbohydrates: 0.1g Proteins: 54g Fat: 47g Fiber: 1g

Instant Pot Serrano Chicken Stir Fry

Serves: 4, Preparation: 10 minutes, Cooking: 15 minutes

Ingredients

2 lbs. chicken breasts, cut small pieces
1 tsp. sea salt
1 tbsp. sesame oil
1 tbsp. ginger, minced
1 tbsp. lemon juice
2 tbsps. coconut oil
1 green onion, minced
2 cloves garlic, minced
8 Serrano peppers, cut in half
1 cup water

Instructions

1. In a bowl, whisk the salt, sesame oil, ginger and lemon juice.
2. Season chicken breast with the mixture.
3. Turn on the Instant Pot and press Sauté button.

4. When the word "Hot" appears on the display, add the coconut oil and sauté the green onion and garlic about 3 minutes. Add halved peppers and sauté for about 2 minutes.
6. Turn off Sauté button; add seasoned chicken, pour water and stir.
7. Lock lid into place and set on the Poultry setting on High Pressure for 10 minutes.
8. When the timer beeps, press "Cancel" and carefully flip the Quick-release valve to let the pressure out. Serve hot.

Nutrition information:

Calories: 359.55 Carbohydrates: 2.5g Proteins: 48g Fat: 17g Fiber: 1g

Instant Pot Tasty Chicken Curry

Serves: 4, Preparation: 10 minutes, Cooking: 10 minutes

Ingredients

2 tbsps. olive oil
1 lb. chicken breast; boneless and skinless, cut in small cubes
Salt and ground black pepper
1/2 tsp. onion powder
1/2 tsp. garlic powder
1 tsp. curry powder
1 1/2 cups coconut cream
1/2 cup water
1 tbsp. chopped parsley, for serving

Instructions

1. Pour the oil to the inner stainless-steel pot in the

Instant Pot.
2. Season the chicken breasts with salt and pepper and place them in Instant Pot.
3. In a bowl, combine together all remaining ingredients and pour over chicken.
4. Lock lid into place and set on the Manual setting for 10 minutes.
5. Use Natural-release for 15 minutes.
6. Serve hot with chopped parsley.

Nutrition information:

Calories: 304 Carbohydrates: 2g Proteins: 25g Fat: 22g Fiber: 0.3g

Slow cooker Chicken Thighs in Coconut Sauce

Serves: 4, Preparation: 10 minutes, Cooking: 4 hours and 20 minutes

Ingredients

1 1/2 lbs. chicken thighs, boneless and skinless
1 red bell pepper, finely chopped
1 green onion, chopped
1 chili pepper, cleaned and finely chopped
2 cloves garlic, minced
1 cup of bone broth
1/2 cup of coconut flakes
2 tbsps. curry powder
Salt and ground pepper to taste
1/4 tsp. ground cinnamon
1/2 cup of coconut milk, unsweetened
1 tbsp. coconut flour
Fresh cilantro, for serving

Instructions

1. Place the chicken thighs, bell pepper, onions, chili pepper and garlic in Crock Pot.
2. Pour broth, and add the coconut flakes, curry powder, salt and pepper, and cinnamon.
3. Cover and cook on Low for 8 - 9 hours or High for 4 hours.
4. In a small bowl, dissolve the coconut flour in coconut milk.
5. Open lid and pour the coconut mixture; stir.
6. Cover again and cook on High for further 20 minutes.
7. Serve hot with fresh chopped cilantro.

Nutrition information:

Calories: 359 Carbohydrates: 5g Proteins: 24g Fat: 28g Fiber: 1.5g

Chicken Cutlets with Spinach Stir-Fry

Serves: 4, Preparation: 5 minutes, Cooking: 15 minutes

Ingredients

2 tbsps. chicken fat
1 spring onion (only green parts), finely chopped
2 medium cloves garlic, thinly sliced
8 chicken breast cutlets; boneless and skinless, cut in pieces
Salt and freshly ground black pepper
3 tbsps. capers, rinsed and chopped
1 lb. fresh spinach, steamed
1/2 cup water
2 tbsps. fresh lemon juice

Instructions

1. Heat the chicken fat in a deep pot, and sauté spring onion and garlic for 3 - 4 minutes.
2. Add chicken cutlets and stir for 4 - 5 minutes.
3. Season with the salt and pepper.
4. Reduce the heat to Medium and add the capers and spinach. Cook and stir until the spinach softens about 3 minutes.
5. Pour water and lemon juice and cook for further 2 - 3 minutes.
6. Serve hot.

Nutrition information:

Calories: 347 Carbohydrates: 5g Proteins: 57g Fat: 15g Fiber: 3g

Squash Spaghetti and Ground Chicken Stir-fry

Serves: 4, Preparation: 5 minutes, Cooking: 25 minutes

Ingredients

1/4 cup olive oil
1 1/4 lbs. squash spaghetti, spiralized
1 lb. ground chicken
1 tbsp. fresh lemon juice (about 2 lemons)
1/2 tbsp. fresh herbs mixture (tarragon, marjoram, oregano)
Salt and freshly ground pepper to taste
1/2 cup shredded mozzarella cheese, for garnish

Instructions

1. Heat the olive oil in a skillet over Medium-high heat.
2. Sauté the squash spaghetti with a pinch of salt for about 8 minutes.
3. Add the ground chicken, fresh lemon juice, fresh herbs and season salt and pepper to taste.
4. Stir, and stir-fry for 8 - 10 minutes over Medium heat.
5. Taste and adjust seasonings; cook for further 5 minutes; gently stir.
6. Serve hot with shredded cheese.

Nutrition information:

Calories: 358 Carbohydrates: 5g Proteins: 35.6g Fat: 22g Fiber:1.6g

Chicken and Zoodle Stir Fry

Serves: 4, Preparation: 15 minutes, Cooking: 7 - 10 minutes

Ingredients

1 lb. chicken breasts; boneless and skinless, cut in slices
2 tbsps. chicken fat
2 cups zucchini, spiralized (or made into ribbons with a vegetable peeler)
Marinade
1 spring onion, finely chopped
2 cloves garlic, minced
1 cup water
1 cup fresh lemon juice
1/3 cup coconut aminos
1/3 cup olive oil
4 green onion, sliced
1 piece of ginger, grated
Salt and ground black pepper to taste

Instructions

1. Place the chicken slices in a container and season with the salt and pepper.
2. In a deep bowl, combine all ingredients for marinade; stir until well combined.
3. Pour the marinade evenly over the chicken; cover and refrigerate for 2 hours.
4. Heat the chicken fat in a large and deep-frying skillet over Medium-high heat.
5. Add the chicken to the skillet and stir-fry about 5 - 7 minutes. Toss in the zucchini ribbons and cook only for 2 minutes. Serve hot.

Nutrition information:

Calories: 327 Carbohydrates: 6g Proteins: 27g Fat: 22g Fiber: 2g

Ground Turkey and Green Beans Stir-fry

Serves: 4, Preparation: 5 minutes, Cooking: 15 minutes

Ingredients

1 tbsp. chicken fat
1 lb. ground turkey
2 cloves garlic, minced
2 spring onions, sliced
1 piece ginger, finely grated
1/2 lb. green beans, boiled
2 zucchinis, cut into slices
2 tbsps. yellow mustard
1/2 cup fresh basil leaves
Salt and ground black pepper

Instructions

1. Heat the chicken fat in a large frying pan.

2. Add turkey and stir-fry for 2 - 3 minutes.
3. Stir the garlic, spring onions and ginger; season with the salt and pepper and stir-fry for 3 -4 minutes.
4. Add green beans and zucchinis, and stir-fry for 3 minutes; stir well.
5. At the end, add mustard and gently toss.
6. Serve hot with fresh basil leaves.

Nutrition information:

Calories: 299 Carbohydrates: 9.8g Proteins: 34g Fat: 16g Fiber: 3.7g

Hungarian Chicken Fillet Stir-fry

Serves: 4, Preparation: 5 minutes, Cooking: 30 minutes

Ingredients

1 tbsp. chicken fat
1 lb. chicken fillet, cut in strips
2 - 3 spring onions, finely chopped
2 cloves garlic
1 green pepper, chopped
1 tomato, grated
Salt and black ground pepper to taste
1 tbsp. fresh parsley, chopped
1 egg, beaten

Instructions

1. Heat the chicken fat in a large pan.
2. Sauté the onion and garlic with a pinch of salt

for 4 - 5 minutes.
3. Add chicken strips and stir for 5 - 6 minutes.
4. Add chopped pepper and grated tomato; season with the salt and pepper.
5. Cover and cook for 12 - 15 minutes over Medium-low heat.
6. Crack one egg in a pan and stir well.
7. Sprinkle with fresh parsley and serve hot.

Nutrition information:

Calories: 67 Carbohydrates: 6.5g Proteins: 6g Fat: 3g Fiber: 2g

Spicy Chicken Stir-Fry

Serves: 4, Preparation: 10 minutes, Cooking: 20 minutes

Ingredients

2 lbs. chicken breasts; boneless and skinless, cut in pieces
1 tsp. sea salt
2 cloves garlic, minced
1 tbsp. almond flour
1 cup water
1 tbsp. sesame oil
1 tbsp. ginger, minced
4 - 5 Serrano peppers, sliced
3 tbsps. olive oil
2 green onions, cut into thin slices

Instructions

1. Place chicken in a large container, and rub with the mixture of salt, garlic, sesame oil, ginger, almond flour and water.
2. Refrigerate for 1 hour.
3. Heat the olive oil in a large skillet over High heat.
4. Add Serrano peppers, ginger and fry for about 2 minutes.
5. Add the chicken, stir, reduce the heat and stir-fry for 5 - 6 minutes.
6. Add chopped green onion, some water, and cook for further 6 - 7 minutes.
7. Adjust salt, stir and serve hot.

Nutrition information:

Calories: 388 Carbohydrates: 2g Proteins: 48g Fat: 20g Fiber: 0.5g

Shredded Turkey with Asparagus Stir-fry

Serves: 4, Preparation: 5 minutes, Cooking: 25 minutes

Ingredients

2 tbsps. chicken fat
2 spring onions, diced
1 tsp. minced garlic
1 red pepper, finely chopped
1/4 lb. button mushrooms, sliced thin
1 cup cooked asparagus, cut into small pieces
1/2 tsp. dried rosemary
Salt and ground black pepper to taste
1 1/2 lbs. turkey breast meat; boneless, shredded
1 cup bone broth

Instructions

1. In a large frying skillet, heat the chicken fat over Medium-high heat.
2. Sauté the onion, garlic and red pepper with a little salt for 4 to 5 minutes.
3. Add mushrooms and asparagus; sauté for 2 - 3 minutes.
4. Stir in rosemary, pepper, and season with the salt to taste.
5. Add shredded turkey meat and stir well.
6. Pour the bone broth, cover and cook for 13 -15 minutes over Medium heat.
7. Taste and adjust seasonings. Serve hot.

Nutrition information:

Calories: 240 Carbohydrates: 7g Proteins: 36g Fat: 8g Fiber: 2.5g

Chapter 9 Pork, Beef & Lamb Recipes

Baked Juicy Pork with Mushrooms

Serves: 8, Preparation: 10 minutes, Cooking Time: 45 minutes

Ingredients

8 pieces of pork, any cut
4 oz. mushrooms
Salt and ground black pepper to taste
1 cup of white wine
1/2 cup of bone broth

Instructions

1. Preheat oven to 425^{0}F.
2. Season pork chunks with the salt and pepper.
3. Place the pork chunks in a large baking sheet.
4. Sprinkle mushrooms over pork evenly.
5. Pour white wine and bone broth over mushrooms and pork.
6. Place in oven and bake for 40 - 45 minutes.
7. The pork is ready when internal temperature reaches 160^{0}F.
8. Serve hot.

Nutrition information:

Calories: 145 Carbohydrates: 1.2g Proteins: 26g Fat: 4g Fiber: 0.2g

Baked Pork Chops with Mozzarella and Bacon Gravy

Serves: 4, Preparation: 10 minutes, Cooking Time: 40 minutes

Ingredients

4 pork chops
1 tsp. nutmeg
Salt and ground pepper to taste
2 tbsp. olive oil
4 slices of bacon, cut in thin strips
1 cup of cream
1 egg beaten
1 cup of shredded mozzarella

Instructions

1. Preheat your oven to 350^{0}F. Brush the pork chops with oil and place them in a baking dish.
2. Generously, season the pork chops with salt and ground pepper. Grill your pork chops for about 25 - 30 minutes, turning once.
3. In a meantime, fry bacon in a skillet strip until crisp.
4. Add cream, pepper, nutmeg and shredded mozzarella. Stir mixture for 5 minutes stirring continuously.
5. When mozzarella melts, remove skillet from the heat.
6. Add beaten egg and stir for 2 - 3 minutes.
7. Remove pork chops from the oven and place on serving platter.
8. Pour with bacon/mozzarella gravy and serve.

Nutrition information:

Calories: 660 Carbohydrates: 3.2g Proteins: 36g Fat: 56g Fiber: 0.1g

Breaded Triple Pork Rolls

Serves: 4, Preparation: 15 minutes, Cooking Time: 35 minutes

Ingredients

6 slices pork loin
6 bacon slices
6 cheese slices
Almond flour for coating
2 large eggs, beaten
Extra virgin olive oil

Instructions

1. Place a slice of bacon and a slice of cheese on top of each pork loin slice.
2. Roll up into a cylinder and secure with toothpicks.
3. Dip bacon in the beaten egg mixture, and then in almond flour.
4. Fry in the large skillet for 6 - 7 minutes or until golden browned on all sides.
5. Drain and serve hot.

Nutrition information:

Calories: 666 Carbohydrates: 1g Proteins: 53g Fat: 50g Fiber: 0g

Pork with Celery in Egg-Lemon Sauce

Serves: 6, Preparation: 10 minutes, Cooking Time: 35 minutes

Ingredients

1 lb. fresh celery root and leaves
Salt and ground white pepper to taste
2 lbs. pork, boneless, cut into cubes
2 scallions, finely chopped
3 cups of warm water
1/2 cup of olive oil
2 eggs
1 lemon

Instructions

1. Rinse the celery root, clean it and cut it into pieces. Wash the celery leaves and chop.
2. Bring water and salt to boil in a large pot and add celery root and leaves.
3. Reduce the temperature to Medium-low and cook for 30 minutes or until soft and tender.
4. Drain and discard cooking liquid.
5. Rinse the meat well, and dry on the kitchen pepper towel.
6. Heat the olive oil in a large skillet and sauté the pork meat with chopped scallions.
7. Add 3 cups warm water, cover and cook until meat softened.
8. Add cooked celery and shake the pot (do not stir) to combine well.
9. In a small bowl, whisk the egg with the lemon juice.
10. Pour the lemon-egg mixture to the pot and gently stir.
11. Remove from the heat and let sit for 5 minutes.
12. Taste and adjust salt and pepper to taste.
13. Serve hot.

Nutrition information:
Calories: 806 Carbohydrates: 4.3g Proteins: 19.5g Fat: 79g Fiber: 1.5g

Keto Barbecue Pork Skillet

Serves: 4, Preparation: 5 minutes, Cooking Time: 15 minutes

Ingredients

1 tsp. sesame oil
1/4 cup Italian dressing
1/4 cup Worcestershire sauce
1 tsp. smoked paprika
1 tsp. apple cider vinegar (preferably non-pasteurized)
6 pork chops, 3/4-inch thick

Instructions

1. In a large skillet, combine together sesame oil, Italian dressing, Worcestershire sauce and smoked paprika and vinegar for 2 minutes over Moderate heat.
2. Add the pork chops, cover with the sauce and simmer for 10 minutes or until chops are tender.
3. Serve hot.

Nutrition information:
Calories: 234 Carbohydrates: 5g Proteins: 31g Fat: 10g Fiber: 0.3g

Pork Sheftalia - Traditional Dish

Serves: 6, Preparation: 20 minutes, Cooking Time: 15 minutes

Ingredients

For the sheftalia

1 1/2 lbs. ground pork
1/3 cup of green onions, finely chopped
3 tbsp. fresh parsley, finely chopped
1 clove garlic, minced
1 tbsp. fresh lemon juice
1 tsp. dried oregano
1 tsp. dried mint
1 tsp. salt and freshly ground black pepper

For the tahini sauce

1/4 cup sesame paste
1/4 cup extra-virgin olive oil
1 tbsp. fresh lemon juice
1 clove garlic, minced
1/2 tsp. salt to taste
1/8 tsp. cayenne pepper (or to taste)
Olive oil

Instructions

1. Combine all ingredients from seftalia in a large bowl; using your hands, combine the mixture well.
2. Divide the pork mixture into 6 portions.
3 Wrap each portion of the pork tightly around a skewer to form a long cylinder.

4. Transfer to a baking sheet, cover, and refrigerate for 4 hours.

Make the tahini sauce

1. Place all ingredients for tahini sauce in your blender, and blend until smooth. Refrigerate until serving.

Grilling

1. Preheat your grill (pellet, gas, charcoal) to 350^{0}F.

2. Brush the sheftalia with oil and grill for 8-12 minutes, turning occasional.

3. Serve hot with tahini sauce.

Nutrition information:

Calories: 409 Carbohydrates: 3.4g Proteins: 21g Fat: 35g Fiber: 1.3g

Easy Pork Roast Casserole

Serves: 5, Preparation: 10 minutes, Cooking Time: 1 hour

Ingredients

2 tbsp. butter
2 lbs. pork roast
1 green onion, chopped
1 tbsp. almond flour
1/2 cup of white wine
1 cup of bone broth
1/2 cup of heavy cream
3 fresh tarragon sprigs
3 slices of Cheddar cheese
Salt and ground pepper to taste

Instructions

1. Heat the butter in a casserole over Medium heat.

2. Brown the roast for 5 - 6 minutes and add chopped green onion.

3. Pour the wine and let simmer for 2 - 3 minutes.

4. Season with the salt and pepper, pour the bone broth, cover and cook for 30 minutes.

5. Add the cream and chopped tarragon and gently stir.

6. Place cheddar slices on the top of meat, cover and cook for further 15 minutes.

7. Serve hot.

Nutrition information:

Calories: 549 Carbohydrates: 2g Proteins: 43.5g Fat: 40g Fiber: 0.1g

Pork and Bacon Baked Casserole

Serves: 4, Preparation: 10 minutes, Cooking Time: 25 minutes

Ingredients

2 lbs. pork loin, cut large strips
Salt and pepper to taste
1 tbsp. lard
1/2 lb. bacon, finely chopped
1 spring onion, finely chopped
2 cloves of garlic, finely chopped
1 cup of white wine
3 bay leaves

Instructions

1. Preheat oven to 350^{0}F.

2. Season the pork strips with the salt and pepper.

3. In a deep and heavy frying skillet, heat the lard over Medium-high heat.

4. Fry the bacon for 2 minutes.

5. Add the green onion and garlic, and sauté for 2 - 3 minutes; stir.

6. Add the pork meat and season with the salt and pepper; stir for 2 minutes.

7. Pour wine, sprinkle with crumbled bay leaves, and season with the salt and pepper.

8. Transfer the mixture in the casserole pan.

9. Place in oven and bake for 20 - 25 minutes. Serve hot.

Nutrition information:

Calories: 376 Carbohydrates: 2g Proteins: 38g Fat: 24g Fiber: 0.2g

Pork with Button Mushrooms Casserole

Serves: 4, Preparation: 10 minutes, Cooking Time: 30 minutes

Ingredients

1 tbsp. almond flour
Salt and freshly ground black pepper
1 1/2 lbs. pork loin chops, cut in strips
2 tbsps. butter

1 green onion, chopped
2 cloves of garlic, finely sliced
1 cup of button mushrooms
1 cup red wine

1/2 cup of water
1 tsp. fresh thyme
1 tbsp. mustard grain
Instructions
1. In a large container, combine the almond flour with thyme and the salt and pepper, and roll the pork strips.
2. Heat the butter in a large casserole dish over

Medium heat and sauté the pork for 2 - 3 minutes.
3. Add all remaining ingredients and sprinkle with the salt and pepper; stir only for 2 - 3 minutes.
4. Bake in the oven for about 20 minutes.
5. Serve hot.
Nutrition information:
Calories: 335 Carbohydrates: 5.5g Proteins: 40g Fat: 17g Fiber: 1g

Instant Pot Pork with Cabbage

Serves: 6, Preparation: 15 minutes, Cooking Time: 5 minutes
Ingredients
3 lbs. pork tenderloin
2 tsps. garlic powder
1 tbsp. kosher salt
1/2 cup bone broth (preferable homemade)
1/2 cup of water
1 small head of cabbage, cut in chunks
Instructions
1. Season salt and garlic powder over pork.
2. Place the pork in your Instant Pot; pour bone broth and water.
3. Lock lid into place and set on the Manual setting on High pressure for 85 minutes.
4. After the pressure-cooking time has finished, use Natural Release, it takes 10 - 25 minutes to depressurize naturally.

5. Open lid and remove the pork to a large bowl.
6. Add the cabbage wedges in your Instant Pot and sprinkle with the salt.
7. Lock lid into place and set on the Manual setting on High for 3 minutes.
8. Use Quick Release and turn the valve from Sealing to Venting to release the pressure.
9. Place cabbage wedges on a large serving platter.
10. Use 2 forks and shred the pork. Spoon the pork over the cabbage and pour with juice from the Pot.
Nutrition information:
Calories: 282 Carbohydrates: 6g Proteins: 50g Fat: 6g Fiber: 3g

Mouth-watering Shredded BBQ Roast

Serves: 8, Preparation: 10 minutes, Cooking Time: 30 minutes
Ingredients
4 lbs. pork roast
1 tsp. garlic powder
Salt and pepper to taste
1/2 cup water
2 can (11 oz.) of barbecue sauce, keto unsweetened
Instructions
1. Season the pork with garlic powder, salt and pepper; place in your Instant Pot.
2. Pour water and lock lid into place; set on the Meat/Stew setting on High Pressure for 30

minutes.
3. When ready, use Quick Release and turn the valve from Sealing to Venting to release the pressure.
4. Remove pork in a bowl, and with two forks shred the meat.
5. Pour BBQ sauce and stir to combine well.
6. Serve.
Nutrition information:
Calories: 362 Carbohydrates: 2.5g Proteins: 34g Fat: 24g Fiber: 3g

Sour and Spicy Spareribs

Serves: 6, Preparation: 15 minutes, Cooking Time: 35 minutes
Ingredients
5 lbs. spare spareribs
Salt and pepper to taste
2 tbsps. tallow
1/2 cup coconut aminos

1/2 cup vinegar
2 tbsps. Worcestershire sauce, to taste
1 tsp. chili powder
1 tsp. garlic powder

1 tsp. celery seeds
Instructions
1. Cut the rack of ribs into equal portions.
2. Season salt and ground pepper your spareribs from all sides.
3. Add tallow in your Instant Pot and place spareribs.
4. In a bowl, combine together all remaining ingredients and pour over spareribs.
5. Lock lid into place and set on the Manual setting on High heat for 35 minutes.
6. When the timer beeps, press "Cancel" and carefully flip the Natural Release for 20 minutes.
7. Open the lid and transfer ribs on a serving platter.
8. Serve hot.
Nutrition information:
Calories: 638 Carbohydrates: 2g Proteins: 36g Fat: 54g Fiber: 0.2g

Spicy Instant Pot Pork Roast

Serves: 8, Preparation: 10 minutes, Cooking Time: 30 minutes
Ingredients
3 lbs. pork shoulder, boneless
Salt and ground black pepper to taste
3 tbsps. olive oil
1 large onion, chopped
2 cloves garlic, minced
2 - 3 chili peppers, chopped
1 tsp. ground coriander
1 tsp. ground cumin
1 ½ cups of bone broth
1/2 cup water
Instructions
1. Season salt and pepper the pork meat.
2. Turn on the Instant Pot and press Sauté button. When the word "hot" appears on the display, add the oil and sauté the onions and garlic about 5 minutes.
3. Add pork and sear for 1 - 2 minutes from all sides; turn off the Sauté button.
4. Add all remaining ingredients into Instant Pot.
5. Lock lid into place and set on the Meat/Stew setting on High heat for 30 minutes.
6. When the timer beeps, press "Cancel" and carefully flip the Natural Release button for 15 minutes. Serve hot.
Nutrition information:
Calories: 397 Carbohydrates: 2.5g Proteins: 36g Fat: 27g Fiber: 0.5g

Slow Cooker Braised Sour Pork Fillet

Serves: 6, Preparation: 10 minutes, Cooking Time: 8 hours
Ingredients
1/2 tsp. dry thyme
1/2 tsp. sage
Salt and ground black pepper to taste
2 tbps. olive oil
3 lbs. pork fillet
1/3 cup of shallots, chopped
3 cloves of garlic, minced
3/4 cup of bone broth
1/3 cup of apple cider vinegar
Instructions
1. In a small bowl, combine thyme, sage, salt and black ground pepper.
2. Rub generously pork from all sides.
3. Heat the olive oil in a large frying pan, and sear pork for 2 - 3 minutes.
4. Place pork in your crock pot and add shallots and garlic.
5. Pour broth in and apple cider vinegar.
6. Cover and cook on Low for 8 hours or on High for 4-5 hours.
7. Remove pork on a plate, adjust salt and pepper, slice and serve with cooking juice.
Nutrition information:
Calories: 328 Carbohydrates: 3g Proteins: 51g Fat: 12.5g Fiber: 0.1g

Pork Stir-fry

Serves: 4, Preparation: 5 minutes, Cooking Time: 30 minutes

Ingredients

2 tbsps. lard
2 spring onion only green part, finely chopped
2 cloves garlic, finely chopped
2 lbs. pork loin, boneless, cut into cubes
Sea salt and black ground pepper to taste
1 green bell pepper, cut into thin strips
1/2 cup water
1/2 tsp. dill seeds
1/2 anise seeds
1/2 tsp. cumin

Instructions

1. Heat the lard in a large frying pot over Medium-high heat.
2. Sauté the spring onions and garlic with a pinch of salt for 3 - 4 minutes.
3. Add the pork and simmer for about 5 - 6 minutes.
4. Add all remaining ingredients and stir well.
5. Cover and let simmer for 15 - 20 minutes
6. Taste and adjust seasoning to taste. Serve.

Nutrition information:
Calories: 479 Carbohydrates: 3g Proteins: 1g Fat: 51.5g Fiber: 1g

Baked Meatballs with Goat Cheese

Serves: 8, Preparation: 15 minutes, Cooking Time: 35 minutes

Ingredients

1 tbsp. beef tallow
2 lbs. ground beef
1 organic egg
1 grated onion
1/2 cup of almond milk, unsweetened
1 cup of red wine
1/2 bunch of chopped parsley
1/2 cup of almond flour
Salt and ground pepper to taste
1/2 tbsp. dry oregano
4 oz. hard goat cheese cut in cubes

Instructions

1. Preheat oven to 400⁰F.
2. Grease a baking pan with tallow.
3. In a large bowl, combine all ingredients except goat cheese.
4. Knead the mixture until ingredients are evenly combined.
5. Make small meatballs and place in a prepared baking dish.
6. Place one cube of cheese on each meatball.
7. Bake for 30 - 35 minutes.
8. Serve hot.

Nutrition information:
Calories: 389 Carbohydrates: 2.2g Proteins: 25.5g Fat: 31g Fiber: 0.5g

Parisian Schnitzel

Serves: 4, Preparation: 15 minutes, Cooking Time: 10 minutes

Ingredients

4 veal steaks; thin schnitzel
Salt and ground black pepper
2 tbsps. butter
3 eggs
4 tbsps. almond flour

Instructions

1. Season steaks with the salt and pepper.
2. Heat butter in a large non-stick frying pan at Medium heat.
3. In a bowl, beat the eggs.
4. Place almond flour in a separate bowl.
5. Roll each steak in almond flour, and then coat in eggs.
6. Fry about 3 minutes per side.
7. Serve immediately.

Nutrition information:
Calories: 355 Carbohydrates: 0.3g Proteins: 54g Fat: 15g Fiber: 0g

Keto Beef Stroganoff

Serves: 6, Preparation: 5 minutes, Cooking Time: 30 minutes

Ingredients

2 lbs. rump or round steak or stew meat
4 tbsps. olive oil
2 green onions, finely chopped
1 grated tomato
2 tbsps. ketchup (without sugar)
1 cup of button mushrooms
1/2 cup of bone broth
1 cup of sour cream
Salt and black pepper to taste

Instructions

1. Cut the meat into strips and sauté in large frying skillet.
2. Add chopped onion and a pinch of salt and cook

meat for about 20 minutes at Medium temperature.
3. Add mushrooms and ketchup and stir for 3 - 5 minutes.
4. Pour the bone broth and sour cream and cook for 3 - 4 minutes.
5. Remove from the heat, taste and adjust salt and pepper to taste.
6. Serve hot.

Nutrition information:

Calories: 353 Carbohydrates: 4.2g Proteins: 37g Fat: 21g Fiber: 1g

Meatloaf with Gruyere

Serves: 6, Preparation: 15 minutes, Cooking Time: 40 minutes

Ingredients

1 1/2 lbs. ground beef
1 cup ground almonds
1 large egg from free-range chickens
1/2 cup grated Gruyere cheese
1 tsp. fresh parsley, finely chopped
1 scallion, finely chopped
1/2 tsp. ground cumin
3 eggs boiled
2 tbsps. butter, melted

Instructions

1. Preheat oven to 350⁰F.
2. Combine all ingredients except eggs and butter in a large bowl.

3. Use your hands, combine well the mixture.
4. Shape the mixture into a roll and place in the middle sliced hard-boiled eggs.
5. Transfer the meatloaf to a 5x9-inch loaf pan greased with melted butter.
6. Place in oven and bake for 40 minutes or until internal temperature of 160⁰F.
7. Remove from the oven and allow rest for 10 minutes.
8. Slice and serve.

Nutrition information:

Calories: 700 Carbohydrates: 5,3g Proteins: 28g Fat: 63g Fiber: 2.6g

Roasted Fillet Mignon in Foil

Serves: 6, Preparation: 15 minutes, Cooking Time: 45 minutes

Ingredients

3 lbs. fillet mignon in one piece
Salt to taste and ground black pepper
1 tsp. of garlic powder
1 tsp. of onion powder
1 tsp. of cumin
4 tbsps. olive oil

Instructions

1. Preheat the oven to 425⁰F.
2. Rinse and clean the filet mignon, removing all fats, or ask your butcher to do it for you.
3. Season with the salt and pepper, garlic powder,

onion powder and cumin.
4. Wrap filet mignon in foil and place in a roasting pan; drizzle with the olive oil.
5. Roast for 15 minutes per pound for medium-rare or to desired doneness.
6. Remove from the oven and allow to rest for 10 -15 minutes before serving.

Nutrition information:

Calories: 165 Carbohydrates: 0.8g Proteins: 52.5g Fat: 12.2g Fiber: 0.2g

Stewed Beef with Green Beans

Serves: 6, Preparation: 10 minutes, Cooking Time: 50 minutes

Ingredients

1/2 cup olive oil
1 1/2 lbs. beef, cut into cubes
2 scallions, finely chopped
2 cups water
1 lb. fresh green beans, trimmed and cut diagonally in half
1 bay leaf
1 grated tomato
1/2 cup fresh mint leaves, finely chopped
1 tsp. fresh or dry rosemary
Salt and freshly ground pepper to taste

Instructions

1. Chop the beef into 1-inch thick cubes.
2. Heat the olive oil in a large pot at High heat. Sauté the beef for about 4 - 5 minutes; sprinkle with a pinch of salt and pepper.
3. Add the scallions and stir and sauté for about another 3 - 4 minutes until softened. Pour water and cook for 2-3 minutes.
4. Add the bay leaf and grated tomato. Cook for about 5 minutes; lower the heat at Medium-low heat. Cover and simmer for about 15 minutes.
5. Add the green beans, rosemary, salt, fresh ground pepper and water enough to cover all ingredients. Gently simmer for 15 - 20 minutes until the green beans are tender.
6. Sprinkle with the mint and rosemary, gently mix and remove from the heat. Serve hot.

Nutrition information:

Calories: 354 Carbohydrates: 6g Proteins: 23g Fat: 26.5g Fiber: 2.7g

Grilled Fillet Mignon with Black Peppercorn

Serves: 6, Preparation: 10 minutes, Cooking Time: 15 minutes

Ingredients

8 beef fillet mignon steaks, 1-inch cut
Sea salt to taste
2 tbsps. olive oil
Cracked black peppercorn to taste

Instructions

1. Preheat your grill (pellet, gas, charcoal) to High according to manufacturer. **Instructions**.
2. Season each fillet with the sea salt.
3. Brush each filet with oil and press some peppercorns in the top side of each steak.
4. Place your fillets in a grill racks, close the lid, and grill for 10-12 minutes for medium-rare turning once.
5. Serve hot.

Nutrition information:

Calories: 586 Carbohydrates: 0 g Proteins: 43g Fat: 46g Fiber: 0 g

Beef and Chicken Meatballs with Curry Sauce

Serves: 4, Preparation: 15 minutes, Cooking Time: 30 minutes

Ingredients

1 lb. ground beef
3/4 lb. ground chicken
1 hot pepper, finely chopped
2 fresh onions, finely chopped
1 tsp. of fresh grated ginger
3 tbsps. fresh coriander, chopped
Ground almonds
Salt and ground black pepper

For curry sauce

3 tbsps. sesame oil
2 spring onions, finely chopped
2 cloves garlic, minced
1 tbsp. curry paste
1 tbsp. cumin

1 grated tomato
2 cups of canned coconut milk
2 tbsps. fresh coriander

Instructions

1. Combine all the ingredients in a bowl; with your hand knead until combine well.
2. Form from the mixture fine meatballs.
3. Heat the oil in a large wok or in a frying skillet.
4. Fry the meatballs for about 10 minutes in total.
5. Remove the meatballs on a plate lined with absorbent paper.

Curry sauce

1. In the wok or frying skillet, sauté the green onions for 3 - 4 minutes; add the garlic, ginger and

curry paste and stir.
2. Add the ground cumin and grated tomato, and cook for 5 minutes, stirring occasionally.
3. Add the coconut milk, season with the salt and bring to boil.
4. Cook, stir for 4 - 5 minutes.
5. Add the meatballs and cook for 5 minutes at Medium-low heat.
6. Add fresh coriander and stir well.
7. Adjust salt and pepper, stir and serve.

Nutrition information:
Calories: 392 Carbohydrates: 7.1g Proteins: 19g Fat: 32g Fiber: 2.7g

Creamy and Peppery Beef Fillets

Serves: 6, Preparation: 10 minutes, Cooking Time: 15 minutes

Ingredients
4 beef fillets (about 2 lbs.)
1 small red bell pepper, thinly chopped
1 red hot chili pepper, finely chopped
2 cloves garlic, finely sliced
2 tbsps. olive oil
1/3 cup of brandy
2 tbsps. butter
1 cup of fresh cream
1/2 cup of bone broth
Salt and ground black pepper

Instructions
1. Sprinkle the beef fillets with the chopped bell pepper, garlic and red hot chili pepper; press deep into the meat. Wrap fillets with a foil and refrigerate for 30 minutes.
2. Heat the oil in a wok or in a large frying pan and fry the fillets for 6 minutes in total for medium-rare.
3. Transfer them on a plate lined with absorbent paper; sprinkle with a pinch of the salt and pepper.
4. In the same wok or the frying pan add brandy, butter, cream and bone broth; stir and cook for 5 minutes, stirring periodically.
5. Return your fillets in a work or skillet and cover with the sauce. Serve.

Nutrition information:
Calories: 629 Carbohydrates: 2.7g Proteins: 31g Fat: 55g Fiber: 0.7g

Perfect Oven Roasted Spareribs

Serves: 6, Preparation: 10 minutes, Cooking Time: 1 hour 25 minutes

Ingredients
3 lbs. beef spareribs with the bone
1 tbsp. fresh butter
2 tbsps. olive oil
2 green onions, finely chopped
2 cloves garlic
3 tbsps. fresh celery, chopped
1 tbsp. grated tomato
2 tbsps. fresh thyme, chopped
1 cup of dry white wine
1/2 cup of bone broth
Salt and freshly ground black pepper

Instructions
1. Preheat the oven to 360°F.
2. Grease one large baking dish with the butter.
3. Season beef spareribs with the salt and pepper.
4. Place meat in a baking dish with the fat side down.
5. Heat the oil in a frying pan and sauté the onions, garlic for 3 - 4 minutes.
6. Add fresh celery, grated tomato and fresh thyme; stir well and cook for 2 - 3 minutes.
7. Pour the wine and bone broth and stir for 3 minutes.
8. Pour the sauce over the meat.
9. Cover with aluminum foil and bake for 1 1/2 hours.
10. Uncover and baste meat with the sauce and roast for further 30 minutes.
11. Allow the meat to cool for 10 - 15 minutes and serve.

Nutrition information:
Calories: 934 Carbohydrates: 2g Proteins: 33.5g Fat: 88g Fiber: 0.8g

Baked Ground Beef and Eggplant Casserole

Serves: 6, Preparation: 15 minutes, Cooking Time: 35 minutes

Ingredients

1 tbsp. beef tallow
1 lb. ground beef
1 spring onion, finely chopped
1 eggplant, diced
1 grated tomato
1/2 tsp. dried parsley flakes
1/2 tsp. dried celery flakes
1 tsp. seasoned salt
1/2 cup water
1 cup cheddar cheese, grated

Instructions

1. Preheat oven to 350^{0}F.

2. In a large casserole dish, heat the tallow and sauté the ground beef, chopped onion for 2 minutes; stir.
3. Add eggplant and stir for 2 minutes.
4. Add all remaining ingredients and give a good stir.
5. Sprinkle with grated cheese and bake for 15 minutes. Serve hot.

Nutrition information:

Calories: 472 Carbohydrates: 8g Proteins: 29g Fat: 36g Fiber: 4.5g

Festive Rosemary Beef Fillet

Serves: 6, Preparation: 15 minutes, Cooking Time: 15 minutes

Ingredients

1/4 cup olive oil
3 1/2 lbs. center-cut beef tenderloin roast
Kosher salt and ground black pepper to taste
2 cloves garlic, finely chopped
2 - 3 tbsps. fresh rosemary, chopped

Instructions

1. Preheat oven to 350^{0}F.
2. Grease one roasting pan with olive oil; set aside.
3. Pat beef roast dry, and generously coat with the salt, pepper, garlic and rosemary.

4. Place meat in a prepared roasting pan.
5. Bake for 25 - 30 minutes per pound or until inserted thermometer for internal temperature reaches 175^{0}F.
6. Remove from oven and allow to rest for 10 -15 minutes.
7. Slice and serve.

Nutrition information:

Calories: 539 Carbohydrates: 0.3g Proteins: 40g Fat: 42g Fiber: 0.3g

Keto Beef Satay

Serves: 4, Preparation: 15 minutes, Cooking Time: 5 minutes

Ingredients

1 lb. beef strips, sliced
1 tsp. turmeric
1/2 tsp. dried chili flakes
1 tbsp. coconut aminos
1 tsp. of stevia granulated sweetener
1/2 tsp. salt
1/2 cup coconut milk
1 tbsp. beef tallow

Instructions

1. Cut beef in strips about 1/4" thick. In a container, combine all remaining ingredients, add

the beef strips and marinate for 2 hours.
2. Remove the beef strips from fridge and drain on a kitchen paper towel: reserve marinade.
3. Heat the tallow in a skillet and fry the beef strips for 5 minutes in total over Medium heat.
4. Pour the marinade over the pork and simmer for 2 minutes.
5. Serve hot.

Nutrition information:

Calories: 570 Carbohydrates: 2g Proteins: 64g Fat: 34g Fiber: 0.2g

Keto Beef Stroganoff

Serves: 6, Preparation: 10 minutes, Cooking Time: 30 minutes

Ingredients

2 tbsps. butter
1/2 cup green onions (scallions), finely chopped
1/2 cup cream cheese, at room temperature
1/2 tsp. of ground garlic
1/2 tsp. dried sage
1 tsp. celery
2 lbs. beef tenderloin, cut into 2-inch strips
1 cup sliced mushrooms
Salt and ground pepper to taste

Instructions

1. Melt butter in medium skillet over Medium heat; add green onion and sauté for 3 minutes. Add cream cheese, ground garlic, sage and celery; stir until combined well. Remove skillet from heat; set aside.
2. Place beef strips with mushrooms in a large frying skillet. Cover and cook for 3 minutes on High heat. Uncover; add the cream cheese mixture and stir well.
3. Cover and cook for 20 -25 minutes over Low heat.
4. Remove from the heat and let sit for 10 minutes before serving.

Nutrition information:

Calories: 506 Carbohydrates: 2g Proteins: 29g Fat: 42g Fiber: 0.4g

Tasty Veal Roast with Herb Crust

Serves: 6, Preparation: 12 minutes, Cooking Time: 2 hours and 15 minutes

Ingredients

3 lbs. veal leg round roast, boneless
1/4 cup ground almonds
2 tbsp. water
1 tbsp. mustard (Dijon, English, or whole grain)
1 tbsp. lemon juice
1/2 tsp. ground pepper
1 tsp. dried thyme
1 tsp. dried basil
1 cup bone broth (or water)
2 tbsps. almond flour
1/4 cup sour cream

Instructions

1. Heat the oven to 350⁰F.
2. Place meat in a roasting pan.
3. In a bowl, stir together ground almonds, water, mustard, lemon juice, basil, thyme, and pepper.
4. Generously spread mixture over the meat.
5. Place a pan in oven and bake for 2-1/2 hours or until inserted thermometer reaches 160⁰F.
6. Transfer meat to a platter; cover and set aside.
7. In a saucepan stir bone broth or water with the flour. Cook and stir until thickened and bubbly, about two minutes.
8. Stir in the sour cream and just heat through.
9. Serve meat with the sauce, and Bon appetite!

Nutrition information:

Calories: 475 Carbohydrates: 2g Proteins: 83g Fat: 15g Fiber: 1g

Beef Prosciutto Casserole

Serves: 8, Preparation: 35 minutes, Cooking Time: 10 minutes

Ingredients

8 beef steaks
1 cup of white wine
8 slices prosciutto
8 leaves of sage
2 tbsps. capers
Salt and freshly ground black pepper
2 tbsps. butter

Instructions

1. Put the steaks in the container; season generously with the salt and pepper and pour in the wine; marinate for 30 minutes; drain and reserve the wine.
2. Preheat the oven to 350⁰F.
3. Place the prosciutto slice and sage leave on each beef steak and fasten with a toothpick or slice into a roll, and then fasten.
4. Grease the casserole dish with the butter and place the steaks.
5. Sprinkle with capers, little fresh pepper, and pour with reserved wine.
6. Bake for 7 - 10 minutes per side.
7. Remove from the oven, and let the meat rest before serving.

Nutrition information:

Calories: 619 Carbohydrates: 1.5g Proteins: 34g Fat: 53g Fiber: 0.2g

Ground Beef and Baby Spinach Casserole

Serves: 4, Preparation: 10 minutes, Cooking Time: 45 minutes

Ingredients

1 lb. ground beef or turkey, beef, lamb, bison
Salt and freshly ground black pepper
1 grated tomato or small dice
2 cups of baby spinach
1 cup sliced black olives
1 tbsp. fresh cilantro, finely chopped
8 eggs
1/2 cup grated cheese (Cheddar or Parmesan)

Instructions

1. Preheat oven to 350⁰F.
2. Place the ground beef in a greased casserole and sprinkle with a pinch of salt and pepper.
3. Add grated tomato, olives and baby spinach over the meat; sprinkle with the little salt and fresh cilantro.
4. In a bowl, whisk the eggs until frothy; add grated cheese and stir. Season it with the salt and pepper and stir.
5. Pour the egg mixture in casserole.
6. Place in the oven and bake for 40 - 45 minutes. Serve hot.

Nutrition information:

Calories: 478 Carbohydrates: 3.5g Proteins: 35g Fat: 36g Fiber: 2g

Instant Pot Tangy Beef Chuck Roast

Serves: 6, Preparation: 10 minutes, Cooking Time: 1 hour and 5 minutes

Ingredients

2 tbsps. olive oil
3 lbs. beef chuck roast, boneless
Seasoned salt and ground black pepper to taste
1 pinch garlic powder
2 spring onions, finely chopped
1 carrot, sliced
1 1/2 cups bone broth
1 1/2 tbsps. Worcestershire sauce

Instructions

1. Season generously the beef roast with seasoned salt and ground black pepper and garlic powder.
2. Press Sauté button on your Instant Pot. When the word "hot" appears on the display, add beef and sear from all sides.
3. Add onions and sliced carrot, turn-off the Sauté button.
4. Pour bone broth and Worcestershire sauce.
5. Lock lid into place and set on the Manual setting for 60 minutes.
6. Naturally release pressure for 5 minutes and quickly release remaining pressure.
7. Remove lid, transfer roast to the large plate and shred the roast. Serve hot.

Nutrition information:

Calories: 756 Carbohydrates: 5g Proteins: 49g Fat: 60g Fiber: 1g

Beef Roast with Herbs and Mustard

Serves: 6, Preparation: 10 minutes, Cooking Time: 8 hours

Ingredients

2 tbsps. beef tallow
2 lbs. beef roast
Salt and black ground pepper to taste
2 tbsps. yellow ground mustard seeds
1 tbsp. fresh parsley, finely chopped
1 tsp. fresh thyme, finely chopped
1 tsp. fresh cilantro chopped
1 tbsp. butter
1 1/2 cups water

Instructions

1. Grease the inner steel pot in the Slow Cooker.
2. Season the beef with the salt and pepper from all sides.
3. Place the beef roast in Slow Cooker and sprinkle with mustard seeds and fresh herbs.
4. Pour the water, add the mustard and sprinkle with parsley-cilantro mix; stir.
5. Cover and cook on Low for 6 - 8 hours.
6. Remove roast from slow cooker on a platter; allow to cool, slice and serve.

Nutrition information:

Calories: 452 Carbohydrates: 0.5g Proteins: 27g Fat: 38g Fiber: 0.3g

Ground Beef with Swiss Chard Stir-fry

Serves: 4, Preparation: 10 minutes, Cooking Time: 20 minutes

Ingredients

1 tbsp. lard or butter
2 green onions only green parts, finely chopped
1 lb. ground beef
1 tsp. garlic powder
1 tsp. ground cumin
1 tsp. oregano
Salt and ground pepper to taste
1 lb. Swiss chard, tender stems and leaves, finely chopped

Instructions

1. In a large pot boil water and cook Swiss chard for 5 - 7 minutes or until soft; transfer in colander to drain.

2. Heat the lard in a large and deep-frying pan.
3. Add the green onions with a pinch of salt, and sauté for 3 - 4 minutes over Medium heat.
4. Add ground beef and stir for 4 -5 minutes.
5. Season with the garlic powder, cumin and oregano; stir well.
6. Add steamed Swish chard and gently stir to combine all ingredients; cover and cook for further 2 - 3 minutes. Serve hot.

Nutrition information:

Calories: 301 Carbohydrates: 5g Proteins: 23g Fat: 21g Fiber: 3g

Ground Beef Kale Stew with Almonds

Serves: 4, Preparation: 5 minutes, Cooking Time: 25 minutes

Ingredients

1 lb. kale, chopped, tough stems discarded
2 tbsps. olive oil
1 lb. ground beef
1/4 tsp. of cinnamon
1 tsp. cumin
1 tsp. oregano
1 tsp. garlic powder
Salt and freshly ground black pepper to taste
1 cup almonds, finely chopped or ground

Instructions

1. Boil water in a large pot; submerge kale and boil for 5 - 6 minutes; transfer kale in a colander to drain.

2. Heat the oil in a large and deep-frying and sauté ground meat for 6 - 7 minutes.
3. Season with the cinnamon, cumin, oregano, garlic powder, and the ground pepper and salt; stir well.
4. Add streamed kale, stir gently, cover and cook for 3 - 4 minutes over Low heat.
5. Taste and adjust seasonings. Sprinkle with ground almonds and serve hot.

Nutrition information:

Calories: 481 Carbohydrates: 8g Proteins: 28g Fat: 38g Fiber: 3.5g

Perfect Keto Beef and Broccoli Stir-Fry

Serves: 4, Preparation: 10 minutes, Cooking Time: 15 minutes

Ingredients

1 lb. pre-cut beef strips, or beef for stir-fry
2 tbsps. almond flour
1/2 cup water
1/2 tsp. garlic powder
2 tbsps. olive oil, divided
4 cups broccoli florets
1 small onion, cut into wedges
1 tsp. ground of fresh ginger

Instructions

1. In a bowl, combine 2 tablespoons of almond flour, 2 tablespoons water and garlic powder until smooth.
2. Pour the mixture over the beef and toss to combine well.

3. In a large skillet heat the oil over Medium-high heat, stir-fry the beef strips for 4 - 5 minutes, or until beef reaches desired doneness. Remove the beef on a plate.
4. Heat some more oil in the same skillet and sauté the onion for 3 - 4 minutes.
5. Add the broccoli; season with the salt and pepper and sauté for about 2 - 3 minutes.
6. Add the chicken again in a skillet, stir and cook along with remaining ingredients for 2 minutes. Serve hot.

Nutrition information:

Calories: 228 Carbohydrates: 1.5g Proteins: 29g Fat: 11g Fiber: 0.5g

Grilled Lamb Skewers

Serves: 6, Preparation: 15 minutes, Cooking Time: 10 minutes

Ingredients

2 lbs. lamb fillet, cut in cubes
Salt to taste
1/2 cup of olive oil
1 tbsp. grated ginger
1 cup of white wine
2 tbsps. wine vinegar
1/4 tsp. of freshly ground black pepper

Instructions

1. Rinse and trim your lamb fillet; cut lamb fillet into 1 1/2-inch cubes. Season the lamb meat generously with salt.
2. In a bowl, whisk the olive oil, ginger, wine, vinegar, and pepper to make the marinade.
3. Add the lamb cube and combine with marinade.

Cover and refrigerate for 2-3 hours or overnight.
4. Preheat your grill (pellet, gas, charcoal) to High according to manufacturer. **Instructions**
5. Remove the lamb from the fridge and pat dry on kitchen paper towel. Thread the meat onto skewers and place on grill.
6. Grill for about 10 minutes in total for medium-rare, turning every 1-2 minutes, until lamb is cooked to desired doneness.
7. Remove skewers from the grill and let sit for 5 minutes. Serve.

Nutrition information:

Calories: 463 Carbohydrates: 1.3g Proteins: 28g Fat: 38.5g Fiber: 0.05g

Grilled Lamb Patties

Serves: 6, Preparation: 15 minutes, Cooking Time: 10 minutes

Ingredients

1 3/4 lbs. ground lamb meat
1/4 cup ground almonds
1 tsp. dried oregano
1 large egg at room temperature
1/2 tsp. garlic powder
1/2 tsp. of onion powder
1 tsp. cumin
2 tsps. chopped fresh rosemary
Cayenne pepper to taste
Sea salt to taste

Instructions

1. Combine all ingredients in a large bowl.
2. Use your hands, combine and knead the mixture until combine well.

3. Wet your hands and form mixture into 6 patties, and place on a plate lined with parchment paper.
4. Place the lamb patties in a fridge for one hour.
5. Preheat your grill (pellet, gas, charcoal) to High according to manufacturer.

Instructions

6. Arrange lamb patties on grill rack and cook for about 4 - 5 minutes per side for medium-rare.
7. Transfer lamb patties to serving plate and let rest for 10 minutes.
8. Serve.

Nutrition information:

Calories: 262 Carbohydrates: 4g Proteins: 39g Fat: 10g Fiber: 1g

Grilled Lamb Chops with Sweet Marinade

Serves: 4, Preparation: 15 minutes, Cooking Time: 15 minutes

Ingredients

3 tbsps. olive oil
1/4 cup stevia granulate sweetener
1 tsp. garlic powder
2 tsps. ground ginger
2 tsps. dried tarragon
1 tsp. ground cinnamon
Salt and ground black pepper to taste
4 lamb chops

Instructions

1. In a bowl, combine the olive oil, stevia, garlic, ginger, tarragon, cinnamon and salt and pepper. Rub lamb chops with mixture, and place in a deep

container. Cover, and refrigerate for 2 hours, preferable overnight.
2. Preheat your grill (pellet, gas, charcoal) to High according to manufacturer instructions.
3. Remove the lamb chops from marinade and place directly on grill grate.
4. Grill for 4-6 minutes per side or until inserted thermometer reaches 135^{0}F internal temperature. Serve hot.

Nutrition information:

Calories: 401 Carbohydrates: 0.3g Proteins: 28g Fat: 32g Fiber: 0.5g

Roasted Lamb Loin with Yogurt Sauce

Serves: 6, Preparation: 15 minutes, Cooking Time: 1 hour and 40 minutes

Ingredients

2 tbsps. olive oil
1 cup of yogurt
1 tbsp. tomato paste
2 tbsps. fresh thyme, chopped
3 cloves garlic, finely chopped
2 lbs. lamb loin
Salt and black pepper, freshly ground
1 bunch of parsley, chopped

Instructions

1. Preheat the oven at 325^{0}F.
2. Combine olive oil, yogurt, tomato paste, thyme and garlic in a bowl and pour in a large baking pan.

3. Season the lamb loin with the salt and pepper and place in a baking pan.
4. Baste the lamb with sauce.
5. Cover with aluminum foil and place in oven.
6. Bake for 1 hour, and then uncover and bake for additional 40 minutes.
7. Sprinkle with chopped parsley and remove from the oven.
8. Before serving, allow to cool for 10 minutes.

Nutrition information:

Calories: 389 Carbohydrates: 4.8g Proteins: 30g Fat: 27g Fiber: 0.8g

Grilled Lamb Chops

Serves: 4, Preparation: 20 minutes, Cooking Time: 10 minutes

Ingredients

8 lamb chops
Roasted red peppers
1 garlic clove, minced
1 tsp. parsley, chopped
3 tbsps. Spanish extra virgin olive oil
Pinch of salt
Black pepper

Instructions

1. Preheat your grill (pellet, gas, charcoal) to High according to manufacturer.

Instructions.

2. Season the lamb chops with the salt and pepper,

and drizzle with the olive oil.
Place the lamb chops on grill and cook for 3- 4 minutes per side for medium-rare.
3. Meanwhile cut the red peppers into strips and add the garlic clove, parsley, Spanish olive oil, salt and black pepper.
4. Season the lamb chops with salt and serve immediately along with the peppers.

Nutrition information:

Calories: 273 Carbohydrates: 1g Proteins: 38g Fat: 13g Fiber: 0.4g

Instant Pot Lamb Chops with Greens

Serves: 4, Preparation: 10 minutes, Cooking Time: 35 minutes

Ingredients

1/4 cup olive oil
2 spring onions, finely chopped
2 cloves of garlic, minced
3 lbs. lamb chops
2 lbs. wild greens
1 tsp. dry rosemary
1 cup water
Salt and ground pepper to taste
Lemon wedges for serving

Instructions

1. Rinse and clean wild greens from any dirt.
2. Press Sauté button on your Instant Pot.
3. When the word "hot" appears on the display, add the oil and sauté green onions and garlic for about 2 - 3 minutes.
4. Add lamb meat and sear for 2 - 3 minutes.

5. Lock lid into place and set on the Manual setting for 25 minutes.
6. Use Quick Release and turn the valve from Sealing to Venting to release the pressure.
7. Add greens, season with the salt and pepper and sprinkle with rosemary. Pour one cup of water and cover.
8. Lock lid into place and set on the Manual setting for 3 minutes.
9. When the timer beeps, press "Cancel" and carefully flip the Quick Release valve to let the pressure out.
10. Serve hot with lemon wedges.

Nutrition information:

Calories: 316 Carbohydrates: 8g Proteins: 35g Fat: 16g Fiber: 5g

Chapter 10 Game Recipes

Drunken Quails with Thyme and Oregano

Serves: 4, Preparation: 15 minutes, Cooking: 35 minutes

Ingredients

4 quails, cleaned (or Cornish game hens)
2 cloves of garlic, minced
1 tbsp. fresh thyme
1 tbsp. oregano, fresh or dry
Freshly ground salt and pepper
2 tbsps. olive oil
1 1/2 cups of white wine
1 lemon juice
Enough water

Instructions

1. Rinse the quails well and cut them with kitchen scissors along the spine.
2. Season with the salt and pepper, and place in a deep container.
3. In a separate bowl, combine all remaining ingredients and pour over the quails.
4. Cover with plastic membrane and refrigerate overnight.
5. Remove birds from the marinade, and pat dry on a kitchen paper.
6. Heat some oil in a large frying skillet and sauté the quails for 4 - 5 minutes, or until get a nice color.
7. Pour some wine and lemon juice, lower the heat, and simmer for 20 minutes.
8. If necessary, add some water and continue cooking for another 10 minutes.
9. Serve instantly.

Nutrition information:

Calories: 353 Carbohydrates: 5g Proteins: 22g Fat: 20g Fiber: 1g

Antelope Steak on Grill

Serves: 4, Preparation: 10 minutes, Cooking: 20 minutes

Ingredients

4 lbs. antelope steak (1/2-inch each) (substitute venison or other game meat if difficult to find)
1/4 tsp. salt and ground pepper
1/4 cup Worcestershire sauce, sugar free
2 tbsps. coconut aminos
1/4 cup olive oil
1/2 cup fresh lemon juice
1/4 tsp. thyme (optional)
1/4 tsp. rosemary
2 cloves garlic, crushed

Instructions

1. In a large container, combine all ingredients for marinade except meat.
2. Submerge the antelope steak and cover evenly with marinade; refrigerate for 12 - 14 hours.
3. Preheat your grill on High.
4. Place the antelope steaks on the grates.
5. Grill for 5 - 7 minutes per side.
6. Lower the heat and cook the antelope steak for further 10 minutes.

Nutrition information:

Calories: 422 Carbohydrates: 4g Proteins: 68g Fat: 16g Fiber: 0.2g

French Marinated Quails

Serves: 4, Preparation: 10 minutes, Cooking: 4 hours

Ingredients

2 spring onions, finely chopped
2 cloves of garlic
4 quails, cleaned (or Cornish game hens)
1 carrot
1 cup of extra virgin olive oil
1 cup of white wine
1 1/2 cups of water
1/4 cup of fresh rosemary, finely chopped
1/2 cup of fresh thyme, chopped
10 -15 grains of black and white pepper
Salt and ground pepper to taste

Instructions

1. Heat the oil in a large skillet and sauté the onion, carrot and garlic for 2 - 3 minutes.
2. Add quails and sear on both sides.
3. Place quails and all remaining ingredients in

Slow Cooker.
4. Cover with liquids (oil, wine and water), add sprinkle with the salt and pepper; stir.
5. Cover and cook for on High for 3 - 4 hours.
6. Allow to cool and transfer in a container;

refrigerate for 3 - 4 days before consuming.
Nutrition information:
Calories: 276 Carbohydrates: 1.5g Proteins: 22g
Fat: 14g Fiber: 1.5g

Bacon Wrapped Pheasant in Wine Sauce

Serves: 4, Preparation: 15 minutes, Cooking: 1 hour and 15 minutes
Ingredients
1 pheasant, cleaned (substitute goose, quail, or Cornish hens)
8 - 10 slice of bacon
1 1/2 cups red wine
1 small glass of cognac
1 cup of very strong black tea
3 tbsps. butter
Salt and ground pepper to taste
Instructions
1. Season the pheasant with the salt and pepper, and wrap breast and thighs with bacon, and fasten with the string.

2. Place the pheasant in a pot and pour it with the wine, cognac, tea and butter into pieces.
3. Cover and cook for 1 hour over Medium-low heat.
4. Remove the pheasant from the pot, cut in a half.
5. Preheat the oven to 360°F.
6. Place the pheasant in baking dish, pour the sauce from the pot, and bake for 15 minutes.
7. Serve hot.
Nutrition information:
Calories: 588 Carbohydrates: 3g Proteins: 30g Fat: 46g Fiber: 0g

Fried Quails with Sesame

Serves: 4, Preparation: 10 minutes, Cooking: 25 minutes
Ingredients
4 big quail (Cornish game hens work as a substitution)
2 tbsps. butter
2 tsps. sesame seeds
2 tbsps. white wine vinegar
1/4 cup garlic-infused oil
Salt and freshly ground pepper
Instructions
1. Season the quails with the salt and pepper.
2. Heat the butter in a deep frying pan and sauté quails for 5 minutes or just to take color.
3. Cover and let it cook for further 10 minutes over Medium heat.

4. In a bowl, stir the vinegar, oil, salt and pepper and sesame seeds.
5. Remove the excess fat from the frying pan with quails.
6. Pour the vinegar over the quails; toss to combine well.
7. Heat the remaining oil in a skillet and fry the quails for 10 minutes from all sides.
8. Serve hot.
Nutrition information:
Calories: 519 Carbohydrates: 1g Proteins: 29g Fat: 44g Fiber: 0.3g

Oven Baked Marinated Quail

Serves: 8, Preparation: 15 minutes; marinade overnight, Cooking: 2 hours
Ingredients
2 spring onions, finely chopped
2 cloves of garlic
8 quail, cleaned
3 cups of dry wine
1 1/2 cups of olive oil
4 medium stalks of celery, chopped
2 cinnamon sticks
15 tsps. ground allspice

4 bay leaves
Salt and ground pepper to taste
Instructions
1. Slice the onions, garlic and celery, and add in a large and deep container.
2. Pour the olive oil, bay leaves, cinnamon sticks, allspice, salt and pepper; toss to combine well, and marinade to cover birds well.

3. Cover and refrigerate overnight.
4. Remove birds on a kitchen towel; strain marinade and reserve.
5. We take care of liquids (wine, olive oil) to cover the quail.
6. Heat the oven to 380 °F.
7. Place the quail in a greased baking dish, and place birds; pour with reserved marinade.
8. Place in the oven and roast for about 2 hours. Serve hot.

Nutrition information:
Calories: 503 Carbohydrates: 6g Proteins: 18g Fat: 41.1g Fiber: 1.5g

Grilled Kangaroo Kebabs

Serves: 4, Preparation: 15 minutes, Cooking: 10 minutes

Ingredients
1 lb. of ground kangaroo meat (substitutes include other game meats, lamb etc.)
3 tbsps. olive oil
1 red onion, finely diced
2 garlic, minced
1 cup mint, chopped
1 cup almonds, roughly chopped
1 cup lemon juice
Zest of 1 medium lemon
Sea salt and freshly ground black pepper

Instructions
1. Preheat your grill to High.
2. In a bowl, combine all ingredients and mix well.
3. Arrange the kangaroo meat onto the skewers.
4. Cook for about 10 minutes, turning occasionally and browning all sides.
5. Serve hot.

Nutrition information:
Calories: 456 Carbohydrates: 6g Proteins: 23g Fat: 38g Fiber: 2g

Instant Pot Venison Roast

Serves: 4, Preparation: 10 minutes, Cooking: 1 hour

Ingredients
1 cup of olive oil
3 lbs. venison roast meat
2 sprigs fresh and organic rosemary
2 tsps. sprigs; fresh, summer savory
2 cups of bone broth
Salt and pepper to taste

Instructions
1. Season the venison roast with the salt and pepper.
2. Pour the olive oil to the inner stainless steel pot in the Instant Pot.
3. Place venison roast and add all remaining ingredients.
4. Lock lid into place and set on the Meat setting for 60 minutes.
5. After the cooking time has finished use Natural-release, it takes 10 - 25 minutes to depressurize naturally.
6. Serve hot.

Nutrition information:
Calories: 410 Carbohydrates: 0.5g Proteins: 60g Fat: 20g Fiber: 0.2g

Marinated Venison Tenderloin on the Grill

Serves: 4, Preparation: 15 minutes, Cooking: 15 minutes

Ingredients
MARINADE
1 tsp. salt and freshly ground black pepper
1 tsp. dried rosemary
1 tsp. sage leaves, finely chopped
1 tsp. red pepper flakes
3 tbsps. fresh lime juice
1 tbsp. hot pepper sauce
3 tbsps. Worcestershire sauce, sugar free
2 tbsps. mustard (Dijon, English, ground stone)

GAME
2 lbs. venison tenderloin

Instructions
1. In a bowl, whisk all ingredients for marinade.
2. Place the venison tenderloin in a large container, and coat with the marinade evenly.
3. Cover and refrigerate for at least 4 hours (preferably overnight).
4. Preheat your grill on High heat.

5. Remove venison tenderloin from marinade and pat dry.
6. Grill the venison tenderloin for about 7 - 8 minutes per side or until reaches 150^{0}F.
7. Remove from grill and let sit 10 - 15 minutes before serving.

Nutrition information:
Calories: 291 Carbohydrates: 4g Proteins: 52g Fat: 6g Fiber: 0.3g

Oven Roasted Marinated Boar

Serves: 6, Preparation: 15 minutes; marinade overnight, Cooking: 3 hours

Ingredients
1 wild boar leg; skinned, about 2 pounds (lean pork is a good substitute)
1 can (6 oz.) of beer
2 spring onions, in moderate frames
2 cloves of garlic, in thin slices
2 tbsps. thyme dry, grated
1 tsp. cumin, powdered
1 tbsp. dry coriander, grated
1 cup of vinegar
1/2 cup of olive oil
Salt and freshly ground pepper
Enough water

Instructions
1. In a deep container, put the boar leg, the vinegar and water to cover the meat.
2. Cover with plastics membrane and leave in the refrigerator for 2 hours.
3. Remove from refrigerator, rinse well and dry on a kitchen towel.
4. Put the boar in the deep pot and add all the other ingredients from the list.
5. Cover with membrane and leave to marinate overnight.
6. Preheat the oven to 360^{0}F.
7. Transfer the boar meat together with the marinade to the baking dish, cover with lid and bake for 1 ½ hours.
8. Lower the oven temperature to 300^{0}F and bake for further 1 1/4 - 1 1/2 hours.
9. Remove the boar meat from the oven, let it cool for a while and cut into thin slices. Serve hot.

Nutrition information:
Calories: 388 Carbohydrates: 4.5g Proteins: 33g Fat: 23g Fiber: 1g

Roasted Gourmet Pheasant

Serves: 4, Preparation: 10 minutes, Cooking: 55 minutes

Ingredients
1 pheasant; cleaned, about 3 lbs.
1 cup of butter, softened
Salt and ground pepper to taste
1 cup of red wine
1 glass of cognac
1/2 cup of fresh parsley
2 bay leaves

Instructions
1. Preheat oven to 450^{0}F.
2. Generously season the pheasant with the salt and pepper.
3. Rub the bird with the butter and place in baking dish breast sides up.
4. Pour it with cognac, wine, and sprinkle fresh parsley and crumble bay leaves.
5. Roast the pheasant for 15 minutes on High temperature.
6. Remove the pheasant on a working surface and lower the heat to 350^{0}F. (wait for about 10 -15 minutes).
7. Return the bird in the oven, and bake for 35 -40 minutes or until internal temperature reaches 155^{0}F to 165^{0}F.
8. Let the pheasant rest for 10 minutes, cut and serve.

Nutrition information:
Calories: 613 Carbohydrates: 0.7g Proteins: 23g Fat: 49g Fiber: 0.3g

Roasted Partridges with Thyme

Serves: 4, Preparation: 10 minutes, Cooking: 3 hours

Ingredients

2 partridges, cleaned (Cornish game hen is a good substitute)
1 cup of salted butter
6 cloves of garlic
1 tsp. nutmeg
1 tsp. pepper, in grains
1 1/3 cups of white dry wine
1 handful of fresh thyme, finely chopped
Salt and ground pepper to taste

Instructions

1. Preheat the oven to 400^{0}F.
2. Place the partridges in a baking dish, season with the salt, and rub them with half of butter.
3. Bake for 1 hour in the oven, with the chest down.
4. Combine, and pour the garlic, nutmeg, pepper, wine, and thyme over the birds.
5. Cover them with aluminum foil and bake for further 2 hours on 340^{0}F.
6. Remove partridges from oven and let them sit for 15 minutes to cool down.
7. Remove bones and cut meat in pieces.
8. Place meat on a platter and pour with the melted butter.
9. Sprinkle with a chopped thyme and serve.

Nutrition information:

Calories: 534 Carbohydrates: 4.5g Proteins: 46g Fat: 30g Fiber: 0.5g

Roasted Wild Rabbit

Serves: 4, Preparation: 10 minutes, Cooking: 1 hour 40 minutes

Ingredients

2 wild rabbits, cut into 8 pieces
1/4 cup olive oil
6 garlic cloves, unpeeled
1 green onion, finely chopped
2 sprigs sage
2 fresh rosemary leaves
2 bay leaves
1 green chili pepper
1 1/2 cups pitted black olives
1 cup white red wine
Chopped flat-leaf parsley

Instructions

1. Heat the oil in a large frying skillet and sauté the rabbit meat for 5 minutes.
2. Add the garlic and onion and stir for 5 minutes over a Medium heat. Add all remaining ingredients and stir well.
3. Preheat oven to 350^{0}F.
4. Bake rabbits uncovered for 1 ½ hours or until meat is tender and comes away from the bone. Top with chopped parsley and serve.
5. Remove rabbits from oven and let them sit for 10 minutes.
6. Serve.

Nutrition information:

Calories: 425 Carbohydrates: 5g Proteins: 53g Fat: 18g Fiber: 1g

Gourmet Rabbit with Rosemary Casserole

Serves: 6, Preparation: 10 minutes, Cooking: 1 hour and 30 minutes

Ingredients

1/4 cup olive oil
2 rabbits, cut into pieces
Salt and pepper to taste
1/2 cup almond flour
4 cloves of garlic, roughly chopped
10 fresh rosemary sprigs
2 cups bone broth

Instructions

1. Preheat the oven to 350⁰F.
2. Season the rabbit generously with the salt and pepper.
3. Toss the rabbit pieces into almond flour and place them in casserole.
4. Sprinkle the rabbit with oil, garlic and rosemary sprigs.
5. Pour the bone broth evenly over the rabbits.
6. Place in the oven and bake for about 1 to 1 1/2 hours or until done.
7. Remove from the oven, let sit for 10 minutes and serve hot.

Nutrition information:

Calories: 364 Carbohydrates: 0.8g Proteins: 60g Fat: 16g Fiber: 0.1g

Wild Boar Tenderloin with Avocado

Serves: 6, Preparation: 10 minutes, Cooking: 25 minutes

Ingredients

2 tsps. lard
1 medium onion, peeled and diced
6 boar tenderloin fillets (pork is a good substitute)
3 ripe avocados; peeled, cut in cubes
1 tbsp. stevia sweetener, granulated (optional)
1 cup white wine
Salt and ground black pepper to taste

Instructions

1. Heat 1 teaspoon of lard in a frying skillet over Medium-high heat.
2. Sauté the onion for 3 - 4 minutes until translucent.
3. Add the avocado and sweetener and stir for 2 minutes.
4. Pour wine, stir and lower the heat to Medium-low.
5. Remove the sauce from the heat and set aside.
6. Heat the remaining lard in a separate frying skillet and fry the tenderloin fillets for 8 - 10 minutes; season with the salt and pepper and stir.
7. Allow fillets to rest 10 minutes and place on a serving plate.
8. Serve warm.

Nutrition information:

Calories: 371 Carbohydrates: 9.5g Proteins: 31g Fat: 19g Fiber: 6g

Chapter 11 Keto Fat Bombs

Absolute Cacao Fat Bombs

Serves: 6, Preparation: 10 minutes

Ingredients

1/2 cup of coconut oil, melted
3/4 cup heavy cream
1/4 cup cacao dry powder, unsweetened
3 tbsps. almond butter
1 tsp. nutmeg, optional
4 drops of natural sweeter stevia, or to taste

Instructions

1. Melt the coconut oil in a microwave for 10 - 15 seconds.

2. Combine all ingredients in a bowl and stir well.
3. Pour the mixture in a cake molds and freeze for two hours or until set.
4. Press out of molds and place on a plate or in a container.
5. Keep refrigerated.

Nutrition information:

Calories: 260 Carbohydrates: 3.5g Proteins: 3g Fat: 26g Fiber: 2g

Zucchini Fat Bomb

Serves: 4, Preparation: 15 minutes

Ingredients

2 tbsps. almond butter
3 large zucchinis, shredded
1 cup fresh basil and chives, finely chopped
1 cup shredded mozzarella
1/2 cup Cheddar cheese
Pinch of salt, optional

Instructions

1. Peel zucchini, and shred in a food processor.
2. Line one baking sheet with parchment paper.

3. In a mixing bowl, combine all ingredients in a compact mixture.
4. For mixture into small balls and place them on a prepared baking sheet.
5. Freeze for 2 - 3 hours in a freezer.
6. Serve. Keep refrigerated.

Nutrition information:

Calories: 116 Carbohydrates: 3g Proteins: 8g Fat: 8g Fiber: 1g

Almonds Gale Fat Bombs

Serves: 4, Preparation: 10 minutes

Ingredients

1 cup coconut oil
1 cup almond butter, unsalted
1/4 cup ground almonds, without salt
1 tsp. vanilla extract
1/4 can natural sweetener, such as stevia, truvia
Pinch of salt

Instructions

1. In a microwave safe bowl, softened the almond butter.

2. Add all ingredients in your fast-speed blender.
3. Blend until thoroughly combined.
4. Make small balls and place on a plate lined with parchment paper.
5. Freeze for about 4 hours or overnight.
6. Serve.

Nutrition information:

Calories: 314 Carbohydrates: 5g Proteins: 6g Fat: 30g Fiber: 2g

Bacon and Basil Fat Bombs

Serves: 6, Preparation: 15 minutes

Ingredients

2 cups of cream cheese from refrigerator
6 slices of bacon, finely chopped
1 small chili pepper, finely chopped
1 tbsp. fresh basil, chopped

1/2 tsp. onion powder
1/4 tsp. garlic powder
Salt and pepper to taste

Instructions

1. Beat the cheese cream in a mixing bowl.
2. Add chopped bacon and stir well with the spoon.
3. Add all remaining ingredients and stir well to combine all ingredients.
4. Make small balls and place on a platter.

5. Refrigerate for 2 - 3 hours and serve.
6. Keep refrigerated.
Nutrition information:
Calories: 275 Carbohydrates: 2g Proteins: 6g Fat: 27g Fiber: 0.03g

Berries and Chia Fat Bombs

Serves: 4, Preparation: 15 minutes
Ingredients
2 cups fresh whipping cream
2 tbsps. fresh butter, softened
1/2 cup of natural granulated sweetener, such as stevia, truvia
1/2 cup frozen berries, thawed (blueberries, raspberries)
1 tbsp. chia
1 tsp. vanilla extract
Instructions
1. Beat the cream with a hand mixer in a bowl

until double in volume and stiff.
2. Add all remaining ingredients and continue to beat until combined completely.
3. Pour the berries mixture in ice cubes tray or in a muffin tray.
4. Freeze for at least 4 hours, preferably overnight.
5. Serve or keep refrigerated.
Nutrition information:
Calories: 76 Carbohydrates: 6.6g Proteins: 3g Fat: 4.2g Fiber: 0.2g

Chilly Tuna Fat Balls

Serves: 6, Preparation: 10 minutes
Ingredients
2 cans tuna, drained
1 medium avocado, cubed
2 tbsps. coconut butter
1/2 cup mayonnaise
2 tbsps. mustard
1 cup Parmesan cheese
1/3 cup ground almonds
1 tsp. garlic powder
Salt and pepper to taste
Instructions
1. Cut medium avocado in half, remove the pit

and skin, and cut the flesh in cubes.
2. Drain and add tuna in a large bawl along with all ingredients; stir well with the spoon.
3. Make the tuna mixture into small balls.
4. Place tuna balls on a plate lined with parchment paper and refrigerate for 2 hours.
5. Serve or keep refrigerated.
Nutrition information:
Calories: 213 Carbohydrates: 6g Proteins: 9g Fat: 17g Fiber: 2.2g

Choco-Peanut Butter Fat Balls

Serves: 4, Preparation: 15 minutes
Ingredients
1/2 cup fresh whipping cream
1 cup of dark chocolate chips (60 %- 69% cacao solid)
1/2 cup of peanut butter, softened
1/4 cup of coconut oil, softened
1/4 cup of butter, softened
2 tbsps. ground peanuts
Instructions
1. In a bowl, beat the cream until stiff peak and double in volume.
2. Melt the chocolate chips in a microwave for

about 45 - 60 seconds; stir every 20 seconds.
3. Fold all ingredients in a whipped cream and beat for 2 - 3 minutes.
4. In a meanwhile, whip together peanut butter, coconut oil and butter.
5. Pour the mixture in molds or in cupcakes holders and freeze for 4 hours.
6. Keep refrigerated.
Nutrition information:
Calories: 300 Carbohydrates: 7g Proteins: 5g Fat: 28g Fiber: 2g

Cinnamon - Nutmeg Fat Bombs

Serves: 6, Preparation: 10 minutes

Ingredients

1 cup almond butter plain, unsalted
1/2 cup unsweetened almond milk, or coconut milk
3/4 cup ground almonds or macadamia nuts, unsalted
1/2 tsp. cinnamon
1 tsp. vanilla extract
1/2 tsp. ground nutmeg, optional
2 tbsps. natural sweetener, such as stevia, truvia

Instructions

1. Add all ingredients in your food processor, and process for 45 - 60 seconds.
2. Add more or less sweetener, or to taste.
3. Grease your hands with oil and form dough into small balls.
4. Place on a baking pan covered with parchment paper and refrigerate for 2 - 3 hours.
5. Serve.

Nutrition information:

Calories: 286 Carbohydrates: 6.5g Proteins: 11g Fat: 24g Fiber: 3.5g

Creamy Green Olive Fat Bombs

Serves: 6, Preparation: 20 minutes

Ingredients

1 lb. cold cream cheese
1 cup whipped cream
1 1/2 cups green olives, pitted
1/2 cup fresh parsley, finely chopped
1 pinch of salt, optional

Instructions

1. Line a platter or baking pan with parchment paper; set aside.
2. Add cream cheese in a bowl and fast whisk with the spoon.
3. In a separate bowl, beat the cream to double in volume.
4. Combine the cream cheese and whipped cream; season with a pinch of salt.
5. Make balls from the cream cheese mixture and insert one olive in a center of each ball.
6. Roll each ball in chopped parsley and coat evenly from all sides.
7. Place the balls on prepared platter and refrigerate for 4 hours or overnight.
8. Serve.

Nutrition information:

Calories: 142 Carbohydrates: 2g Proteins: 2g Fat: 14g Fiber: 0.5g

Creamy Lime Fat Bombs

Serves: 10, Preparation: 10 minutes

Ingredients

3/4 cup coconut oil
1/2 cup whipping cream (yields 2 cups, whipped)
1/2 cup cream cheese
1 tsp. pure lime extract
10 drops natural sweetener, such as stevia, truvia

Instructions

1. In a bowl, beat the cream with a hand mixer.
2. Add all remaining ingredients and continue to beat for 45 - 60 seconds.
3. Pour the mixture into a silicone tray and freeze for several hours.
4. When hard enough, remove from the freezer, and from silicone tray and serve.

Nutrition information:

Calories: 233 Carbohydrates: 1g Proteins: 1g Fat: 25g Fiber: 0g

Eggs with Gorgonzola Fat Bombs

Serves: 6, Preparation: 10 minutes

Ingredients

2 eggs, boiled
1/4 cup butter, softened
1 cup cream cheese full fat
3/4 cup Gorgonzola - blue cheese, grated

Instructions

1. First, boil the eggs in a saucepan; remove from heat and set aside for 10 minutes.
2. In a meantime, line a baking pan with

parchment paper.

3. Combine cream cheese, butter and grated Gorgonzola. Add the chopped eggs and stir well.

4. Make 6 - 8 balls and place them on a prepared pan.

5. Refrigerate for 2 - 3 hours and serve.

Nutrition information:
Calories: 283 Carbohydrates: 2g Proteins: 8g Fat: 27g Fiber: 0g

Lemon Coconut Fat Bombs

Serves: 5, Preparation: 10 minutes

Ingredients
1/2 cup coconut oil, melted and cooled
1/4 cup heavy cream
1/4 cup cream cheese, full fat
1 lemon, freshly squeezed
1 lemon zest, finely grated fresh
1 tsp. pure lemon extract
1/4 cup natural sweetener, such as stevia, erythritol
1/2 cup coconut shredded, unsweetened

Instructions
1. Melt the coconut oil in a microwave oven for 10 - 15 seconds. Set it aside to cool for 2 - 3 minutes.
2. Whisk melted coconut oil with heavy cream, and with the cream cheese.

3. Pour the lemon juice and lemon zest and stir. Add stevia sweetener and stir well until sweetener dissolve completely.

4. At the end, add pure lemon extract and stir.

5. Pour the mixture in a candy molds or ice cube tray.

6. Freeze for 2 hours, and then remove your fat bombs on a platter.

7. Keep refrigerated.

Nutrition information:
Calories: 177 Carbohydrates: .5g Proteins: 1g Fat: 17g Fiber: 1g

Maca and Vanilla Protein Fat Bombs

Serves: 5, Preparation: 15 minutes

Ingredients
1 cup coconut oil, melted
1/2 cup coconut butter
1/2 cup coconut shreds
1/2 cup raw almonds, peeled and finely chopped
2 tbsps. maca root powder
1 scoop of vanilla protein powder
1 tsp. vanilla extract
1/4 cup of natural sweetener (stevia, honey etc.) or to taste

Instructions
1. Melt the coconut butter in a microwave oven for 10 seconds; let it cool for 2 - 3 minutes.

2. Add melted coconut oil along with all other ingredients from the list above in a food processor.

3. Process until the mixture is well combined.

4. Make small balls and place on a platter lined with parchment paper.

5. Freeze for 2 hours, remove from freezer and serve.

6. Keep refrigerated in a container.

Nutrition information:
Calories: 386 Carbohydrates: 7g Proteins: 4g Fat: 38g Fiber: 2g

Minty Chocolate Fat Bombs

Serves: 4, Preparation: 10 minutes

Ingredients
1/2 cup coconut oil, melted
1/4 cup fresh butter, softened
2 tbsps. cocoa dry powder
1/4 cup natural sweetener, such as stevia
2 tbsps. fresh mint leaves, finely chopped

Instructions
1. Stir all ingredients in a deep bowl.

2. Pour the mixture into silicon cases or ice cube trays and freeze for 4 hours.

3. Store in a container and keep refrigerated.

Nutrition information:
Calories: 246 Carbohydrates: 2g Proteins: 1g Fat: 26g Fiber: 1g

Monk Fruit Candy Fat Balls

Serves: 5, Preparation: 15 minutes

Ingredients

1 cup coconut oil, softened
1 cup almond butter
2 tbsps. avocado oil
1/2 cup cocoa powder, unsweetened
1/2 cup coconut shreds
2 tbsps. monk fruit sweetener or to taste

Instructions

1. In a small saucepan over Medium-low heat, combine and stir the coconut oil, almond butter and avocado oil.
2. Add cocoa powder, coconut shreds and monk fruit sweetener; stir until all ingredients are combined well.
3. Pour the mixture in a freezer-safe container and freeze for 1 1/2 - 2 hours.
4. Remove the mixture from the freezer, and for into small balls.
5. Place balls on a plate and return in freezer for further 1 hour.
6. Serve immediately or keep balls refrigerated.

Nutrition information:

Calories: 416 Carbohydrates: 3g Proteins: 2g Fat: 44g Fiber: 2g

Spicy Pepperoni Fat Bombs

Serves: 5, Preparation: 15 minutes

Ingredients

2 cups of cream cheese from the fridge
1 cup of whipped cream, cold from fridge
4 slices pepperoni sausages, finely chopped
3 slices bacon, cut into pieces
1 chili pepper
1 tsp. fresh thyme, chopped fine
1/4 tsp. hot paprika or smoked paprika
1 pinch salt and pepper or to taste
1/4 tsp. garlic powder
1/4 tsp. onion powder

Instructions

1. Beat the cream cheese in a mixing bowl with the whisker.
2. Add whipped cream and continue to beat for 30 - 45 seconds.
3. Add chopped pepperoni sausages and bacon and stir well.
4. Add all remaining ingredients and give a good stir.
5. Form the mixture into 12 balls and place them on a plate lined with parchment paper.
6. Refrigerate balls for 3 hours.
7. Serve immediately or keep refrigerated.

Nutrition information:

Calories: 201 Carbohydrates: 2g Proteins: 5g Fat: 20g Fiber: 0.2g

Rumichino Almond Fat Bombs

Serves: 4, Preparation: 10 minutes

Ingredients

1/2 cup of refined coconut oil, melted
3/4 cup almond butter
3/4 cup fresh butter, softened
3 tbsps. cocoa powder, unsweetened
1/2 cup natural sweetener, such as stevia, truvia
2 tbsps. strong rum

Instructions

1. Melt the almond butter in a microwave oven for 15 - 20 seconds.
2. Pour the coconut oil in a bowl and whisk along with almonds butter and fresh butter.
3. Add all remaining ingredients and whisk for 35 - 40 seconds to combine well.
4. Pour the mixture into molds and freeze for 2 hours or more.
5. Serve or store in container and keep refrigerated.

Nutrition information:

Calories: 302 Carbohydrates: 4g Proteins: 4g Fat: 30g Fiber: 2g

Spicy Chocolate Fat Bombs

Serves: 4, Preparation: 10 minutes

Ingredients

3/4 cup fresh butter, softened
3/4 cup coconut oil, softened
3/4 cup almond butter
1/4 cup cocoa dry powder, unsweetened (80% cacao solid)
1/4 cup natural sweetener like stevia or to taste
2 pinch of cayenne pepper or to taste

Instructions

1. Softened coconut oil and fresh butter in a microwave safe bowl; heat in a microwave oven for several seconds.
2. Add all ingredients in a bowl and stir with a spoon.
3. Pour the mixture into small cupcakes holders, muffin tin, etc.
4. Place in a freezer for 2 hours and serve.
5. Keep refrigerated in a container.

Nutrition information:

Calories: 338 Carbohydrates: 4g Proteins: 4g Fat: 34g Fiber: 2.3g

Strawberry Fat Bombs coated with Ground Nuts

Serves: 4, Preparation: 10 minutes

Ingredients

1/3 cup butter, softened
1/2 cup coconut oil
2 tbsps. strawberry extract
2 tbsps. cocoa dry powder, unsweetened
1/2 cup ground nut mixture, such as walnuts, hazelnuts, almonds

Instructions

1. In a saucepan heat butter, coconut oil and cocoa powder over Moderate heat; stir.
2. Remove from heat and pour strawberry extract; stir. Set aside to completely cool.
3. Make small balls and roll in ground nut mixture.
4. Place balls on a plate covered with parchment paper and freeze for at least 2 hours.
5. Keep refrigerated.

Nutrition information:

Calories: 250 Carbohydrates: 2g Proteins: 2g Fat: 26g Fiber: 1g

Vanilla Coconut - Nuts Fat Bombs

Serves: 4, Preparation: 10 minutes

Ingredients

1/2 cup coconut oil, melted and cooled

3 cups coconut shreds, unsweetened

1 cup natural sweetener such as stevia, erythritol

2 tsps. vanilla

1 pinch of salt, optional

Toppings

2 tbsps. shredded coconut

2 tbsps. chopped nuts such macadamia, almonds, Brazilian

Instructions

1. Add Ingredients from the list above in your food processor.

2. Process until the mixture is compact and blended well.

3. Grease your hands with coconut oil and form balls.

4. Place fat balls on a platter lined with parchment paper and sprinkle with coconut shreds and chopped nuts.

5. Refrigerate for two hours and serve.

Nutrition information:

Calories: 249 Carbohydrates: 4g Proteins: 2g Fat: 25g Fiber: 3g

Sweet Cream Cheese Muffin Bombs

Serves: 4, Preparation: 10 minutes

Ingredients

1/4 cup coconut butter, softened on room temperature

2 cups cream cheese (full fat), softened

1 cup heavy whipping cream

3/4 cup natural sweetener, such as stevia, truvia, erythritol

1 1/2 tsps. vanilla extract

1 pinch of sea salt

Instructions

1. Prepare 2 muffin tins with 6 paper liners.

2. Add all ingredients in your blender; blend for 35 -50 seconds.

3. Pour the mixture in a prepared muffin tin evenly.

4. Freeze for 3 - 4 hours and serve.

5. Store in a container and keep refrigerated.

Nutrition information:

Calories: 247 Carbohydrates: 2.5g Proteins: 3g Fat: 25g Fiber: 0g

Chapter 12 Smoothies & Juice

Almonds & Blueberries Smoothie

Serves: 2, Preparation: 5 minutes

Ingredients

1/4 cup ground almonds, unsalted
1 cup fresh blueberries
Fresh juice of 1 lemon
1 cup fresh kale leaves
1/2 cup coconut water
1 cup water
2 tbsps. plain yogurt (optional)

Instructions

1. Dump all ingredients in your high-speed blender, and blend until your smoothie is smooth.
2. Pour the mixture in a chilled glass.
3. Serve and enjoy!

Nutrition information:

Calories: 110 Carbohydrates: 8g Proteins: 2g Fat: 7g Fiber: 2g

Almonds and Zucchini Smoothie

Serves: 2, Preparation: 5 minutes

Ingredients

1 cup zucchini; cooked and mashed, unsalted
1 1/2 cups almond milk
1 tbsp. almond butter (plain, unsalted)
1 tsp. pure almond extract
2 tbsps. ground almonds or macadamia almonds
1/2 cup water
1 cup ice cubes, crushed (optional, for serving)

Instructions

1. Dump all ingredients from the list above in your fast-speed blender; blend for 45 - 60 seconds or to taste.
2. Serve with crushed ice.

Nutrition information:

Calories: 322 Carbohydrates: 6g Proteins: 6g Fat: 30g Fiber: 3.5g

Avocado with Walnut Butter Smoothie

Serves: 2, Preparation: 5 minutes

Ingredients

1 avocado, diced
1 cup baby spinach
1 cup coconut milk (canned)
1 tbsp. walnut butter, unsalted
2 tbsps. natural sweetener, such as Stevia, Erythritol, Truvia, etc.

Instructions

1. Place all ingredients into food processor or a blender; blend until smooth or to taste.
2. Add more or less walnut butter.
3. Drink and enjoy!

Nutrition information:

Calories: 364 Carbohydrates: 7g Proteins: 8g Fat: 35g Fiber: 5.5g

Baby Spinach and Dill Smoothie

Serves: 2, Preparation: 5 minutes

Ingredients

1 cup of fresh baby spinach leaves
2 tbsps. fresh dill, chopped
1 1/2 cups of water
1/2 avocado, chopped into cubes
1 tbsp. chia seeds (optional)
2 tbsps. natural sweetener, Stevia or Erythritol (optional)

Instructions

1. Place all ingredients into fast-speed blender. Beat until smooth and all ingredients united well.
2. Serve and enjoy!

Nutrition information:

Calories: 136 Carbohydrates: 8g Proteins: 7g Fat: 10g Fiber: 9g

Blueberries and Coconut Smoothie

Serves: 5, Preparation: 5 minutes

Ingredients

1 cup of frozen blueberries, unsweetened
1 cup Stevia or Erythritol sweetener
2 cups coconut milk (canned)
1 cup of fresh spinach leaves
2 tbsps. shredded coconut (unsweetened)
3/4 cup water

Instructions

1. Place all ingredients from the list in food-processor or in your strong blender.
2. Blend for 45 - 60 seconds or to taste.
3. Ready for drink! Serve!

Nutrition information:

Calories: 190 Carbohydrates: 8g Proteins: 3g Fat: 18g Fiber: 2g

Collard Greens and Cucumber Smoothie

Serves: 2, Preparation: 15 minutes

Ingredients

1 cup collard greens
A few fresh pepper mint leaves
1 big cucumber
1 lime, freshly juiced
1/2 cup avocado, sliced
1 1/2 cups water
1 cup crushed ice
1/4 cup of natural sweetener, Erythritol or Stevia (optional)

Instructions

1. Rinse and clean your collard greens from any dirt.
2. Place all ingredients in a food processor or blender.
3. Blend until all ingredients in your smoothie is combined well.
4. Pour in a glass and drink. Enjoy!

Nutrition information:

Calories: 123 Carbohydrates: 8g Proteins: 4g Fat: 11g Fiber: 6g

Creamy Dandelion Greens and Celery Smoothie

Serves: 2, Preparation: 10 minutes

Ingredients

1 handful of raw dandelion greens
2 celery sticks
2 tbsps. chia seeds
1 small piece of ginger, minced
1/2 cup almond milk
1/2 cup water
1/2 cup plain yogurt

Instructions

1. Rinse and clean dandelion greens from any dirt;

add in a high-speed blender.
2. Clean the ginger; keep only inner part and cut in small slices; add in a blender.
3. Add all remaining ingredients and blend until smooth.
4. Serve and enjoy!

Nutrition information:

Calories: 58 Carbohydrates: 5g Proteins: 3g Fat: 6g Fiber: 3g

Dark Turnip Greens Smoothie

Serves: 2, Preparation: 10 minutes

Ingredients

1 cup of raw turnip greens
1 1/2 cups of almond milk
1 tbsp. almond butter
1/2 cup of water
1/2 tsp. cocoa powder, unsweetened
1 tbsp. dark chocolate chips
1/4 tsp. cinnamon
A pinch of salt
1/2 cup of crushed ice

Instructions

1. Rinse and clean turnip greens from any dirt.
2. Place the turnip greens in your blender along with all other ingredients.
3. Blend it for 45 - 60 seconds or until done; smooth and creamy.
4. Serve with or without crushed ice.

Nutrition information:

Calories: 131 Carbohydrates: 6g Proteins: 4g Fat: 10g Fiber: 2.5g

Butter Pecan and Coconut Smoothie

Serves: 2, Preparation: 5 minutes

Ingredients

1 cup coconut milk, canned
1 scoop butter pecan powdered creamer
2 cups fresh spinach leaves, chopped
1/2 banana, frozen or fresh
2 tbsps. Stevia granulated sweetener to taste
1/2 cup water
1 cup ice cubes, crushed

Instructions

1. Place ingredients from the list above in your high-speed blender.
2. Blend for 35 - 50 seconds or until all ingredients combined well.
3. Add less or more crushed ice.
4. Drink and enjoy!

Nutrition information:

Calories: 268 Carbohydrates: 7g Proteins: 6g Fat: 26g Fiber: 1.5g

Fresh Cucumber, Kale and Raspberry Smoothie

Serves: 3, Preparation: 10 minutes

Ingredients

1 1/2 cups of cucumber, peeled
1/2 cup raw kale leaves
1 1/2 cups fresh raspberries
1 cup of almond milk
1 cup of water
Ice cubes, crushed (optional)
2 tbsps. natural sweetener (Stevia, Erythritol, etc.)

Instructions

1. Place all ingredients from the list in a food processor or high-speed blender; blend for 35 - 40 seconds.
2. Serve into chilled glasses.
3. Add more natural sweeter if you like. Enjoy!

Nutrition information:

Calories: 70 Carbohydrates: 8g Proteins: 3g Fat: 6g Fiber: 5g

Fresh Lettuce and Cucumber-Lemon Smoothie

Serves: 2, Preparation: 10 minutes

Ingredients

2 cups fresh lettuce leaves, chopped (any kind)
1 cup of cucumber
1 lemon, washed and sliced
1/2 avocado
2 tbsps. chia seeds
1 1/2 cups water or coconut water
1/4 cup Stevia granulate sweetener (or to taste)

Instructions

1. Add all ingredients from the list above in the high-speed blender; blend until completely smooth.
2. Pour your smoothie into chilled glasses and enjoy!

Nutrition information:

Calories: 51 Carbohydrates: 4g Proteins: 2g Fat: 4g Fiber: 3.5g

Green Coconut Smoothie

Serves: 2, Preparation: 10 minutes

Ingredients

1 1/4 cups coconut milk (canned)
2 tbsps. chia seeds
1 cup of fresh kale leaves
1 cup of spinach leaves
1 scoop vanilla protein powder
1 cup of ice cubes
Granulated Stevia sweetener (to taste; optional)
1/2 cup of water

Instructions

1. Rinse and clean kale and the spinach leaves from any dirt.
2. Add all ingredients in your blender.
3. Blend until you get a nice smoothie.
4. Serve into chilled glass.

Nutrition information:

Calories: 179 Carbohydrates: 5g Proteins: 4g Fat: 18g Fiber: 2.5g

Instant Coffee Smoothie

Serves: 2, Preparation: 10 minutes

Ingredients

2 cups of instant coffee
1 cup almond milk (or coconut milk)
1/4 cup heavy cream
2 tbsps. cocoa powder, unsweetened
1-2 handful of fresh spinach leaves
10 drops of liquid Stevia

Instructions

1. Make a coffee; set aside.
2. Place all remaining ingredients in your fast-speed blender; blend for 45 - 60 seconds or until done.
3. Pour your instant coffee in a blender and continue to blend for further 30 - 45 seconds.
4. Serve immediately.

Nutrition information:

Calories: 142 Carbohydrates: 6g Proteins: 5g Fat: 14g Fiber: 3g

Keto Blood Sugar Adjuster Smoothie

Serves: 2, Preparation: 10 minutes

Ingredients

2 cups of green cabbage
1/2 avocado
1 tbsp. apple cider vinegar
Juice of 1 small lemon
1 cup of water
1 cup of crushed ice cubes, for serving

Instructions

1. Place all ingredients in your high-speed blender or in a food processor and blend until smooth and soft.
2. Serve in chilled glasses with crushed ice.
3. Enjoy!

Nutrition information:

Calories: 74 Carbohydrates: 7g Proteins: 2g Fat: 6g Fiber: 4g

Lime Spinach Smoothie

Serves: 2, Preparation: 5 minutes

Ingredients

1 cup water
1 lime juice (2 limes)
1 green apple; cut into chunks, core discarded
2 cups fresh spinach, roughly chopped
1/2 cup fresh chopped fresh mint
1/2 avocado
Ice, crushed
1/4 tsp. ground cinnamon
1 tbsp. natural sweetener, of your choice (optional)

Instructions

1. Place all ingredients in your high-speed blender.
2. Blend for 45 - 60 seconds or until your smoothie is smooth and creamy.
3. Serve in a chilled glass.
4. Adjust sweetener to taste.

Nutrition information:

Calories: 112 Carbohydrates: 8g Proteins: 4g Fat: 10g Fiber: 5.5g

Protein Coconut Smoothie

Serves: 2, Preparation: 10 minutes

Ingredients

1 1/2 cups of coconut milk, canned
1 cup of fresh spinach, finely chopped
1 scoop vanilla protein powder
2 tbsps. chia seeds
1 cup of ice cubes, crushed
2-3 tbsps. Stevia granulated natural sweetener (optional)

Instructions

1. Rinse and clean your spinach leaves from any dirt.
2. Place all ingredients from the list above in a blender.
3. Blend until you get a smoothie like consistently.
4. Serve into chilled glass and it is ready to drink.

Nutrition information:

Calories: 377 Carbohydrates: 7g Proteins: 10g Fat: 38g Fiber: 2g

Strong Spinach and Hemp Smoothie

Serves: 3, Preparation: 10 minutes

Ingredients

1 cup almond milk
1 small ripe banana
2 tbsps. hemp seeds
2 handful fresh spinach leaves
1 tsp. pure vanilla extract
1 cup of water
2 tbsps. natural sweetener, such as Stevia, Truvia, etc.

Instructions

1. First, rinse and clean your spinach leaves from any dirt.
2. Place the spinach in a blender or food processor along with remaining ingredients.
3. Blend for 45 - 60 seconds or until done.
4. Add more or less sweetener.
5. Serve.

Nutrition information:

Calories: 75 Carbohydrates: 7g Proteins: 4g Fat: 6g Fiber: 3g

Total Almond Smoothie

Serves: 2, Preparation: 15 minutes

Ingredients

1 1/2 cups of almond milk
2 tbsps. almond butter
2 tbsps. ground almonds
1 cup of fresh kale leaves (or to taste)
1/2 tsp. cocoa powder
1 tbsp. chia seeds
1/2 cup of water

Instructions

1. Rinse and carefully clean kale leaves from any dirt.
2. Add almond milk, almond butter and ground almonds in your blender; blend for 45 - 60 seconds.
3. Add kale leaves, cocoa powder and chia seeds; blend for further 45 seconds.
4. If your smoothie is too thick, pour more almond milk or water.
5. Serve.

Nutrition information:

Calories: 228 Carbohydrates: 7g Proteins: 8g Fat: 11g Fiber: 6g

Ultimate Green Mix Smoothie

Serves: 2, Preparation: 15 minutes

Ingredients

Handful of spinach leaves
Handful of collard greens
Handful of lettuce, any kind
1 1/2 cups of almond milk
1/2 cup of water
1/4 cup of Stevia granulated sweetener
1 tsp. pure vanilla extract
1 cup crushed ice cubes (optional)

Instructions

1. Rinse and carefully clean your greens from any dirt.
2. Place all ingredients from the list above in your blender or food processor.
3. Blend until done or 45 - 30 seconds.
4. Serve with or without crushed ice.

Nutrition information:

Calories: 73 Carbohydrates: 4g Proteins: 5g Fat: 7g Fiber: 1g

Chapter 13 Ice Cream & Dessert

Athletes Matcha & Chia Granita

Serves: 4, Preparation: 10 minutes

Ingredients

1/2 cup water
1 cup coconut milk, unsweetened
1-2 tsps. chia seeds, soaked for 20 - 30 minutes
2 scoops vanilla protein powder
2 tbsps. coconut oil
1 tsp. cinnamon, ground
1 tsp. Matcha powder

Instructions

1. Place all ingredients in your high-speed blender; blend until your mixture gets a smooth consistency.

2. Pour the mixture in a freezer-safe container and freeze for 6 hours.

3. Remove container from the freezer and stir vigorously to smooth granita.

4. Serve on chilled glasses.

Nutrition information:

Calories: 54 Carbohydrates: 5g Proteins: 2g Fat: 5g Fiber: 2g

Cayenne Strawberry Popsicle

Serves: 4, Preparation: 10 minutes

Ingredients

14 oz. fresh strawberries, finely chopped
1 cup Stevia granulate sweetener (or to taste)
2 tbsps. lemon juice, freshly squeezed
1/4 cup water
Cayenne pepper to taste
1 pinch of salt

Instructions

1. Add all ingredients in a blender and blend until smooth.

2. Pour the mixture evenly in a Popsicle mold or a cup.

3. Insert sticks into each mold.

4. Place molds in a freezer and freeze for at least 4 hours.

5. Before serving, place molds under lukewarm water.

Nutrition information:

Calories: 20 Carbohydrates: 4g Proteins: 0.5g Fat: 1g Fiber: 1g

Coco - Strawberry Ice Cream

Serves: 4, Preparation: 20 minutes

Ingredients

2 cups almond milk, unsweetened
1 cup frozen strawberries
1 tbsp. chia seeds, soaked for 10 minutes
1 scoop chocolate protein powder
1 tbsp. MCT oil (sub liquid coconut oil or omit)
1 cup ground Macadamia or Brazilian nuts
1 tbsp. raw cocoa powder

Instructions

1. Place all ingredients into your high-speed powered blender; blend on High until all ingredients combined well.

2. Pour the mixture in a safe-freezer container and freeze for 6 hours or overnight.

3. Remove the ice cream from freezer for about 10 - 15 minutes before serving.

4. If you notice the ice crystal, just place the ice cream in a mixing bowl, and beat with a mixer for 3 - 4 minutes.

5. Serve in chilled glasses.

Nutrition information:

Calories: 113 Carbohydrates: 6g Proteins: 5g Fat: 10g Fiber: 3g

Creamy Strawberry Ice Cream

Serves: 4, Preparation: 10 minutes, Cooking: 15 minutes

Ingredients

1 lb. fresh chopped strawberries
Juice of 1 small lemon
1 cup of Stevia sweetener
1 pinch of salt
1 1/2 cups of yogurt
1/2 cup of almond milk, unsweetened

Instructions

1. Put the strawberries in a saucepan with lemon juice, sweetener and salt, and heat, stirring, until fruit softens.
2. Remove the saucepan from heat and allow strawberries to cool.
3. Add yogurt and almond milk and gently stir with wooden spatula.
4. Pour the ice cream mixture in a container, wrap with plastic membrane and freeze for 6 hours.
5. Serve in a chilled glasses or bowls.

Nutrition information:

Calories: 45 Carbohydrates: 4g Proteins: 3g Fat: 7g Fiber: 1g

Dark Parfait Ice Cream

Serves: 4, Preparation: 25 minutes

Ingredients

5 egg yolks
1/2 cup of Stevia granulated sweetener
1 cup of heavy cream
3 eggs whites, beaten to a meringue
3/4 cup almonds (unsalted) or hazelnuts, macadamia
6 oz. dark chocolate chips (60% - 69% cocoa solid)

Instructions

1. Whisk egg yolks with Stevia in a saucepan.
2. Place the saucepan over double boiler and stir until egg yolks mixture begin to thicken.
3. Remove the mixture in a mixing bowl, and let it cool for 5 minutes.
4. Beat with the mixer for 2 - 3 minutes.
5. Add cream and gently stir with wooden spatula.
6. Add meringue and almonds; stir well to combine all ingredients.
7. Melt the chocolate chips and add in a bowl; stir gently to combine well.
8. Pour the mixture in freezer safe bowl or container and freeze overnight.
9. Remove the ice cream from the freezer 10 - 15 minutes before serving.

Nutrition information:

Calories: 160 Carbohydrates: 7g Proteins: 6g Fat: 14g Fiber: 2g

Frozen Keto Chocolate Mousse

Serves: 4, Preparation: 15 minutes

Ingredients

2 tbsps. coconut powder, unsweetened
4 cups of heavy cream
1/2 cup Stevia granulate sweetener (or to taste)
1 tbsp. MCT oil (or liquid coconut oil or omit)
1 pinch of salt
1 tbsp. pure vanilla extract
Shredded coconut, unsweetened

Instructions

1. In a mixing bowl, beat the coconut powder and heavy cream for about 2 - 3 minutes,
2. Add the remaining ingredients and beat with the mixer on Low speed for further 3-4 minutes.
3. Pour the mixture in a container and freeze for 6 hours.
4. Remove the ice cream mixture from freezer every hour; place the ice cream in a mixing bowl and beat with the mixer.
5. Remove the ice cream in container and freeze again.
6. This process will avoid making of ice crystals.
7. Serve and enjoy!

Nutrition information:

Calories: 317 Carbohydrates: 4.5g Proteins: 2g Fat: 33g Fiber: 1g

Frozen Red Wine Pops

Serves: 6, Preparation: 15 minutes, Cooking: 10 minutes

Ingredients

2 cups of fresh cream
1 cup of almond milk (unsweetened)
1/2 cup Stevia granulated sweetener (or to taste)
6 fresh egg yolks
1/2 cup red dry wine

Instructions

1. In a saucepan, cook the cream, almond milk and Stevia sweetener over low heat; stir.
2. Add egg yolks and stir for 5 minutes.
3. Transfer the mixture in a freezer-safe container and pour the wine; stir well.
4. Freeze the mixture for 2 hours.
5. Remove the ice cream mixture from the freezer and stir well with a hand mixer.
6. Pour the mixture in a Popsicle molds and insert the sticks.
7. Store Popsicle in a freezer until froze.
8. Ready to Serve and enjoy!

Nutrition information:

Calories: 220 Carbohydrates: .5g Proteins: 4g Fat: 20g Fiber: 0g

Homemade MCT Ice Cream

Serves: 6, Preparation: 5 hours and 10 minutes

Ingredients

1/2 cup of MCT oil (medium-chain triglyceride)
1 cup unsweetened almond milk
6 whole eggs
6 egg yolks
1 vanilla pod
1 tsp. Stevia glycerite (alcohol-free and a zero-calorie)
1 tsp. salt
5 tbsps. unsweetened cocoa powder

Instructions

1. Place all ingredients in a mixing bowl and beat with a hand mixer.
2. Pour the ice cream mixture in a freezer-safe bowl and freeze for one hour.
3. Then, pour the mass into the ice cream maker and work according to the manufacturer's instructions.
4. Keep in freezer for 4 - 5 hours.
5. Serve in chilled glasses or bowl.
6. Enjoy!

Nutrition information:

Calories: 223 Carbohydrates: 2.5g Proteins: 8g Fat: 22g Fiber: 1g

Iced Blueberry Granita

Serves: 4, Preparation: 10 minutes, Cooking: 15 minutes

Ingredients

1 1/4 cups of water
Juice of ½ of a medium lemon
1 lb. blueberries (frozen)
1 cup of natural granulated sweetener, such Stevia
1 tsp. vanilla extract

Instructions

1. Make syrup in a saucepan, combine water, Stevia sweetener and lemon juice over Medium-low heat.
2. Stir until becomes a thick syrup.
3. Remove from heat and let it cool on room temperature.
4. Place blueberries in a large bowl, and sprinkle with Stevia.
5. Pour the syrup in and stir.
6. Stir vanilla extract and pour the mixture in a freezer-safe container; freeze for 4 hours.
7. Serve in chilled bowls or glasses.

Nutrition information:

Calories: 45 Carbohydrates: 7g Proteins: 1g Fat: 1g Fiber: 2g

Coconut Raspberry Ice Cream

Serves: 4, Preparation: 15 minutes, Cooking: 45 minutes

Ingredients

4 cups fresh raspberries
1 1/2 cups of natural sweetener (Stevia, Truvia, Erythritol, etc.)
2 tbsps. water
2 cups thick coconut cream

Instructions

1. In a saucepan, stir raspberries, sweetener and water over Medium heat.
2. Reduce heat and cook, stirring, for 10 - 12 minutes or until raspberries melt.
3. Remove from heat and set aside to cool down.
4. Beat the coconut cream in a bowl with a mixer (on High).
5. Pour the syrup in a mixing bowl and continue to beat for 45 - 60 seconds.
6. Place mixture in a freezer-safe bowl, and place in a freezer for 4 hours.
7. Every 30 - 45 minutes remove the ice cream in a mixing bowl and beat with a mixer.
8. This process will prevent ice crystallization.
9. Serve and enjoy!

Nutrition information:

Calories: 160 Carbohydrates: 7g Proteins: 2g Fat: 17g Fiber: 4g

Lemon Granita

Serves: 4, Preparation: 10 minutes

Ingredients

4 fresh lemons, juice about 3/4 cup
1 ½ cups of natural sweetener (Stevia, Erythritol, etc.)
3 cups water
2 lemons; peeled, pulp

Instructions

1. In a saucepan, heat all ingredients over Medium heat.
2. Remove from heat and let it cool on room temperature.
3. Pour the mixture in a baking dish, wrap with plastic membrane and freeze for 6 - 8 hours.
4. Remove granita from the freezer, scratch with big fork and stir.
5. Serve in chilled glasses and enjoy!
6. Keep in freezer.

Nutrition information:

Calories: 13 Carbohydrates: 3g Proteins: 1g Fat: 1g Fiber: 0.2g

Low Carb Blackberry Ice Cream

Serves: 4, Preparation: 10 minutes

Ingredients

3/4 lb. frozen blackberries, unsweetened
1 1/4 cups of caned coconut milk
1/4 cup of granulated Stevia sweetener or to taste
2 tbsps. almond flour
1 pinch of ground vanilla
1 tbsp. MCT oil

Instructions

1. Put all the ingredients in a blender. Make sure blackberries are still frozen.
2. Blend until the mixture is creamy.
3. Pour the blackberry mixture in a container and freeze overnight.
4. Serve in chilled glasses or bowls.

Nutrition information:

Calories: 83 Carbohydrates: 5g Proteins: 1g Fat: 8g Fiber: 2.5g

Chocolate Coconut Ice Cream

Serves: 4, Preparation: 15 minutes

Ingredients

2 cans (11 oz.) of frozen coconut milk
2 scoops powdered chocolate protein
4 tbsps. Stevia sweetener
2 tbsps. cocoa powder

Instructions

1. In a high-speed blender, stir the frozen coconut milk.
2. Blend for 30 - 45 seconds and then add the remaining ingredients.
3. Blend again until get a thick cream.

4. Pour the mixture in a container and store in freezer for 4 hours.
5. To prevent forming ice crystals, beat the mixture every 30 minutes.

6. Ready! Serve in chilled glasses.
Nutrition information:
Calories: 135 Carbohydrates: 3g Proteins: 4g Fat: 15g Fiber: 1g

Chocolate Peppermint Popsicle

Serves: 4, Preparation: 20 minutes
Ingredients
3 cups coconut milk (canned), divided
2 gelatin sheets
3 cups packed peppermint leaves
1 cup Stevia granulate sweetener
1/4 tsp. pure peppermint extract
3/4 cup of dark chocolate (60%- 69% of cacao solid), melted
Instructions
1. Soak gelatin in a little coconut milk for 10 minutes.
2. In a saucepan, heat the coconut milk and peppermint leaves; cook for 3 minutes stirring constantly.
3. Add gelatin and stir until completely dissolved.

4. Remove the saucepan from heat, cover and set aside for 20 - 25 minutes.
5. Strain the mint mixture through a colander into the bowl and add the Stevia sweetener; stir well. Pour the peppermint extract and stir.
6. Place bowl in the freezer for about one hour.
7. Remove from freezer and stir melted dark chocolate.
8. Pour into Popsicle molds, insert sticks in each mold, and freeze overnight.
9. Remove Popsicle from the mold and serve.
Nutrition information:
Calories: 231 Carbohydrates: 8g Proteins: 3g Fat: 22g Fiber: 1g

Perfect Strawberry Ice Cream

Serves: 6, Preparation: 20 minutes
Ingredients
2 lbs. strawberries
2 1/4 cups of water
2 tbsps. coconut butter, softened
1 1/2 cups of natural granulated sweetener (Stevia, Truvia, Erythritol, etc.)
2 egg whites
Juice of 1 large lemon
Instructions
1. Heat strawberries, water, coconut butter and Stevia sweetener in a saucepan over Medium-low heat.
2. When strawberries softened, remove the saucepan from heat, and allow it to cool on room temperature.

3. Whisk the egg whites until stiff; add the lemon juice and stir.
4. Add the egg whites mixture to strawberry mixture and gently stir with wooden spatula.
5. Refrigerate the ice cream mixture for 2 hours.
6. Pour cold ice cream mixture into ice cream maker, turn on the machine, and do according to manufacturer's directions.
7. In the case that you do not have ice cream maker, pour the mixture in a container and freeze for 8 hours.
Nutrition information:
Calories: 50 Carbohydrates: 6g Proteins: 1g Fat: 5g Fiber: 2g

Raskolnikov Vanilla Ice Cream

Serves: 4, Preparation: 10 minutes, Cooking: 20 minutes
Ingredients
3 sheets of gelatin, sugar-free
2 US pints of cream
1/2 vanilla stick
1/2 cup Stevia granulated sweetener
4 egg yolks
3 tbsps. vodka

Instructions
1. Soak gelatin in some water (about 1 cup per 1 sheet of gelatin)
2. Heat the cream in a saucepan along with vanilla stick and Stevia sweetener; stir.
3. Add the egg yolks and continue to stir for

further 2 - 3 minutes.

4. Remove from heat, add gelatin and stir well.

5. Pour vodka and stir again; allow the mixture to cool.

6. Pour the mixture in a container and refrigerate for at least 4 hours.

7. Remove the mixture in an ice cream maker; follow manufacturer's instructions.

8. Or, pour the mixture in a freeze-safe container and freeze overnight.

9. Beat every 45 minutes with the mixture to prevent ice crystallization.

10. Serve and enjoy!

Nutrition information:
Calories: 118 Carbohydrates: 4g Proteins: 3g Fat: 10g Fiber: 0g

Traditional Spanish Cold Cream with Walnuts

Serves: 4, Preparation: 5 minutes, Cooking: 3 hours

Ingredients

3 cups of almond milk

3 cups of heavy cream

1 cup of ground walnuts

3/4 cup of natural sweetener (Stevia, Erythritol, etc.) or to taste

1 cinnamon stick

Instructions

1. Add all ingredients from the list above in your Slow Cooker.

2. Cover and cook on High for 3 hours.

3. During cooking, stir several times with wooden spoon.

4. If your cream is too dense, add more almond milk.

5. Store cream in glass container and refrigerate for 4 hours.

6. Remove cream from the refrigerator 15 minutes before serving.

Nutrition information:
Calories: 193 Carbohydrates: 5g Proteins: 8g Fat: 20g Fiber: 2g

Chocolate Ice Cream

Serves: 4, Preparation: 15 minutes

Ingredients

1 can (15 oz.) coconut milk

1/2 cup cocoa powder

1/4 cup natural sweetener (Stevia, Truvia, Erythritol, etc.)

1 tsp. vanilla extract

Chopped nuts or shredded coconut, for serving (optional)

Instructions

1. Combine all ingredients in a bowl.

2. Use an electric mixer and beat the mixture until all ingredients combine well.

3. Transfer the mixture in a freezer-safe bowl and freeze for 4 hours.

4. To prevent ice crystallization, beat the ice cream with the mixer every hour.

5. Serve garnished with sliced nuts or shredded coconuts.

Nutrition information:
Calories: 204 Carbohydrates: 7g Proteins: 4g Fat: 21g Fiber: 4.5g

Cinnamon Ice Cream

Serves: 8, Preparation: 10 minutes, Cooking:15 minutes

Ingredients

1 1/2 cups almond milk (or coconut milk)

1 cinnamon stick

1 1/2 cups natural granulated sweetener (Stevia, Truvia, Erythritol, etc.)

1 1/2 tbsps. lemon peel

8 egg yolks, from free-range chicken

1 pinch of salt

1 1/2 tbsps. ground cinnamon

1 cup cream

Instructions

1. In a saucepan, heat almond milk, cinnamon stick, Stevia sweetener and lemon peel.

2. Bring to boil, reduce the heat and stir over low heat for 10 minutes,

3. In a bowl, beat the egg yolks with the pinch of salt until frothy. Place the egg mixture in a glass bowl over the double boiler and stir until thickened.

4. Remove the cinnamon and lemon peel, pour the almond milk in egg yolk mixture; continue to until the mixture becomes thick.
5. Remove the mixture from heat, add ground cinnamon, stir; set aside and allow it to cool on room temperature.
6. In a bowl, beat the cream until double in volume.

7. Combine the cream with egg mixture and gently stir with wooden spatula.
8. Place the ice cream in the freezer until frozen or for at least 6-8 hours.
9. Serve and enjoy!
Nutrition information:
Calories: 181 Carbohydrates: 6g Proteins: 4g Fat: 17g Fiber: 2g

Vanilla Coconut Ice Cream

Serves: 4, Preparation: 10 minutes
Ingredients
15 oz. coconut cream
2 tbsps. coconut butter, softened
1/2 cup of Stevia sweetener or to taste
1 pinch of salt
2 tsps. vanilla extract
1 tsp. vanilla powder
Instructions
1. Place all ingredients to the mixing bowl and beat for 3 - 4 minutes.
2. Pour the mixture in a container, cover with

membrane and freeze for 4 - 5 hours.
3. After one hour, remove the mixture, place in a mixing bowl and beat it again for 3 - 4 minutes.
4. Repeat this process every half an hour in order to get smooth ice cream without the ice crystals.
5. When done, serve the ice cream in chilled bowls or glasses and serve.
Nutrition information:
Calories: 210 Carbohydrates: 3g Proteins: 3g Fat: 7g Fiber: 2g

Coconut Ice Cream

Serves: 4, Preparation: 10 minutes
Ingredients
4 cups of coconut cream or full-fat coconut milk
2 tbsps. coconut aminos
2 tbsps. coconut extract
1/2 cup of natural sweetener Stevia or to taste
1/2 cup of coconut flakes, for serving (optional)
Instructions
1. In a large bowl, stir all ingredients.
2. Pour the ice cream mixture in container and freeze for 8 hours.

3. Stir every hour to avoid ice cream crystallization.
4. When done, remove the ice cream from freezer.
5. Serve in chilled glasses and sprinkle with coconut flakes.
Nutrition information:
Calories: 361 Carbohydrates: 6g Proteins: 4g Fat: 37g Fiber: 3g

Crock Pot Zucchini Goat Cheese Cake

Serves: 4, Preparation: 15 minutes, Cooking: 2 hours
Ingredients
Non-stick cooking spray, for greasing
6 zucchinis, grated
1 handful fresh mint, roughly chopped
2 eggs
1 tbsp. almond flour
1/2 tsp. baking soda
3/4 cup goat cheese, crumbled
Instructions
1. Grease the bottom and sides of your crock pot; set aside.

2. Grate the zucchinis and squeeze out all the excess water; place in a large bowl.
3. Add eggs, crumbled goat cheese, almond flour, baking soda and mint; stir thoroughly.
4. Pour batter in your prepared crock pot.
5. Cover and cook on Low for 2-3 hours.
6. Allow cake to cool, slice and serve.
Nutrition information:
Calories: 117 Carbohydrates: 2g Proteins: 8g Fat: 10g Fiber: 0.3g

"Stroganoff" Queso Fresco Cheese

Serves: 4, Preparation: 5 minutes, Cooking: 12 minutes

Ingredients

2 tbsps. olive oil
1 chopped green onion
1 cup of fresh button mushrooms
1 grated tomato
1 lb. fresco cheese, cut into cubes
1 cup of fresh heavy cream
Salt to taste
Worcestershire sauce to taste
Mustard (Dijon, English, ground stone) to taste
Ketchup to taste

Instructions

1. Heat the oil in a large skillet and sauté the onion until soft.
2. Add mushrooms and gently stir for 2 - 3 minutes.
3. Add grated tomato, and season with the salt, Worcestershire sauce, ketchup and mustard.
4. Bring to boil; add cheese cubes and stir well.
5. Cook just for one minute, to avoid the cheese melting.
6. Add the heavy cream and stir.
7. Remove from the heat and allow it to cool for 5 minutes.
8. Serve.

Nutrition information:

Calories: 469 Carbohydrates: 5.7g Proteins: 19.5g Fat: 48g Fiber: 0.7g

Dark Nutty Chocolate Sauce

Serves: 4, Preparation: 5 minutes, Cooking: 4 hours or 2 hours

Ingredients

4 cups of almond milk
2 cups fresh cream
1 1/2 cups grated dark chocolate (70% - 80% cacao solid)
1 tsp. espresso coffee (two shoots)
2 tbsps. ground almonds
1/2 tsp. ground cinnamon
Pinch of ground red pepper (optional)
Natural sweetener (Stevia, Truvia, Erythritol, etc.) to taste

Instructions

1. Place all ingredients in your crock pot.
2. Cover and cook on Low for 4 hours or High for 2 hours.
3. Open lid and give a good stir.
4. Allow cream to cool before serving.
5. Keep refrigerated.

Nutrition information:

Calories: 263 Carbohydrates: 9g Proteins: 3.5g Fat: 22g Fiber: 2g

Irresistible Keto Lemon Cake

Serves: 4, Preparation: 15 minutes, Cooking: 3 hours and 30 minutes

Ingredients

1/3 cup almond butter, melted
2 cups almond flour
3/4 tsp. baking soda
1 pinch of salt (optional)
1 cup of natural sweetener (Stevia, Truvia, Erythritol, etc.)
3 medium lemons
2 eggs

Instructions

1. Line your Crock Pot with parchment paper.
2. In a bowl, combine the almond butter, almond flour, sweetener, baking soda and a pinch of salt (optional).
3. In a separate bowl, whisk eggs; add lemons.
4. Combine the flour mixture with egg mixture and stir until all ingredients combined.
5. Pour the batter into crock pot.
6. Cover and cook on Low setting for 3 - 3 1/2 hours.
7. Transfer cake to the plate, let it cool completely, cut in bars and serve.

Nutrition information:

Calories: 236 Carbohydrates: 6g Proteins: 835g Fat: 22g Fiber: 3g

Keto Blueberry Topping

Serves: 4, Preparation: 10 minutes, Cooking: 2 hours and 15 minutes

Ingredients

3/4 cup natural sweetener (Stevia, Truvia, Erythritol, etc.)
2 tbsps. water
2 tbsps. butter
1 cup fresh blueberries (or frozen blueberries)
Juice from 1 medium lemon
Zest from 1 lemon

Instructions

1. Heat the sweetener and water in a saucepan over Low heat. Stir approximately 3 to 5 minutes until make nice, smooth syrup.
2. Add butter and stir to get smooth and shiny surface.
3. Add blueberries in your crock pot and pour syrup evenly to cover blueberries.
4. Sprinkle the lemon zest, and drizzle with fresh lemon juice; gentle stir.
5. Cover and cook on Low for 2 hours.
6. Open the lid and give a good stir.
7. Keep refrigerated.

Nutrition information:

Calories: 76 Carbohydrates: 6.5g Proteins: 0.5g Fat: 7g Fiber: 4g

Sinless Raspberries Cake

Serves: 6, Preparation: 15 minutes, Cooking: 2 hours 30 minutes or 1 hour 30 minutes

Ingredients

6 large eggs
1/4 cup natural sweetener (Stevia, Truvia, Erythritol, etc.)
1 tsp. cinnamon
1/4 cup olive oil
2 cups fresh raspberries

Instructions

1. Line the bottom of your Crock Pot with parchment paper; set aside.
2. Beat eggs with a hand mixer in a bowl; add the sweetener, oil and cinnamon.
3. Pour the egg mixture in prepared crock pot.
4. Sprinkle the raspberries over the egg mixture evenly.
5. Cover and cook on High for 1 hour and 30 minutes, or on Low for 2 hours and 30 minutes.
6. Remove the cake from the Crock Pot, allow to cool, slice and serve.

Nutrition information:

Calories: 173 Carbohydrates: 5g Proteins: 15g Fat: 7g Fiber: 3g

Strawberry Sauce

Serves: 4, Preparation: 5 minutes, Cooking: 3 hours

Ingredients

2 lbs. fresh strawberries
1 1/2 cups natural sweetener (Stevia, Truvia, Erythritol, etc.)
2 tbsps. vanilla extract
1 1/4 cups water
1/2 lemon juice
2 cinnamon sticks

Instructions

1. Place all ingredients in your Slow Cooker and stir well.
2. Cover and cook on Low for 3 hours.
3. Open lid and give and good stir.
4. Allow sauce to cool completely.
5. Remove cinnamon sticks and store into glass jar; keep refrigerated.

Nutrition information:

Calories: 35 Carbohydrates: 6g Proteins: 1g Fat: 11g Fiber: 1g

Chapter 14 Keto Grilling Recipes

Grilled Beef Fillet with Fresh Herbs

Serves: 4, Preparation: 15 minutes, Cooking: 10 minutes

Ingredients

2 lbs. beef eye fillet
Salt and freshly ground black pepper to taste
1/4 cup oregano leaves, fresh and chopped
1/4 cup parsley, fresh and chopped
2 tbsps. rosemary leaves, fresh and chopped
2 tbsps. basil, fresh and chopped
1/4 cup olive oil

Instructions

1. Season beef fillets with the salt and pepper; place in a shallow container.
2. In a bowl, combine all remaining ingredients and rub the meat from all sides.
3. Cover and refrigerate overnight.
4. Remove meat from the fridge to room temperature 20 minutes before you put it on the grill.
5. Preheat your grill (pellet, gas, charcoal) to High according to manufacturer instructions.
6. Place fillets on a grill and cook for about 8-10 minutes per side or to your preference for doneness.
7. When ready, let meat rest for 10 minutes and serve warm.

Nutrition information:

Calories: 591 Carbohydrates: 4g Proteins: 46g Fat: 54g Fiber: 3.5g

Grilled Chicken Breast with Stone-Ground Mustard

Serves: 4, Preparation: 15 minutes, Cooking: 15 minutes

Ingredients

4 chicken breasts, boneless and skinless
4 garlic cloves, minced
1/4 cup stone-ground mustard (gluten-free)
3 tbsps. olive oil
1 tbsp. fresh herb mix
Sea salt and ground black pepper to taste

Instructions

1. Place the chicken breasts in a shallow container.
2. In a bowl, combine all remaining ingredients and pour over the chicken.
3. Cover the container and refrigerate for 4 - 6 hours.
4. Preheat your grill (pellet, gas, charcoal) to High according to manufacturer instructions.
5. Remove the chicken from the fridge.
6. Grill the chicken breasts for 10 - 12 minutes per side; flip them 3 - 4 times.
7. Serve hot.

Nutrition information:

Calories: 366 Carbohydrates: 1.5g Proteins: 50g Fat: 17g Fiber: 0.1g

Grilled Chicken in Sour Marinade

Serves: 4, Preparation: 15 minutes, Cooking: 10 minutes

Ingredients

4 lbs. chicken breasts, boneless
6 lemons, in slices
2 tbsps. onion, minced
1 tbsp. garlic, minced
1/4 cup olive oil
1/2 tsp. nutmeg, grated
1/4 tsp. cinnamon
Salt and freshly ground black pepper to taste

Instructions

1. In a large container, place chicken breasts and lemon slices.
2. In a small bowl, combine all remaining ingredients.
3. Pour the mixture evenly over the chicken. Refrigerate for 2 - 3 hours or overnight.
4. Preheat your grill (pellet, gas, charcoal) to High according to manufacturer instructions.
5. Grill your chicken and lemon slices on direct heat for about 9 -10 minutes per side (internal temperature 165⁰F).
6. Serve hot.

Nutrition information:

Calories: 338 Carbohydrates: 7g Proteins: 49.5g Fat: 14g Fiber: 1g

Grilled Chicken Thighs in Bacon-Whiskey Marinade

Serves: 4, Preparation: 25 minutes, Cooking: 20 minutes

Ingredients

For the sauce

4 slices of bacon, cut into cubes
2 green onions, finely chopped
1 tbsp. chopped garlic
1/2 cup of mustard
3 tbsps. coconut aminos
2 tbsps. cinnamon
1/2 cup of whiskey
2 tbsps. Worcester sauce
1 - 2 drops of Tabasco (optional)
4 chicken thighs, skinless

Instructions

1. For the sauce, in a medium skillet, fry bacon for about 5 - 6 minutes over Medium heat.
2. Lower the heat, add the onion and garlic and sauté for 4 - 5 minutes.
3. Add the remaining ingredients, stir and cook for 5 minutes.
4. Remove the sauce from heat and let it cool down.
5. In a large plastic bag, add the chicken legs and drop the half of the sauce; shake to combine well。
6. Refrigerate the chicken to marinate overnight.
7. Remove the chicken from marinade.
8. Preheat your grill (pellet, gas, charcoal) to Medium according to manufacturer instructions.
9. Grill the chicken breasts for about 20 minutes; flip every 5 - 6 minutes.
10. Brush the chicken with the rest of the sauce, and grill for further 15 minutes.
11. Let the chicken sit for 10 minutes before servings.

Nutrition information:

Calories: 573 Carbohydrates: 6.5g Proteins: 36g Fat: 7g Fiber: 3g

Grilled Chops in Citrus Sesame Marinade

Serves: 6, Preparation: 15 minutes, Cooking: 8 minutes

Ingredients

3 tbsps. sesame oil
3/4 cup coconut aminos (from coconut sap)
2 garlic cloves, minced
1 tbsp. chili sauce
1 tbsp. Stevia granulated sweetener
1/4 cup lemon juice, fresh
Salt and ground black pepper to taste
6 pork chops, bone-in

Instructions

1. In a bowl, combine the sesame oil, coconut aminos, garlic, chili sauce, Stevia, salt and pepper, and fresh lemon juice.
2. Place the marinade in a large resalable plastic bag along with pork; seal the bag and refrigerate overnight。
3. Remove the pork from the marinade, and pat dry on kitchen paper.
4. Preheat your grill (pellet, gas, charcoal) to High according to manufacturer instructions.
5. Place the pork chops on a grill and cook for 4 minutes per side.
6. Transfer the pork chops on a platter and let sit for 10 minutes. Serve warm.

Nutrition information:

Calories: 328 Carbohydrates: 4g Proteins: 29g Fat: 22g Fiber: 0.3g

Grilled Cuttlefish

Serves: 6, Preparation: 15 minutes, Cooking: 10 minutes

Ingredients

1/2 cup of olive oil
1 tbsp. lemon juice
1 tsp. ground ginger
1 tsp. oregano
2 pinches of salt
1 tsp. five spice powder
8 large cuttlefishes, cleaned
2 - 3 lemons, for serving

Instructions

1. In a deep container add the cuttlefishes.
2. In a bowl, combine all remaining ingredients and pour evenly over cuttlefish.
3. Cover and marinate for about 2 hours.
4. Remove the cuttlefish from marinade and pat dry them on kitchen paper.
5. Preheat your grill (pellet, gas, charcoal) to High

according to manufacturer instructions.
6. Place the cuttlefish on grill and grill the cuttlefish 3-5 minutes on each side (depend of the size).

7. Serve hot with lemon wedges and lemon juice.
Nutrition information:
Calories: 301 Carbohydrates: 4g Proteins: 28g Fat: 19.5g Fiber: 2g

Grilled Lamb Chops with Tomato Marinade

Serves: 8, Preparation: 15 minutes, Cooking: 8 - 10 minutes
Ingredients
8 lamb chops
For marinade / sauce
1 small white onion, cut into pieces
1 grated tomato
1 cup extra virgin olive oil
4 cloves of garlic
2 tbsps. red wine vinegar
1 tbsp. sweet paprika
1 tbsp. dried thyme
1 tbsp. coriander
2 tsps. cumin
2 tsps. salt
1 tsp. cayenne pepper
1 tsp. grated black pepper
Instructions
1. Combine the marinade ingredients and stir well.

2. Place the lamb chops in a shallow container next to each other, and cover with marinade.
3. Wrap the container with plastic membrane and refrigerate for 6 hours.
4. Remove the lamb chops 30 minutes before grilling; place them on a kitchen towel to pat dry.
5. Preheat the grill for direct baking on High heat.
6. Place the lamb chops on grill, and cook, with lid closed, for about 4 minutes per side for medium-rare; turn them twice.
7. Remove from the grill, let it rest for 5 minutes and serve hot.
Nutrition information:
Calories: 460 Carbohydrates: 4.5g Proteins: 28g Fat: 36g Fiber: 1.5g

Grilled Marinated Goat Skewers

Serves: 6, Preparation: 15 minutes, Cooking: 15 minutes
Ingredients
3 lbs. goat chops, cut into large pieces
4 cloves garlic (minced)
2 tsps. sweet paprika
1 tsp. ground chili
2 tsps. ground cumin
2 tsps. dried oregano
1/4 cup olive oil
1/4 cup white vine
1 tsp. fresh basil, finely chopped
1 tsp. fresh mint, finely chopped
Kosher or sea salt to taste
1 lemon juice (freshly squeezed)
Instructions
1. Place the goat chops in a shallow container.
2. In a bowl, combine all remaining ingredients

and pour evenly over chops.
3. Cover and refrigerate overnight.
4. Remove chops from fridge 30 minutes before grilling. Pat dry the meet on a kitchen paper towel. Thread the meat cubes onto the skewers.
5. Preheat your grill (pellet, gas, charcoal) to High according to manufacturer instructions.
6. Put skewers directly on grill grate and grill for 5 - 6 minutes from each side (Medium Rare – 145⁰F, Medium – 160⁰F, Well Done – 170⁰F), turning occasionally, until done.
Nutrition information:
Calories: 388 Carbohydrates: 4g Proteins: 45g Fat: 37g Fiber: 1g

Grilled Marinated Pancetta Strips

Serves: 6, Preparation: 15 minutes, Cooking: 8 - 10 minutes

Ingredients

5 - 6 lbs. pancetta, cut in strips
2 tbsps. salt and black pepper or to taste
1 tsp. smoked pepper
1 clove garlic, minced
1/2 tsp. fresh oregano
1 tbsp. allspice (ground)
2 tbsps. olive oil
1/2 cup of white wine
2 - 3 lemons, sliced for serving

Instructions

1. Place pancetta strips in a large container.
2. In a bowl, combine all remaining ingredients, and pour evenly over the pancetta strips.
3. Cover and shake the container; refrigerate it overnight.
4. Remove pancetta from fridge for at least half an hour before grilling.
5. Preheat your grill (pellet, gas, charcoal) to High according to manufacturer instructions.
6. Place pancetta strips on a grill and cook each side for 3 - 4 minutes or until done.
7. Remove grilled pork pancetta strips on a serving platter and let it sit for 10 minutes.
8. Serve with the lemon wedges.

Nutrition information:

Calories: 319 Carbohydrates: 4g Proteins: 0.5g Fat: 26g Fiber: 1.5g

Grilled Pork Chops with Ginger-Garlic

Serves: 4, Preparation: 15 minutes, Cooking: 14 - 16 minutes

Ingredients

4 pork chops
1/2 cup fresh cilantro, chopped
3 tbsps. fresh mint, more for garnish
2 tbsps. minced fresh ginger
2 tbsps. minced garlic
2 tsps. grated lime zest
1/2 cup bone broth (or water)
1/4 cup coconut aminos (from coconut sap)
2 tbsps. sesame oil
Salt and freshly ground black pepper to taste
Lime wedges for serving

Instructions

1. Season pork chops with the salt and pepper, and place in a shallow container.
2. In a bowl, combine all remaining ingredients and pour evenly over chops; refrigerate overnight.
3. When you're ready to grill the chops, remove them from the marinade and discard the liquid.
4. Preheat your grill (pellet, gas, charcoal) to High according to manufacturer instructions.
5. Set the chops directly over the heat. Cook them for about 2 minutes per side, and then remove the chops at a side. Cover the grill and cook the chops indirectly for further 4-6 minutes per side.
6. Transfer the chops to a clean platter and let them rest for 5 minutes before serving. Serve with the lime wedges.

Nutrition information:

Calories: 514 Carbohydrates: 4g Proteins: 52g Fat: 33g Fiber: 1g

Grilled Pork Ribs with Sweet Mustard Sauce

Serves: 6, Preparation: 15 minutes, Cooking: 30 minutes

Ingredients

5 lbs. pork ribs
1/4 cup coconut aminos
3 tbsps. sesame oil
2 tbsps. mustard (Dijon, English, ground stone)
2 tbsps. Stevia sweetener
1/2 cup water
2 garlic cloves, minced

Instructions

1. Cut the ribs into serving-sized portions and place them in a large container.
2. Combine all remaining ingredients and pour the sauce over the pork ribs.
3. Refrigerate for 6 hours or overnight.
4. Drain ribs and reserve marinade.
5. Preheat your grill (pellet, gas, charcoal) to High according to manufacturer instructions.
6. Place the ribs on a grill (bone-side down), close the lid and cook for 30 - 35 minutes on 300°F.
7. Remove ribs to a plate, let them sit for 5 minutes and serve hot.

Nutrition information:

Calories: 588 Carbohydrates: 4g Proteins: 36g Fat: 57g Fiber: 0.3g

Grilled Sea bass with Hot Sauce

Serves: 4, Preparation: 10 minutes, Cooking: 5 - 6 minutes

Ingredients

1 lbs. sea bass fillets
1 cup mayonnaise
1/2 cup of ground stone mustard
1/4 tsp of liquid smoking
Juice of 1 medium lemon
2 tbsps. hot sauce
2 cloves garlic, minced

Instructions

1. Rinse and clean the fish; pat dry on kitchen paper.
2. In a bowl, combine all remaining ingredients and rub evenly the fish.
3. Preheat your grill (pellet, gas, charcoal) to Medium-high according to manufacturer instructions.
4. Place fish fillets on a grill and cook for about 5 - 6 minutes per side.
5. Serve hot.

Nutrition information:

Calories: 253 Carbohydrates: 8g Proteins: 24g Fat: 14g Fiber: 0.5g

Grilled Spicy Shrimp with Coriander

Serves: 4, Preparation: 15 minutes, Cooking: 2 - 4 minutes

Ingredients

1 cup of olive oil
1 tbsp of ground red hot peppers
1 tbsp of coconut aminos
1 tsp of salt
2 lbs of large shrimps, cleaned
2 tbsps of chopped fresh coriander leaves

Instructions

1. In a large bowl, combine the olive oil, hot peppers with coconut aminos and salt.
2. Add the shrimps and make sure to cover it evenly with the mixture.
3. Cover with membrane and marinate at room temperature for 30 minutes or in the refrigerator for 1 hour.
4. Prepare the grill for direct baking at High temperature.
5. Remove the shrimp from the bowl and remove any marinade.
6. Thread shrimp onto skewers, three per skewer.
7. Grill shrimp, with lid closed, for 2 to 4 minutes, turning only once.
8. Remove shrimp from the grill and sprinkle with the chopped coriander.
9. Serve hot.

Nutrition information:

Calories: 334 Carbohydrates: 4g Proteins: 34g Fat: 20g Fiber: 1g

Lemon Marinated Grilled Salmon

Serves: 4, Preparation: 15 minutes, Cooking: 10 -12 minutes

Ingredients

Juice and zest of 2 large lemons, freshly squeezed
1/4 cup of olive oil
3 clove garlic, minced
1 tsp smoked paprika (mild)
Salt and freshly ground black pepper
2 lbs. salmon fillets with skin

Instructions

1. Combine the lemon juice and zest, olive oil, garlic, smoked paprika, and the salt and pepper.
2. Pour the mixture over the salmon fillets.
3. Cover and refrigerate for 2 hours.
4. Preheat your grill (pellet, gas, charcoal) to High according to manufacturer instructions.
5. Place the salmon fillets on grill (skin side down), and cover. Cook for 10 - 12 minutes or to preference.
6. Serve warm.

Nutrition information:

Calories: 459 Carbohydrates: 4g Proteins: 45g Fat: 28g Fiber: 1g

Grilled Steak with Ginger and Sesame

Serves: 4, Preparation: 15 minutes, Cooking: 10 - 12 minutes

Ingredients

3 tbsps of oil
2 tbsps of grated fresh ginger
1 tsp of salt
1-1 / 2 tsp of ground black pepper
2 bone-in steaks (about 4lbs.)

For the sauce

2 tbsps of sesame oil
4 tbsps of sesame seeds
1 tsp of salt
1 tsp freshly ground black pepper
1 tbsp of fresh lemon juice

Instructions

1. In a bowl, stir the oil, ginger, salt and pepper.
2. Rub the steaks with the ginger mixture and leave them at room temperature for about 15 to 30 minutes before baking.

3. Preheat your grill (pellet, gas, charcoal) to High according to manufacturer instructions.
4. Heat non-stick saucepan over Moderate heat and sauté sesame oil and seeds, salt and black pepper for 4 - 5 minutes; stir with a wooden spoon. Place the sauce in a bowl and set aside.
5. Bake the steaks in Medium heat with the lid closed, about 5 - 6 minutes per side, turning 1 or 2 times.
6. Your steak is ready when a meat thermometer reads 140ºF.
7. Serve hot.

Nutrition information:

Calories: 657 Carbohydrates: 2g Proteins: 54g Fat: 52g Fiber: 1g

Grilled Swordfish Stuffed with Fresh Herbs

Serves: 4, Preparation: 15 minutes, Cooking: 16 minutes

Instructions

1 swordfish (well-cleaned)
2 lemon juice
2 tbsps of freshly chopped herbs (thyme, oregano, onions, dill)
1 onion (small), finely chopped
1 small tomato, chopped
1 clove of garlic
1 tbsp of butter, softened
Salt and pepper to taste
Olive oil

Instructions

1. Preheat your grill (pellet, gas, charcoal) to High according to manufacturer instructions.
2. Wash the fish and dry it.

3. Whisk the lemon juice, onion, tomato, fresh herbs, garlic, butter and the salt and pepper to taste.
4. Fill the fish with the lemon-herbs mixture; rub the fish with a little salt and brush the fish with the olive oil.
5. Place the fish on a grill and lower the heat to Moderate.
6. Grill for 8 minutes per side, turning once. Serve hot.

Nutrition information:

Calories: 371 Carbohydrates: 4.5g Proteins: 45g Fat: 18g Fiber: 1g

Grilled Chicken Skewers

Serves: 6, Preparation: 15 minutes, Cooking: 14 – 15 minutes

Ingredients

3 lbs of chicken fillet, cut in pieces
2 cloves of garlic, finely chopped
3 tbsps of olive oil
1 lemon zest and juice
1/2 tsp of salt and pepper
1/4 tsp of coriander
1/4 tsp of cinnamon
1/4 tsp of turmeric
1/4 tsp of nutmeg
Lemon wedges, for serving

Instructions

1. Rinse the fillet, pat dry on a kitchen paper, and cut in pieces.
2. Peel and chop the garlic.
3. Place the chicken pieces in a bowl.
4. Combine the olive oil, garlic, lemon, salt, pepper, coriander, cinnamon, turmeric and nutmeg, and pour over chicken.
5. With your hands mix the chicken with marinade, cover and refrigerate for 4 hours or overnight.
6. Drain the chicken and thread onto skewers.
7. Preheat your grill (pellet, gas, charcoal) to High according to manufacturer instructions.
8. Place skewers on grill and cook for 5 - 7 minutes each side.
9. Serve hot with lemon wedges.

Nutrition information:

Calories: 332 Carbohydrates: 3g Proteins: 49g Fat: 13g Fiber: 3g

Ribeye with Chili Sauce and Garlic

Serves: 4, Preparation: 15 minutes, Cooking: 20 - 30 minutes

Ingredients

4 ribeye steaks (12 ounces each), cleaned

For spread

2 tbsps. extra virgin olive oil
2 tsps of chili powder
2 tsps of coarse salt
1 tbsp of ground red hot paprika
2 cloves of garlic, grated
1 tsp of ground black pepper

For the sauce

1 medium chopped tomato
1 cup of spring onions, finely chopped
1 chili pepper, sliced
1 cup fresh coriander leaves, chopped
2 tbsps of fresh lime juice
3 tsps of coarse salt
1 tsp of grated black pepper
1 tsp of cumin
1 clove of garlic, grated

Instructions

1. Stir all ingredients for the spread.
2. Rub the spread on both sides of the rib eye and allow to sit for 15 to 20 minutes before grilling.
3. In the meantime, combine all ingredients for the sauce; set aside.
4. Preheat your grill (pellet, gas, charcoal) to High according to manufacturer instructions.
5. Bake ribeye on a High heat (direct baking with the lid closed) for about 4 - 6 minutes on each side for medium-rare.
6. Remove the steaks from the grill and let them rest for 10 minutes.
7. Serve warm with the sauce.

Nutrition information:

Calories: 611 Carbohydrates: 8g Proteins: 46g Fat: 51g Fiber: 8g

Simple Grilled Marinated Chicken Fillets

Serves: 8, Preparation: 15 minutes, Cooking: 15 - 20 minutes

Ingredients

6 - 8 chicken fillets, boneless

MARINADE

3/4 cup of olive oil

1/2 cup of fresh lemon juice

1 tsp of lemon zest

1 tsp of oregano, fresh or dry

2 tbsps of bone broth

Salt and ground black pepper

Instructions

1. Clean the fillets and add score marks.

2. Whisk with a fork all marinade ingredients to combine and pour over the chicken fillets.

3. Cover with saran wrap and refrigerate for 6-8 hours or overnight.

4. Remove the chicken from the fridge 1 hour before grilling.

5. Preheat your grill (pellet, gas, charcoal) according to manufacturer's instructions.

6. Bake for 4 minutes from one side, turn them out, and grill for another 4 minutes.

7. Then turn them on and continue firing on the other side for 6-8 minutes.

8. The chicken is ready when internal temp. reach 165F. Serve hot.

Nutrition information:

Calories: 446 Carbohydrates: 1.5g Proteins: 38g Fat: 32g Fiber: 0.2g

Stuffed Chicken Breasts with Olives and Feta

Serves: 4, Preparation: 20 minutes, Cooking: 15 - 20 minutes

Ingredients

4 chicken breasts

1 green onion, finely chopped

2 cloves of garlic

2 tsps. fresh thyme

1 sprig of rosemary

12 black olives, pitted

1/2 cup crumbled feta cheese

12 slices of bacon

3 tbsps of olive oil

Salt and ground pepper

Instructions

1. Clean and chop the onion and garlic.

2. Remove the leaves of thyme and rosemary from the stems and chop them very well.

3. Finally, clean olives and crumble feta cheese, and place into a bowl.

4. Place all remaining ingredients in a bowl and combine well.

5. Open the chicken breasts and fill with the mixture.

6. Then, wrap the breasts in rolls and wrap them with bacon.

7. Preheat your grill (pellet, gas, charcoal) to High according to manufacturer instructions.

8. Place wrapped chicken breasts on the grill and bake for about 15 - 20 minutes, turning them occasionally until the chicken reaches internal temperature of 150 ° F.

9. Serve hot.

Nutrition information:

Calories: 577 Carbohydrates: 4g Proteins: 5g Fat: 44g Fiber: 1g

Chapter 15 Keto – International

Chinese

Sweet Pork and Mushrooms

Serves: 6, Preparation: 15 minutes, Cooking: 20 minutes

Ingredients

1/2 lb. pork loin, boneless
2 cups of coconut aminos (from coconut saps)
1 cup of white wine
1 tbsp. Stevia
1 1/2 cups of avocado oil
1 large onion, finely chopped
1 lb. fresh mushrooms
Salt and ground pepper to taste

Instructions

1. Rinse and cut mushrooms in thin strips.
2. Cut the onion in half and finely cut in cubes.
3. Cut the pork into thin strips.
4. Heat the oil in a large wok or frying skillet over High-moderate heat.
5. Sauté the onion with a pinch of salt for two minutes stirring continuously.
6. Add mushrooms and continue to sauté for further 3 minutes; stir.
7. Remove all ingredients in a bowl; set aside.
8. In a same wok or frying skillet, heat the oil and fry the pork stirring continuously for 4 - 5 minutes or until meat is no longer pink.
9. Remove the mushrooms mixture to wok, pour the wine, Stevia and continue to cook, stirring continuously, for further 3 - 4 minutes.
10. Taste and adjust salt and pepper; stir. Serve hot.

Nutrition information:
Calories: 380 Carbohydrates: 5g Proteins: 12g Fat: 32.5g Fiber:1g

Braised Veggies with Coconut Aminos

Serves: 4, Preparation: 5 minutes, Cooking: 20 minutes

Ingredients

1 tbsp. avocado oil
2 green onions, finely chopped
11 oz. celery (stalks), sliced
1/2 cup water
11 oz. white mushrooms, sliced
1/2 cup cauliflower rice
2 tbsps. coconut aminos
Salt to taste

Instructions

1. Heat the avocado oil in a wok or in a frying skillet.
2. Add the chopped onions and sprinkle with a little salt; sauté for 3 - 4 minutes, stir.
3. Add sliced celery stalks and pour 1/2 cup water; simmer for 6 - 8 minutes.
4. Add white mushrooms and season with little salt; stir for 2 - 3 minutes.
5. Add cauliflower rice and coconut aminos and cook, stirring, for further 3 - 4 minutes. Serve hot.

Nutrition information:
Calories: 111 Carbohydrates: 1.5g Proteins: 4g Fat: 6g Fiber: 3.5g

Breaded Pork with Sweet-Sour Sauce

Serves: 4, Preparation: 15 minutes, Cooking: 15 minutes

Ingredients

1 lb. pork; without bone, cut in strips
1/2 tsp. salt, or to taste
1/4 cup almond flour
2 egg yolks
Olive oil, for frying
1 onion, cut into cubes
1 large tomato, finely chopped
1 tsp. mustard
1 green pepper, finely chopped
2 tbsps. Stevia sweetener
1/2 cup of fresh lemon juice

Instructions

1. Heat the oil in a wok over High heat.
2. Season pork strips with the salt evenly.
3. Roll the pork in almond flour, then in beaten egg yolks, and again in the almond flour.
4. Fry the pork strips in hot oil for 5 - 7 minutes.
5. Remove the pork on a plate covered with kitchen paper to drain.
6. In a meantime, in a same wok sauté the onion with a little salt.
7. Add the chopped tomato and stir for 2 - 3 minutes.
8. Add mustard, green pepper, Stevia sweetener and some salt; stir for 2 - 3 minutes.
9. Remove the sauce from heat and pour the lemon juice; stir well.
10. Place the pork on a serving plate, pour the sauce over the meat and serve.

Nutrition information:
Calories: 469 Carbohydrates: 7g Proteins: 12g Fat: 47g Fiber: 2.5g

Chinese Chicken with Bamboo and Lemongrass

Serves: 4, Preparation: 5 minutes, Cooking: 25 minutes

Ingredients
2 tsps. sesame oil
2 tbsps. coconut oil
1 lb. chicken fillet, cut into chunks
1 onion, finely chopped
2 medium carrots, sliced
2 cloves of garlic, minced
1 piece of fresh ginger, cleaned and cut
1 tbsp. fresh lemongrass
Bamboo slices (canned, unsalted)
2 fresh onions, sliced
1 chili pepper, finely chopped
Fresh coriander, finely chopped
Salt and black pepper to taste

Instructions
1. Heat the coconut and sesame oil in a wok over Moderate-strong fire.
2. Add the chicken with little salt and sauté for 3 - 4 minutes.
3. Put the onion in the wok and continue to sauté for further 2 - 3 minutes; stir.
4. Add the carrots and garlic and stir for 2 - 3 minutes.
5. Add ginger, lemongrass, chili and bamboo slices; continue to stir for further 3 minutes.
6. At the end, add fresh onions, coriander, and adjust salt and pepper to taste; cook for 3 - 4 minutes. Serve hot.

Nutrition information:
Calories: 108 Carbohydrates: 8g Proteins: 3g Fat: 7g Fiber: 2.5g

Five Spice Broccoli (Chinese)

Serves: 2, Preparation: 10 minutes, Cooking: 15 minutes

Ingredients
1 lb. broccoli flower
2 - 3 tsps. avocado oil
2 1/2 cups of water
Kosher salt to taste
1 tbsp. five spice powder

Instructions
1. Cut the broccoli into small pieces; rinse it and drain in a strainer.
2. Heat the avocado oil in a wok over High temperature.
3. Add the broccoli with a pinch of salt and sauté for 2 - 3 minutes.
4. Pour water and cook for 5 minutes; stir occasionally.
5. Remove broccoli to a serving plate, and sprinkle with five spice powder.
6. Serve immediately.

Nutrition information:
Calories: 55 Carbohydrates: 4g Proteins: 8g Fat: 3g Fiber: 1g

Fried Sweet-Sour Chicken Fillets

Serves: 4, Preparation: 10 minutes, Cooking: 5 - 6 minutes

Ingredients
1 1/2 lbs. chicken fillets, sliced
Salt to taste
1/2 cup fresh lemon juice
1/4 cup coconut flour
2 tbsps. Stevia sweetener, granulated
1/2 cup of olive oil, for frying

Instructions

1. Place your chicken in a bowl, and season with salt to taste.
2. Pour the lemon juice over the chicken and stir well.
3. In a separate small bowl combine coconut flour and Stevia sweetener.
4. Add coconut flour mixture to the bowl with the chicken; stir well.
5. Heat the oil in a wok and fry the chicken fillets for about 5 - 6 minutes.
6. Stir continuously to prevent sticking. Serve hot.

Nutrition information:
Calories: 381 Carbohydrates: 6g Proteins: 37g Fat: 21g Fiber: 0.5g

Instant Pot Duck and Celeriac Soup

Serves: 4, Preparation: 5 minutes, Cooking: 35 minutes

Ingredients

1 - 2 tbsps. duck fat
2 big celery roots, cut in cubes
4 - 5 cups of water
1 lb. duck meat; boneless, cut in small pieces
2 cups of mushrooms, sliced
2 green onions, chopped (only green parts)
Salt and pepper to taste

Instructions

1. Use a sharp knife to remove the tough skin of celery roots; cut in cubes.
2. Add the duck fat to your Instant Pot.
3. Add celery roots and all remaining ingredients and stir well.
4. Lock lid into place and set on the Poultry setting for 30 - 35 minutes.
5. When ready, use Natural Release about 15 - 20 minutes.
6. Taste and adjust salt and pepper to taste. Serve.

Nutrition information:
Calories: 155 Carbohydrates: 6g Proteins: 18g Fat: 6g Fiber: 2g

Marinated Pork Chops with Avocado Oil

Serves: 4, Preparation: 10 minutes, Cooking: 10 - 15 minutes

Ingredients

1/4 cup avocado oil
3 cloves of garlic, minced
1/2 cup lemon juice
1/2 cup coconut aminos
4 pork chops

Instructions

1. In a bowl, combine all ingredients except for pork chops. Set the pork in a baking pan and pour marinade over pork. Refrigerate for at least 4 hours or overnight.
2. Remove the pork chops from marinade and place on a kitchen paper to drain (reserve marinade).
3. Heat the marinade in wok over Medium heat to simmer.
4. Cook the pork chops for 10 minutes over Medium heat.
5. Serve hot with marinade.

Nutrition information:
Calories: 361 Carbohydrates: 3g Proteins: 34g Fat: 15g Fiber: 0.3g

Spicy Marinated and Fried Chicken

Serves: 3, Preparation: 10 minutes, Cooking: 5 minutes

Ingredients

1 1/2 lbs. chicken fillet, cut into strips
Two pinches of salt (or to taste)
1 yogurt
1 tbsp. coriander (crushed seeds)
2 tbsps. coconut milk
1 tbsp. palm sugar or Stevia sweetener
1 tbsp. curry powder
1 tsp. ginger powder
1 tsp. garlic powder
1 tsp. hot mustard
Olive oil, for frying

Instructions

1. Season your chicken with a salt from all sides.
2. Place the chicken in a large resealable Ziploc bag and add all remaining ingredients.
3. Shake the bag to combine all ingredients

evenly.
4. Refrigerate your marinated chicken for at least 3 hours.
5. Heat the oil in a wok or in a large frying skillet over Moderate-high heat.
6. Remove the chicken from the bag, but do not clean the marinade.
7. Fry the chicken for 3 - 4 minutes per side or until done. Serve.

Nutrition information:
Calories: 211 Carbohydrates: 7g Proteins: 9g Fat: 18g Fiber: 1g

Stir Fry Vegetable Omelet with Mustard

Serves: 4, Preparation: 5 minutes, Cooking: 15 minutes

Ingredients
3 whole eggs, from free-range chickens
3 egg whites
2 tbsps. coconut oil
2 cups of mushrooms, of your choice
2 small red chili peppers
1 grated carrot
2 cups of grated cabbage
1 small zucchini, sliced
1/2 tsp. cumin
1 tsp. curry
1/3 tsp. garlic powder
3 tbsps. stone-ground mustard
1 tbsp. sesame, for garnish

Instructions
1. Beat the eggs and egg whites together in a bowl; set aside.
2. Heat the coconut oil in a wok over High heat.
3. Sauté the mushrooms and chili peppers with a pinch of salt.
4. Add carrot, cabbage, and zucchini and cook, stirring, for 4 - 5 minutes.
5. Then, add the egg mixture and stir well; cook for about 2 - 3 minutes; stir.
6. Season with cumin, curry, garlic powder, mustard and little salt; stir.
7. Remove from heat, serve and sprinkle with sesame.

Nutrition information:
Calories: 194 Carbohydrates: 7g Proteins: 12g Fat: 13g Fiber: 4g

Mediterranean

Artichokes Stuffed with Gruyere and Capers

Serves: 4, Preparation: 20 minutes, Cooking: 1 hour

Ingredients
1/2 cup of olive oil
1 chopped onion
2 cloves garlic, chopped
2 tsps. fresh thyme, chopped
1 tsp. fresh fennel seeds
3/4 cup of finely ground almonds
1 cup of grated Gruyere cheese
2 tbsps. capers
4 large artichokes; cleaned, without stalks
3 cups of white dry wine
3 cups of water or bone broth
Salt and ground pepper

Instructions
1. Preheat the oven to 400⁰F.
2. Heat 3 tablespoon of oil in frying pan over Medium heat.
3. Add the onion and sauté until soft for about 4 - 5 minutes.
4. Add the garlic, thyme, fennel and stir for 2 minutes.
5. Transfer to a bowl and allow to cool.
6. Add ground almonds, 1 cup of cheese, caper, and season with the salt the pepper; stir well.
7. With a spoon, take 2 tablespoons of the filling and place it in the center of each artichoke.
8. Put the artichokes in greased baking dish.
9. Sprinkle the artichokes with some oil and 1 cup of cheese.
10. Pour the wine and water or bone broth.
11. Cover with an aluminum foil and bake for about 1 hour.
12. Serve warm.

Nutrition information:
Calories: 459 Carbohydrates: 9g Proteins: 13g Fat: 38g Fiber: 7g

Baked Zucchini and Feta Omelet

Serves: 6, Preparation: 10 minutes, Cooking: 35 minutes

Ingredients

1/4 cup of olive oil
3 cloves of garlic, finely chopped
3 zucchinis, sliced
1 bunch of parsley
10 eggs
1 cup feta, crumbled
Sea salt and freshly ground pepper to taste

Instructions

1. Preheat the oven to 360^{0}F.
2. Grease a large baking dish and set aside.
3. Heat the olive oil in a frying skillet over Medium heat. Sauté the garlic with the pinch of salt, stir gently, for 3 - 4 minutes.
4. Add zucchinis and cook for further 3 - 4 minutes.
5. Transfer the zucchini mixture in a prepared baking dish.
6. Whisk the eggs with parsley, little salt and pepper and stir crumbled feta. Pour the egg mixture evenly over zucchinis.
7. Bake for about 25 - 30 minutes.
8. Allow to cool for 5 minutes, slice and serve.

Nutrition information:

Calories: 285 Carbohydrates: 5g Proteins: 16g Fat: 23g Fiber: 1g

Cretan Lamb Kiofta

Serves: 4, Preparation: 15 minutes, Cooking: 15 minutes

Ingredients

2 1/2 lbs. ground lamb meat
1 large onion, grated
4 cloves of garlic, minced
1 tsp. cumin
1 tsp. paprika
1 tsp. myrtle pepper (or allspice)
1 tsp. turmeric
3/4 cup chopped parsley
3/4 cup chopped mint leaves
1/2 cup of fresh rosemary leaves
Salt and pepper to taste

Instructions

1. In a large bowl, combine all the ingredients.
2. Knead it with your hands until get a compact mixture.
3. Form the meat mixture into meatballs.
4. Line a platter with parchment paper, place meatballs, cover and refrigerate for 1 hour.
5. If you want you can grill your meatballs, or you can fry them in a frying skillet, 15 minutes in total. Serve hot.

Nutrition information:

Calories: 214 Carbohydrates: 1.5g Proteins: 27g Fat: 10g Fiber: 1,5g

Fried Mustard Mussels

Serves: 4, Preparation: 5 minutes, Cooking Time: 15 minutes

Ingredients

4 tbsps. olive oil
2 fresh spring onions, chopped
1/2 green pepper, chopped into small pieces
1 tsp. oregano
1 1/2 lbs. mussels with shells, freshly cleaned
1 cup water
1/4 cup yellow mustard
Freshly ground pepper to taste
2 lemons; juice, zest and slices

Instructions

1. Heat the oil in a large frying pan over Medium-high heat.
2. Add chopped onion, pepper, and oregano; sauté for 2-3 minutes.
3. Add the mussels and water; toss the pan and cover.
4. Cook until all mussels opened.
5. Once opened, they are juicy and delicious.
6. Dissolve mustard with little water and pour over mussels. Cook for 1 minute and sprinkle with freshly ground pepper.
7. Serve with lemon juice and lemon zest.

Nutrition information:

Calories: 300 Carbohydrates: 8g Proteins: 22g Fat: 20g Fiber: 3,5g

Fried Sardines with Caper

Serves: 4, Preparation: 10 minutes, Cooking Time: 5 minutes

Ingredients

1 lb. canned sardines
2 tbsps. wine vinegar
1 tsp. fresh oregano
1/2 cup olive oil
1/2 cup caper
2 limes, sliced

Instructions

1. Place sardines on the plate; sprinkle with the vinegar and oregano.

2. Place sardines in refrigerator for about 30 minutes.
3. Heat the oil in a large frying pan, and fry sardines for 2 minutes per side.
4. Serve sardines on the plate with lime and capers.

Nutrition information:

Calories: 506 Carbohydrates: 2g Proteins: 30g Fat: 42g Fiber: 1g

Grilled Sea Bream with Thyme

Serves: 4, Preparation: 15 minutes, Cooking Time: 20 minutes

Ingredients

2 sea bream fish
3 tbsps. olive oil
Salt to taste
1 lemon
2 tsps. fresh chopped thyme

Instructions

1. Preheat your grill (charcoal, gas, and pellet).

2. Clean fish and rub with the oil, lemon, and the salt and fresh thyme mixture.
3. Grill the fish for 7 - 8 minutes per side.
4. Serve hot.

Nutrition information:

Calories: 313 Carbohydrates: 2.5g Proteins: 42g Fat: 15g Fiber: 1,5g

Grilled Seafood Basket

Serves: 5, Preparation: 10 minutes, Cooking Time: 1 hour and 10 minutes

Ingredients

2 lbs. octopus tentacles
1 lb. squid
2 tbsps. garlic-infused olive oil
1 lemon juice fresh
1 lemon slices
Sea salt and pepper
Capers for serving

Instructions

1. Preheat the grill to 400°F.
2. Season the octopus tentacles and squid with the salt.

3. Transfer the seafood on the grill.
4. Turn the octopus every 15 minutes and the squid / threshing once in 25 minutes.
5. Remove the squid after 40 minutes, and the octopus is ready after 1 hour and 10 minutes.
6. Sprinkle with olive oil and serve hot with lemon slices, fresh lemon juice and capers.

Nutrition information:

Calories: 260 Carbohydrates: 1.5g Proteins: 41g Fat: 10g Fiber: 0.2g

Haddock Napolitano (Italian)

Serves: 4, Preparation: 10 minutes, Cooking Time: 40 minutes

Ingredients

1/4 cup of virgin olive oil
2-3 clove of garlic, whole but crushed
1 red hot chili pepper
1 tomato, grated
1/2 cup of black olives, pitted
2 tbsps. caper
2 tbsps. almonds, chopped
1 1/2 lbs. haddock

1 tsp. fresh oregano
1 tbsp. fresh parsley, finely chopped

Instructions

1. In a drying pan, heat the olive oil over Medium-high heat.
2. Fry the haddock with skin side down for about 2 minutes per side.
3. Remove the fish from the pan, and place on a

plate; set aside.
4. Heat the oil in a separate skillet and sauté the garlic for 2 - 3 minutes.
5. Add the hot pepper, grated tomato and the capers; cook and stir for 3 - 4 minutes.
6. Add the almonds, black olives, and gently stir.
7. Cover and cook the sauce for 15 minutes over low heat.
8. Preheat the oven to 360⁰F.
9. In a greased baking dish, put the pieces of haddock and pour them with the sauce, remove the garlic.
10. Bake for about 10 minutes.
11. Sprinkle fish with oregano and bake for further 2 minutes.
12. Serve immediately with fresh parsley.

Nutrition information:
Calories: 201 Carbohydrates: 6.5g Proteins: 30g Fat: 6g Fiber: 3g

Mediterranean "Horta" Greens Patties

Serves: 4, Preparation: 15 minutes, Cooking Time: 5 minutes

Ingredients
1 1/2 cups chervil, fine substitute would be fresh parsley or tarragon
1/2 lb. fresh spinach
1 fresh onion, chopped
1 tbsp. mint leaves, freshly chopped
2 tbsps. anise
1/2 tsp. baking powder
Salt and ground black pepper
1 large egg
1/2 cup almond flour
Oil for frying

Instructions
1. Rinse and chop the chervil and spinach and put them in a bowl with the remaining ingredients. Knead well the mixture and make small patties.
2. In a large frying skillet, heat the oil and fry patties for 2 minutes per each side.
3. Transfer the patties on a platter lined with kitchen paper. Serve hot.

Nutrition information:
Calories: 165 Carbohydrates: 6g Proteins: 6g Fat: 13g Fiber: 3g

Mediterranean Octopus "Meatballs"

Serves: 6, Preparation: 15 minutes, Cooking Time: 50 minutes

Ingredients
2 lbs. octopus, cleaned
1/4 cup of extra virgin olive oil
3 tbsps. chopped spring onion
2 tbsps. dill fresh dill, finely chopped
3 tbsps. fresh parsley, finely chopped
1/2 cup red wine
1 cup water
1 bay leaf
1 large egg
1 cup almond flour
Salt and freshly ground pepper to taste
Olive oil for frying

Instructions
1. Rinse the octopus thoroughly.
2. Heat the olive oil in a pot over Medium-high heat.
3. Cover the pot and sauté for 10 minutes, or until changes color (red).
4. Add the wine, water, bay leaf and cover the pot again; bring to boil and cook for 35 minutes.
5. Allow the octopus to cool and cut into large pieces.
6. Place the octopus in a blender and mince.
7. Pour the octopus into a bowl and add all remaining ingredients.
8. From the mixture make balls.
9. Heat the oil in a frying skillet and fry the octopus balls for 3 - 4 minutes over Medium heat.
10. Remove octopus balls into place lined with kitchen paper. Serve warm.

Nutrition information:
Calories: 356 Carbohydrates: 6g Proteins: 29g Fat: 24g Fiber: 1.5g

Oven Baked Oysters and Mushrooms Frittata

Serves: 6, Preparation: 5 minutes, Cooking Time: 30 minutes

Ingredients

2 cups button mushroom, sliced
1/2 cup onion, chopped fine
1 tbsp. fresh butter
10 oysters, well drained
6 eggs
1 cup almond milk
1/4 tsp. paprika
1/4 tsp. pepper
2 tbsps. cooked, crumbled bacon

Instructions

1. Preheat oven to 400⁰F.
2. Heat the butter in a skillet over Medium heat.
3. Sauté mushrooms and onion for 2 - 3 minutes.

Drain oysters and add to the mushroom mixture.
4. Cook for 1 - 2 minutes. Remove pan from heat and set aside.
5. In a bowl, beat eggs, almond milk, paprika and pepper.
6. Pour mixture over oyster mixture in skillet, and sprinkle with crumbled bacon.
7. Bake for 20 minutes or until set.
8. Cut into slices and serve.

Nutrition information:

Calories: 146 Carbohydrates: 3g Proteins: 11g Fat: 10g Fiber: 0.5g

Roasted Asparagus with Garlic and Feta

Serves: 4, Preparation: 15 minutes, Cooking Time: 25 minutes

Ingredients

1 lb. fresh asparagus
1/2 cup of olive oil
3 cloves garlic
1 lemon zest + juice
1 tbsp. dry oregano
1 tsp. hot pepper, ground
1 tsp. salt and ground pepper
3/4 cup of feta cheese
3 tbsps. fresh thyme leaves, finely chopped

Instructions

1. Preheat the oven to 400⁰F.
2. Clean the asparagus by cutting the hard place on its base (it is like wood), peel off from the waist and down.
3. Heat 2 tablespoon of oil in a frying pan over Medium heat.

4. Add the garlic, lemon zest, oregano, and ground hot pepper; stir and sauté until the garlic is golden brown.
5. Remove from the heat.
6. In a large bowl put the asparagus with the remaining olive oil, salt, pepper and stir well.
7. Add the garlic mixture from the pan and stir well.
8. Add the asparagus in oiled baking dish, and sprinkle with feta cheese, and with the thyme.
9. Put in the oven and bake for 10-15 minutes.
10. Remove from the oven, sprinkle with the lemon juice and serve.

Nutrition information:

Calories: 380 Carbohydrates: 8.5g Proteins: 11g Fat: 33.5g Fiber: 5g

Roasted Lamb Chops with Rosemary

Serves: 4, Preparation: 10 minutes, Cooking Time: 45 minutes

Ingredients

1/2 cup of almond flour
1 1/2 cups fresh rosemary
2 tbsps. minced garlic
2 tbsps. olive oil
1 tsp. yellow mustard
Salt and ground pepper to taste
4 lamb chops

Instructions

1. Preheat the oven to 400⁰F.
2. In a deep bowl, combine almond flour, garlic, rosemary, and the salt and pepper.

3. Pour the olive oil and mustard and stir well.
4. Season the lamb chops with the garlic-rosemary mixture.
5. Place the lamb chops in oiled baking dish.
6. Bake for 20 minutes, and then turn chops over, reduce heat to 360⁰F, and bake for further 20 - 25 minutes.
7. Serve hot.

Nutrition information:

Calories: 479 Carbohydrates: 4g Proteins: 28g Fat: 39g Fiber: 02g

Spicy Seafood "Meatballs"

Serves: 6, Preparation: 15 minutes, Cooking Time: 10 minutes

Ingredients

1 lb. octopus, ground
1 lb. squid, ground
3 tbsps. ground almonds
1 bunch of parsley, finely chopped
2 -3 drops of hot pepper sauce
Salt and freshly ground pepper
1 cup olive oil for frying
2 lemon slices and juice

Instructions

1. Cut octopus and squid into small pieces and blend in food processor or blender until minced well.
2. Transfer the minced seafood into bowl.
3. Add ground almonds, chopped parsley, red hot sauce, and little salt and pepper; knead the mixture until combine well.
4. Cover and refrigerate for 1 hour.
5. Remove the seafood mixture from the fridge and make balls.
6. Heat the oil in a frying skillet pan.
7. Fry your seafood "meatballs" until golden from one side.
8. Flip and fry from the other side for 1 minutes.
9. Drain on a kitchen pepper and serve immediately.

Nutrition information:

Calories: 524 Carbohydrates: 6g Proteins: 35g Fat: 40g Fiber: 0.5g

Zucchini with Scrambled Eggs

Serves: 4, Preparation: 10 minutes, Cooking Time: 10 minutes

Ingredients

6 medium-sized zucchinis
2 green onions, chopped
10 fresh eggs
Sea salt to taste
1/4 cup olive oil

Instructions

1. Rinse and peel zucchini; cut into thin slices and sprinkle with little salt.
2. Heat the oil in a skillet over Medium heat.
3. Sauté onions with a pinch of salt; add zucchini slices and sauté for 2 - 3 minutes, gently stir.
4. In a bowl, whisk eggs and pour over garlic and zucchini.
5. Cook the omelet 2 minutes, and then use the spatula to turn omelet; cook for one minute and remove from the heat.
6. Serve hot.

Nutrition information:

Calories: 313 Carbohydrates: 6g Proteins: 16g Fat: 25g Fiber: 1g

Mexican

Hot Strawberry Ice Cream

Serves: 4, Preparation: 10 minutes, Cooking Time: 15 minutes

Instructions

1 lb. strawberries, fresh or frozen
1 1/2 cups stevia powdered sweetener
2 tbsps. water
2 cups whipped cream
1/2 tsp. cayenne pepper powder
1 tbsp. pure vanilla extract
Chopped almonds for decoration

Instructions

1. Combine the strawberries, stevia sweetener and 2 tablespoons of water in a saucepan.
2. Heat over Medium heat and bring to a boil.
3. Reduce heat to Low and stir for 3 - 4 minutes.
4. Remove from heat and add whipped cream; stir with spatula.
5. Add cayenne pepper powder and stir well.
6. Finally, pour the vanilla extract and give a good stir; set aside to cool.
7. Place the mixture in a freezer-safe bowl and freeze for 4 hours or overnight.
8. Let the ice cream at room temperature for 10 - 15 minutes before serving.
9. Serve decorated with chopped almonds.

Nutrition information:

Calories: 177 Carbohydrates: 5g Proteins: 10g Fat: 13g Fiber: 1.5g

Albóndigas (Keto Adaption)

Serves: 7, Preparation: 15 minutes, Cooking Time: 25 minutes

Ingredients

1 lb. ground beef
1/2 lb. minced pork
2 cloves garlic
3 eggs
1 tbsp. cumin, rosemary, thyme mixture
2 - 3 tbsps. almond flour
Salt and pepper to taste
Olive oil for frying

SAUCE

2 - 3 tbsps. olive oil
3 cloves of garlic, sliced
2 ripe tomatoes, peeled
1/2 cup of bone broth
Fresh thyme, finely chopped
Salt and ground black pepper to taste

Instructions

1. In a bowl, add pork and beef meat, garlic, eggs, the salt and pepper and spices.
2. Knead with your hands to combine well.
3. Oil your hands and make meatballs from dough.
4. Roll each meatball in almond flour and place on a plate.
5. Cover the plate with plastic membrane and refrigerate meatballs.
6. Make a sauce: Heat the oil in a deep pan and sauté the garlic with a pinch of salt.
7. Add tomato pulp and season with the salt and pepper; stir with wooden spoon.
8. Add thyme and bone broth and stir.
9. Reduce heat and cook your sauce covered over Low heat for 8 - 10 minutes.
10. In a meantime, fry your meatballs just 2 - 3 minutes to get a color.
11. Add meatballs in a sauce and cook for 10 minutes.
12. Serve hot.

Nutrition information:

Calories: 443 Carbohydrates: 5g Proteins: 22g Fat: 38g Fiber: 1.5g

Mexican Basil Avocado Pops

Serves: 6, Preparation: 15 minutes

Ingredients

2 large avocados
1/4 can stevia natural sweetener, or to taste
2 lemons, juice
3 cup of coconut milk
1 1/4 cups of water
20 fresh basil leaves, finely chopped

Instructions

1. Place all ingredients in your fast-speed blender.
2. Blend until smooth or for about 30 - 45 seconds.
3. Pour the avocado mixture in Popsicle molds and insert wooden sticks in every mold.
4. Freeze until completely frozen. Serve and enjoy!

Nutrition information:

Calories: 215 Carbohydrates: 6.5g Proteins: 9g Fat: 17g Fiber: 4g

Enchiladas - Keto Version

Serves: 4, Preparation: 10 minutes, Cooking Time: 50 minutes

Ingredients

1/4 cup of olive oil
1 onion, finely chopped
1 chili pepper, finely chopped
2 cloves of garlic, sliced
1 small tomato, finely chopped
2 - 3 tbsps. fresh water
1 chicken fillet boneless
1 green pepper, finely chopped
2 tbsps. grated Gouda cheese
2 tbsps. grated mozzarella cheese

Salt and ground black pepper to taste

Instructions

1. Heat the oil over Medium heat, and sauté the onion, chili pepper, garlic and the tomato for 3 minutes.
2. Season with the salt and pepper and remove from heat.
3. Transfer the chili pepper mixture in a blender and pour little water; blend for 20 - 30 seconds.
4. Sprinkle generously the salt and pepper over

chicken fillet.

5. Brush the chicken fillet with chill mixture, wrap in saranwrap and marinate for 3 hours in the refrigerator.

6. Preheat your oven to 360⁰F.

7. Place marinated chicken in oiled baking dish.

8. Sprinkle the green pepper over chicken, place in oven and bake for 25 minutes.

9. Remove chicken from the oven and sprinkle with grated mozzarella and Gouda cheese.

10. Bake for further 10 - 15 minutes or until cheese melt.

11. Serve hot.

Nutrition information:

Calories: 217 Carbohydrates: 6g Proteins: 7g Fat: 18g Fiber: 1.5g

Baked Mexican Meatballs with Anejo Cheese

Serves: 6, Preparation: 5 minutes, Cooking Time: 30 minutes

Ingredients

1 1/2 lbs. ground beef

1 onion, chopped fine

2 cloves garlic

1 cup shredded Anejo cheese (or Parmesan, Cotija)

1 tbsp. fresh butter

1¼ tsps. chili powder

1 tsp. ground coriander

1¼ tsps. ground cumin

2 eggs

Sea salt and freshly ground pepper to taste

Instructions

1. Preheat oven to 350⁰F.

2. Heat the butter in a frying pan and sauté onions

and garlic for 3 minutes until translucent; season with the salt, stir and set aside.

3. In a bowl, whisk the eggs with a pinch of salt. Add the spices, salt, and pepper and stir.

4. Add onions and grated cheese; stir well.

5. Add beef and combine until all ingredients are well combined.

6. Make a meatballs and place on oiled baking pan.

7. Bake for 18 - 20 minutes. Serve hot.

Nutrition information:

Calories: 417 Carbohydrates: 3g Proteins: 27g Fat: 33g Fiber: 1g

Cold Mexican Coffee with Cinnamon

Serves: 4, Preparation: 10 minutes

Ingredients

4 cups espresso-style coffee

3/4 cup whipped cream

1 tbsp. liquid stevia or to taste

2 tbsps. cocoa powder, unsweetened

1 tsp. ground cinnamon

1/2 cup ice cubes, crushed

Instructions

1. Combine all ingredients in your blender; blend for 30 - 45 seconds.

2. Pour coffee into cups, sprinkle with cinnamon and serve.

Nutrition information:

Calories: 128 Carbohydrates: 3g Proteins: 2g Fat: 12g Fiber: 1,5g

Fajitas (Keto adaption)

Serves: 4, Preparation: 10 minutes, Cooking Time: 15 minutes

Ingredients

1 1/2 lbs. pork fillet, cut into thin strips

1 tsp. garlic powder

1 tsp. cayenne pepper

1 tsp. cumin

2 - 3 tbsps. tequila

1/4 cup of olive oil

1 red pepper, chopped

1 green pepper, finely chopped

2 onions, chopped

2 tbsps. ketchup

2 tbsps. mustard

Salt and ground black pepper

Instructions

1. Combine pork with garlic powder, red hot pepper, cumin and tequila; refrigerate for one hour to marinate.

2. Heat the oil in a large frying skillet and sauté pork along with peppers and onion; season with

the salt and pepper and cook for 3 - 4 minutes stirring from time to time.

3. Add the ketchup and mustard and stir well.

4. Cover and simmer on low heat for 5 - 7 minutes.

Serve hot.

Nutrition information:
Calories: 574 Carbohydrates: 7g Proteins: 15g Fat: 54g Fiber: 2g

Keto Guacamole Dip

Serves: 4, Preparation: 15 minutes

Instructions

2 ripe avocados, cut in small cubes
1 small onion, chopped
1 ½ tbsps. lime, juice
Zest from 1 lime
3 tbsps. olive oil
4 - 5 sprigs of fresh cilantro leaves
2 red hot peppers, stems and seeds removed, sliced
Coarse salt to taste
1/4 cup of fresh chopped coriander for serving (optional)

Instructions

1. Peel avocados and remove the pit; cut into small cubes.
2. Dump all ingredients in your food processor or into high-speed blender.
3. Blend until combined well or for about 30 - 45 seconds.
4. Taste and adjust salt and seasonings to taste.
5. Place in a glass bowl, sprinkle with coriander and refrigerate until serving.

Nutrition information:
Calories: 288 Carbohydrates: 8g Proteins: 10g Fat: 24g Fiber: 6g

Keto Serrano Avocado Dip

Serves: 8, Preparation: 15 minutes

Ingredients

4 large avocados
Fresh juice of 2 limes
2 cloves of garlic, finely chopped
1 small tomato, cut into cubes
1 Serrano chili pepper, sliced
Salt and ground black pepper to taste
2 tbsps. mustard
3 tbsps. grated Parmesan cheese

Instructions

1. Cut avocados in the middle, remove the stalk

and, with a spoon, remove the flesh and place it in a bowl.
2. With a fork, melt the avocado, add the lime juice, garlic, salt, pepper, mustard, tomato, and chili pepper; mix gently.
3. Refrigerate in a glass bowl for at least 1 hour. Serve.

Nutrition information:
Calories: 196 Carbohydrates: 7g Proteins: 6g Fat: 16g Fiber: 0.2g

Spicy Coconut - Pork Tenderloin Stew

Serves: 4, Preparation: 10 minutes, Cooking Time: 25 minutes

Ingredients

1 1/2 lbs. pork tenderloin
Salt and ground pepper to taste
1 tbsp. chili powder or to taste
2 tbsps. olive oil
3 fresh onions, finely chopped
1 onion, finely chopped
1 cup of red wine
1/2 cup of coconut water (optional)

Instructions

1. Season the pork with the salt and a chili powder and refrigerate for 3 - 4 hours.
2. When done, remove meat from the fridge.
3. Heat the oil in a frying pan and sauté the onion

and fresh onion for 3 -4 minutes; stir.
4. Add marinated pork and sauté for 3 minutes; stir.
5. Pour the red wine and stir.
6. Cover and cook on Low heat for about 15 minutes.
7. Pour the coconut water, stir and remove from heat.
8. Serve immediately.

Nutrition information:
Calories: 429 Carbohydrates: 8g Proteins: 52g Fat: 21g Fiber: 3g

Bacon Cooked in a Red Onion Peels (Siberia, Russia)

Serves: 6, Preparation: 5 minutes, Cooking Time: 25 minutes

Ingredients

2 cloves of garlic, sliced
Red onion peel (from 5 - 6 onions)
About 1/2 cup of salt
4 bay leaves, crumbled
4 whole cloves
6 grains of black pepper
Water for cooking
2 lbs. bacon

Instructions

1. In a large pot full of salted water, boil the garlic, red onion peel, bay leaves, cloves, and black pepper for 10 minutes.
2. Add the bacon, cover and boil for 10 - 12 minutes.
3. Remove from the heat and let it rest 15 minutes (uncovered).
4. Remove the bacon and wrap in aluminum foil; refrigerate for 1 hour.
5. Remove from the fridge, slice and serve.

Nutrition information:
Calories: 282 Carbohydrates: 3g Proteins: 18g Fat: 22g Fiber: 2g

Baked Creamy Chicken with Vodka (Russia)

Serves: 6, Preparation: 15 minutes, Cooking Time: 40 minutes

Ingredients

4 chicken fillets, boneless
2 tsps. allspice
1/4 cup of olive oil, softened
1 clove of garlic, crushed
1 spring onion, chopped
2 tbsps. vodka
1/2 cup of water
1 tbsp. fresh tomato, grated
Salt and ground pepper to taste
1 cup cream
1/2 cup of goat cheese, softened
1 tbsp. fresh parsley, chopped

Instructions

1. Season the chicken with allspice, and with the salt and pepper.
2. Heat the oil in a large frying skillet over High-moderate heat.
3. Sauté the chicken just until get nice golden color.
4. Remove the chicken from the skillet and place in a greased baking dish.
5. Preheat the oven to 360^{0}F.
6. In a same frying skillet add little oil and sauté the onion and garlic with a pinch of salt for 3 - 4 minutes.
7. Add water, tomato pulp, cream goat cheese, and stir for 2 - 3 minutes over Medium heat; stir frequently.
8. Remove the sauce from heat and pour vodka; stir well.
9. Pour the sauce over the chicken evenly.
10. Place in oven and bake for 30 minutes.
11. Serve hot with chopped parsley.

Nutrition information:
Calories: 459 Carbohydrates: 2.5g Proteins: 38g Fat: 33g Fiber: 0.3g

Roasted Sour Duck with Horseradish & Ginger

Serves: 8, Preparation: 15 minutes, Cooking Time: 1 hour and 15 minutes

Ingredients

1 duck (about 4 - 5 lbs.)
Salt and ground pepper to taste
1 tsp. cumin
1 tsp. marjoram
1 tsp. horseradish
1 tsp. ground ginger
1 tsp. allspice
1 tsp. stevia granulated sweetener

1 tbsp. duck fat

Instructions

1. Combine cumin, marjoram, horseradish, ginger, allspice, stevia sweetener in a bowl.
2. Rinse and clean duck from fat inside, and season with the salt and pepper.
3. Rub the duck generously with the spice mixture inside and outside.

4. Wrap the duck in a foil.
5. On the stove place a large pot half-filled with water.
6. Take the colander in a pot and place the duck.
7. Bring to boil, and then cook the duck for 55 minutes.
8. Preheat the oven to 380^{0}F.
9. Remove the duck from the foil and cut in half.
10. Unwrap and place the duck in greased baking dish.
11. Bake for 15 -20 minutes.
12. Remove from oven and let it cool for 10 minutes. Serve.

Nutrition information:
Calories: 652 Carbohydrates: 0.5g Proteins: 54.5g Fat: 48g Fiber: 0.2g

Fried Turmeric Salmon

Serves: 4, Preparation: 10 minutes, Cooking Time: 15 minutes

Ingredients
2 salmon fillets, without skin
2 tbsps. olive oil
1 tsp. turmeric
1/2 tsp. smoked paprika
1/4 tsp. sea salt and black pepper, freshly ground
1 tbsp. coconut aminos (from coconut sap)
1 lemon, fresh juice

Instructions
1. Rinse and pat dry salmon on absorb paper.
2. Rub each fillet generously with salt, ground pepper, smoked paprika, turmeric.
3. Heat a large frying pan over Medium heat.
4. Fry the salmon fillets on both sides until golden brown, 4-5 minutes per side.
5. Remove salmon from the heat, and sprinkle with coconut aminos sauce, and drizzle with lemon juice. Serve.

Nutrition information:
Calories: 347 Carbohydrates: 1.5g Proteins: 40g Fat: 20g Fiber: 0.2g

Keto "Peking" Duck

Serves: 4, Preparation: 10 minutes, Cooking Time: 35 minutes

Ingredients
1/4 cup duck or chicken fat
3 scallions (only green parts), finely chopped
2 lbs. duck breasts, boneless
1 tsp. ground paprika
1/2 cup water
1 tsp. fresh ginger, grated
1/2 tsp. five spice powder
1/4 tsp. ground nutmeg
2 whole star anises
Salt and freshly ground pepper to taste

Instructions
1. Preheat the oven to 375^{0}F.
2. Rinse and pat dry the chicken breast; season with the salt and paprika.
3. Heat the duck or chicken fat in frying skillet, and sauté scallions with little salt for 5 - 6 minutes.
4. Add the duck breast, and sauté for 5 minutes; add water and spices and stir well.
5. Transfer the duck mixture to the oven and bake for 15 - 20 minutes.
6. Remove from the oven, cover and let sit for 15 minutes before serving.

Nutrition information:
Calories: 379 Carbohydrates: 2g Proteins: 45.5g Fat: 21g Fiber: 1g

Sautéed Duck Gizzards with Spices

Serves: 4, Preparation: 5 minutes, Cooking Time: 1 hour and 40 minutes

Ingredients
1 lb. duck gizzards
1/2 cup of duck fat (or lark)
4 leeks, finely chopped
1 tsp. fresh ginger, grated
1/2 tsp. cumin, grated
1/2 tsp. dry mustard
1/2 tsp. chili powder
1/4 tsp. turmeric ground
Salt and ground pepper to taste
Water

Instructions
1. Rinse the gizzards, pat dry and cut in pieces. In a frying pan add 1 of tablespoon coconut oil and add the gizzards.

2. Heat the fat in a wok or frying skillet over High heat; sauté gizzards with the salt and pepper.
3. Add chopped gizzards and sauté for 5 minutes.
4. Add all spices and pour water; stir well. Pour enough water to cover gizzards.
5. Cover and cook for 1 1/2 hours (or until done)

over Medium-low heat.
6. Serve hot.
Nutrition information:
Calories: 312 Carbohydrates: 7.5g Proteins: 21g Fat: 22g Fiber: 1.5g

Shashimi Coriander and Sesame Breaded Salmon

Serves: 4, Preparation: 15 minutes, Cooking Time: 10 minutes
Ingredients
1 bunch of fresh coriander, finely chopped
1 1/2 lbs. fresh salmon (filleted, boneless)
1/4 cup white sesame
1/4 cup black sesame
2 tbsps. coconut aminos
2 tbsps. olive oil
Lime juice
Instructions
1. Finely chop fresh coriander and place in a bowl.
2. Cut the salmon into 4 - 5 pieces and roll in coriander covering all sides.

3. Roll the salmon in a sesame seeds mixture.
4. Heat the oil in a frying skillet and fry the salmon for 7 - 10 minutes or until golden brown.
5. Remove salmon on a plate with absorbent paper.
6. Place on a serving plate, pour coconut aminos, sprinkle with lime juice and serve.
Nutrition information:
Calories: 409 Carbohydrates: 3g Proteins: 39g Fat: 26.5g Fiber: 1.2g

Snails in Parsley Sauce

Serves: 4, Preparation: 15 minutes, Cooking Time: 20 minutes
Ingredients
2 tbsps. olive oil
2 spring onions, finely chopped
1 green pepper, chopped into small pieces
3 garlic cloves
1 grated tomato
1 lb. snails, canned (sub scallops or clams)
1/2 cup red wine
1/2 cup water
1 bunch of parsley, finely chopped
1/2 cup lemon juice, freshly squeezed
Coarse salt and freshly ground black pepper
Instructions

1. Heat the oil in a frying pan, sauté spring onions, garlic and green pepper. Add grated tomato and pour the wine and water; stir.
2. Add snails and chopped parsley; stir.
3. Season salt and pepper and pour the wine; stir.
4. Cover and cook for about 15-20 minutes over Low heat.
5. Serve with lemon juice.
Nutrition information:
Calories: 293 Carbohydrates: 5g Proteins: 21g Fat: 21g Fiber: 1.5g

Spicy Beef with Nuts

Serves: 6, Preparation: 10 minutes, Cooking Time: 30 minutes
Ingredients
2 lbs. beef fillets, cut into strips
2 scallions, finely chopped
2 cloves of garlic, minced
2 green peppers, cut into thin strips
3 tbsps. almonds, chopped
1/2 cup of coconut aminos
1 cup of beef broth
3 tbsps. sesame oil
1 tsp. cumin

1 tsp. cinnamon
1 tsp. coriander
1 tsp. allspice
1/2 cup of hot water
Salt and ground black pepper
Instructions
1. Cut the beef into thin strips.
2. In a large skillet or wok, heat sesame oil.
3. Add beef strips and cook, stirring, just for 2 - 3

minutes.

4. Transfer beef on a plate and set aside.

5. In a same skillet or wok heat the oil and sauté scallions, garlic, pepper and ground almonds; season with the salt and pepper and stir for 3 - 4 minutes.

6. Add beef, bone broth, coconut aminos, spices, water, the salt and pepper, and bring to boil.

7. Reduce heat to Moderate-low, cover and cook for 20 - 25 minutes; stir occasionally.

8. Serve hot.

Nutrition information:

Calories: 452 Carbohydrates: 4g Proteins: 37g Fat: 32g Fiber: 2g

Spicy Chicken in Pakistani Way

Serves: 4, Preparation: 10 minutes, Cooking Time: 25 minutes

Ingredients

3 tbsps. olive oil

1 onion, finely chopped

1 clove of garlic

1 tsp. freshly ground ginger

2 - 3 tbsps. yogurt

1 tsp. ground coriander

1 tsp. chili powder

1 tsp. turmeric

3 tbsps. ground mustard

Salt to taste

1/2 cup water

1 lb. chicken boneless cut in slices

1 tsp. garam masala

10 grains of black pepper

4 - 6 whole cloves

Fresh chopped parsley to taste

Instructions

1. Heat the oil in a wok or in a frying skillet and sauté the onion and garlic with a pinch of salt.

2. Add the ginger, yogurt, coriander, chili, curcuma and ground mustard, salt and water; stir to combine well, and cook for 2 - 3 minutes.

3. Add sliced chicken and stir for 2 minutes.

4. Add the remaining ingredients, lower heat to Moderate-low, and cook for 15 - 17 minutes. Serve hot with chopped parsley.

Nutrition information:

Calories: 157 Carbohydrates: 4g Proteins: 6g Fat: 13g Fiber: 1.5g

Arab Fattoush Salad

Serves: 8, Preparation: 15 minutes

Ingredients

1 grated tomato (medium)

1/4 cup almonds, chopped

1 medium hot pepper

1 cucumber (medium)

1/2 lettuce head (medium)

1 cup fresh onions slices

2 tbsps. fresh parsley

1 tsp. fresh mint

Dressing

1 tbsp. lemon juice fresh

4 tbsps. olive oil

Salt and black pepper to taste

1 tsp. cumin

Instructions

1. Rinse the tomato and cut into cubes.

2. Rinse, peel and cut the cucumber in cubes.

3. Clean the pepper from the seeds and cut into cubes.

4. Finely chop the onions, parsley and mint.

5. Finally, clean the leaves of lettuce from any dirt and chop them into bite sized pieces.

6. Add all ingredients in a large salad bowl and stir.

7. Beat the olive oil with the lemon juice, cumin, and salt and pepper to taste.

8. Pour the salad with the sauce, toss to combine well, cover and refrigerate one hour before serving.

Nutrition information:

Calories: 130 Carbohydrates: 7g Proteins: 3g Fat: 10g Fiber: 2.5g

Middle Eastern

Serves: 6, Preparation: 15 minutes, Cooking Time: 6 minutes

Ingredients

1 tbsp. red ground paprika
Salt and ground pepper to taste
Juice of 1 lemon
1/2 cup olive oil for marinade
2 lbs. anchovies
1 1/4 cups of almond flour
5 - 6 large fig leaves
1 cup olive oil for frying

Instructions

1. Combine the paprika, salt, pepper, lemon juice and olive oil; stir well.
2. Place anchovies in a large container and pour marinade over the fish evenly.
3. Cover the container and place in fridge for 1 hour.
4. Rinse and pat dry the fig leaves.
5. Remove anchovies from marinade and roll each fish in almond flour.
6. Heat the oil in a frying skillet and place the anchovies.
7. Cover fish with fig leaves.
8. Cook anchovies for 2 - 3 minutes per side.
9. Flip fish once, one by one, and cove again with fig leaves.
10. Remove fig leaves and serve immediately.

Nutrition information:

Calories: 496 Carbohydrates: 1.5g Proteins: 1g Fat: 54g Fiber: 0.5g

Arabian Baba Ghanoush Eggplant Salad

Serves: 6, Preparation: 15 minutes, Cooking Time: 45 minutes

Ingredients

1 large eggplant
4 cloves of garlic, unpeeled
2 tbsps. lemon juice
3 tbsps. tahini or ground sesame seeds
1/2 tsp. ground cumin
1/4 tsp. salt or to taste
Olive oil for serving
Fresh parsley or coriander for serving
Ground red paprika for serving

Instructions

1. Preheat oven to 400⁰F.
2. Pick the eggplant with a fork; place it on a baking sheet along with the garlic.
3. Bake the eggplant for 45 minutes, but remove after 30 minutes, peel them and continue to bake.
4. When the eggplant is ready, remove it from the oven and leave it for 10 minutes to cool.
5. Add the eggplant, garlic and tahini in a food processor and pulse until smooth.
6. Transfer the eggplant mixture to a bowl and season with the salt the pepper, cumin, and fresh lemon juice; stir well.
7. Serve with olive oil and ground red paprika.

Nutrition information:

Calories: 114 Carbohydrates: 3g Proteins: 3g Fat: 10g Fiber: 3.5g

Baked Mustard-Almond Breaded Fillet

Serves: 4, Preparation: 5 minutes, Cooking Time: 55 - 65 minutes

Ingredients

2 lbs. beef fillet, cleaned
Salt and black ground pepper
2 - 3 tbsps. ground mustard seeds
1 tbsp. yellow mustard
1 tsp. turmeric powder
4 tbsps. almond flour
1/2 cup of olive oil

Instructions

1. Season your fillet with the salt and pepper, mustard powder, yellow mustard, oil and sprinkle with turmeric.
2. Roll each fillet in almond flour, place on a plate and refrigerate for one hour.
3. Preheat the oven to 400⁰F.
4. Place the fillet in oiled baking pan and bake for about 55 - 65 minutes.
5. Remove from the oven and let sit for 10 minutes. Serve hot.

Nutrition information:

Calories: 701 Carbohydrates: 1.5g Proteins: 41g Fat: 59g Fiber: 0.6g

Cyprian Lamb Riffi

Serves: 6, Preparation: 10 minutes, Cooking Time: 50 - 60 minutes

Ingredients

1/2 cup of olive oil
3 lbs. lamb chops
1 tbsp. salt or to taste
1 cup of water
4 bay leaves
2 cloves of minced garlic
Juice of 1 large lemon

Instructions

1. Heat the oil in the saucepan over Medium-high heat.
2. Season the lamb chops with the salt and brown evenly on all side.
3. Pour the water and place the bay leaves and garlic between the lamb chops.
4. Reduce heat to Low and cook covered for 40 - 45 minutes.
5. Check if your lamb is well cocked, and if not, pour some boiling water and cook for further 10 - 15 minutes.
6. Remove the lamb chops on a serving platter. Serve hot with fresh lemon juice.

Nutrition information:

Calories: 615 Carbohydrates: 1.5g Proteins: 42g Fat: 49g Fiber: 0.1g

Egyptian Spinach with Coriander Sauce

Serves: 4, Preparation: 10 minutes, Cooking Time: 20 minutes

Ingredients

3/4 lb. fresh spinach
2 tbsps. olive oil
1 onion, finely chopped
1 leek, finely chopped
3 cloves of garlic
3 cups of water
4 tbsps. grated tomato
1 cup fresh coriander, finely chopped
1 tbsp. fresh butter
Salt and ground pepper to taste

Instructions

1. Put the spinach in boiled salted water and cook for 3 to 5 minutes.
2. Remove from heat and place in colander.
3. In a frying skillet heat the oil, add the onion garlic and leek; sauté for 2-3 minutes.
4. Pour water and grated tomato, coriander, the salt and pepper to taste; stir.
5. Transfer spinach, stir, cover and cook for 6 - 8 minutes over Low heat.
6. Transfer the spinach mixture to your high-fast blender, add butter and blend for 30 seconds.
7. Taste and adjust salt and pepper. Serve.

Nutrition information:

Calories: 145 Carbohydrates: 5.5g Proteins: 5g Fat: 11g Fiber: 4g

Grilled Spicy Kebabs

Serves: 4, Preparation: 10 minutes, Cooking Time: 10 minutes

Ingredients

1 lb. minced beef and lamb (or only beef)
1 small onion, finely chopped
2 cloves of garlic, minced
2 tbsps. fresh parsley
2 tbsps. fresh mint
1 tsp. cumin
1 tsp. ground sweet paprika
1 tsp. vinegar
1 tbsp. cold water
1 tbsp. sesame oil
1 pinch of nutmeg
1 pinch of cayenne pepper
Salt and freshly ground pepper
Fresh chopped parsley for garnish

Instructions

1. In a bowl, add all ingredients from the list above and knead vigorously for 5-7 minutes.
2. Cover the bowl with a plastic membrane and refrigerate for 2 hours.
3. Take a small amount of minced meat to our palm and stab it on a skewer.
4. Place on a grill and cook for 3-4 minutes on each side.
5. Garnish with chopped parsley. Serve with yogurt or tzatziki.

Nutrition information:

Calories: 343 Carbohydrates: 4g Proteins: 21g Fat: 27g Fiber: 0.6g

Halloumi with Basil Sauce

Serves: 4, Preparation: 10 minutes, Cooking Time: 5 minutes

Ingredients

1 lb. Halloumi cheese, cut into sticks (sub with other firm cheese or tofu)
Basil sauce
1 1/2 fresh basil leaves
1 cup of olive oil
1 tsp. ground almonds
2 cloves of garlic
1/4 cup grated Parmesan

Instructions

1. Fry the Halloumi sticks in a skillet for 1-2 minutes. Remove from heat and set aside.

Basil sauce

1. Place all the ingredients in the blender and blend until the mixture is completely smooth.
2. Serve Halloumi stick with basil sauce and enjoy!

Nutrition information:
Calories: 696 Carbohydrates: 3g Proteins: 27g Fat: 64g Fiber: 0.4g

Keto Lahmajoun Dish

Serves: 4, Preparation: 10 minutes, Cooking Time: 20 minutes

Ingredients

3/4 lbs. ground beef
2 tbsps. olive oil
1 tomato, peeled and grated
3 tbsps. tomato juice, unsweetened
1 spring onion, finely chopped
2 cloves of garlic, chopped
Pinch of cayenne pepper
1 tbsp. cumin
1 tsp. ground sweet paprika
1/2 bunch of parsley, finely chopped
2 tbsps. fresh mint, finely chopped
Salt and ground pepper to taste
Yogurt for serving

Instructions

1. In a large frying skillet heat the olive oil.
2. Sauté the ground beef with a pinch of salt until it changes a color.
3. Add the onion, garlic and season with cumin, paprika and chili.
4. Continue the sauté for 1 minute and add the tomato and tomato juice.
5. Season the salt the pepper, stir, and cover; let it simmer for about 15 minutes.
6. Finally, add fresh parsley and mint and stir.
7. Serve hot with Greek yogurt.

Nutrition information:
Calories: 256 Carbohydrates: 3g Proteins: 25g Fat: 16g Fiber: 1g

Mousahan Chicken

Serves: 6, Preparation: 10 minutes, Cooking Time: 45 minutes

Ingredients

3 lbs. boneless skinless chicken breast
2 small onions, finely chopped
1/2 cup of olive oil
1/2 cup of dry sumac spice or lemon zest
1/2 tbsp. spices mix (cloves, basil, thyme)
10 cardamom seeds
3 bay leaves
1 cinnamon stick
Salt and ground black pepper to taste
Enough water

Instructions

1. Cut the chicken into 4 pieces, and season generously with the salt.
2. Place the chicken in a pot and add water until totally covered.
3. Add all remaining ingredient and simmer for about 25 minutes over Low heat.
4. Preheat the oven to 360⁰F.
5. Remove the chicken from the saucepan and lay in an oiled baking dish.
6. Sprinkle with the salt and pepper and add little sumac; bake for about 20 minutes. Serve hot.

Nutrition information:
Calories: 236 Carbohydrates: 6g Proteins: 8g Fat: 20g Fiber: 2.5g

Sardines Saganaki

Serves: 4, Preparation: 10 minutes, Cooking Time: 10 - 12 minutes

Ingredients

2 lbs. fresh sardines, cleaned
2 tbsps. mustard
Juice of 3 large lemons
1/4 cup of olive oil
2 - 3 tbsps. water
4 cloves of garlic
1 hot pepper, finely chopped
Salt to taste
1 tbsp. fresh chopped parsley

Instructions

1. Season sardines with the salt; set aside.
2. In a bowl, beat the mustard with the lemon juice; set aside.
3. Cut the garlic and the hot pepper into small pieces.
4. Heat the oil in a frying skillet and sauté garlic and hot pepper with a pinch of salt.
5. Add sardines and water; toss the skillet to combine well.
6. Cover and cook (without stirring) for 10 minutes over Medium-low heat.
7. Add the mustard-lemon juice mixture, shaking the pan gently.
8. Put the sardines on a platter, sprinkle with chopped parsley and serve.

Nutrition information:

Calories: 157 Carbohydrates: 1.5g Proteins: 4g Fat: 15g Fiber: 0.5g

Sephardic Eggs Haminados

Serves: 10, Preparation: 10 minutes, Cooking Time: 15 minutes

Ingredients

20 eggs
Onion peels
1 cup of vegetable oil
Salt and ground pepper to taste
4 cups of water

Instructions

1. In a saucepan pour water, salt and pepper, oil and add onion peels.
2. Add eggs in saucepan and cover with onion peels.
3. Cook on Medium heat for 15 minutes.
4. Remove from heat, cover and let sit for 2 hours.
5. Rinse eggs, peel and place on a platter. Serve.

Nutrition information:

Calories: 244 Carbohydrates: 0.8g Proteins: 13g Fat: 21g Fiber: 0.05g

Shakshuka - Baked Eggs in Sauce (Keto version)

Serves: 6, Preparation: 5 minutes, Cooking Time: 25 minutes

Ingredients

1/4 cup of olive oil
2 green onions, thinly sliced
1 bell pepper, seeded and thinly sliced
2 - 3 cloves of garlic, minced
Pinch of cayenne, or to taste
1 tsp. ground cumin
2 tomatoes, peeled and coarsely chopped
Salt and ground pepper to taste
6 large eggs
1 1/2 cups of feta cheese, crumbled
Fresh cilantro and basil leaves, finely chopped for serving

Instructions

1. Preheat oven to 400⁰F.
2. Heat the oil in a large heat-proof skillet over Medium heat.
3. Sauté the onion and pepper with the pinch of salt for 3 - 4 minutes; stir occasionally.
4. Add the garlic, cayenne and cumin and stir for further 2 minutes.
5. Add the tomato and stir for 6 - 8 minutes until mixture has thickened.
6. Finally, add crumbled feta cheese and stir.
7. Crack the eggs into skillet, one by one, and sprinkle with pinch of salt and pepper.
8. Place skillet to oven and bake for 8 minutes or until eggs are set.
9. Remove skillet from oven, sprinkle with fresh cilantro and basil and serve.

Nutrition information:

Calories: 399 Carbohydrates: 6.5g Proteins: 19g Fat: 33g Fiber: 2g

Shish Taouk - Lebanese Marinated Chicken

Serves: 4, Preparation: 10 minutes, Cooking Time: 40 minutes

Ingredients

2 lbs. chicken breast, cut in cubes

For the marinade:

1/2 cup fresh tomato juice

2 tbsps. mayonnaise

1 tbsp. olive oil

Juice of 1-2 lemons

1 tsp. garlic powder

1 tsp. fresh thyme

Salt and black pepper to taste

1/2 tsp. hot ground paprika

1/2 tsp. fresh ginger

1/2 tsp. fresh coriander

1/2 tsp. white pepper

1/2 tsp. cinnamon

Instructions

1. Stir all marinade ingredients until combined well.
2. Put the chicken into large bowl, cover evenly with marinade and refrigerate overnight.
3. Preheat oven to 350⁰F.
4. Remove chicken from the fridge and place in an oiled baking dish.
5. Bake for about 30 - 35 minutes.
6. Serve hot.

Nutrition information:

Calories: 324 Carbohydrates: 5g Proteins: 49g Fat: 12g Fiber: 1g

Turkish Tas Kebap

Serves: 6, Preparation: 5 minutes, Cooking Time: 1 hour and 40 minutes

Ingredients

2 lbs. beef shoulder; boneless, cut into small pieces

2 large onions, finely chopped

2 cloves of garlic, minced

1/3 cup of olive oil

2 tbsps. fresh parsley, finely chopped

2 small ripe tomatoes, peeled and mashed

1 cup of white dry wine

1 tsp. cinnamon

1 tsp. dried oregano

1 bay leaf

2 - 3 whole cloves

Salt and black ground pepper to taste

Instructions

1. In a deep frying pan, heat the olive oil to

Moderate heat and sauté the meat for 2 minutes per side.
2. Transfer meat to a plate, cover and set aside.
3. In the same frying skillet, sauté the onion and garlic with a pinch of salt for 5 - 7 minutes; stir.
4. Return the meat to the skillet.
5. Add all remaining ingredients from the list and stir well: cover and cook for 1 1/2 hours over Low heat.
6. Remove the cloves and bay leaves from the pot. Serve hot.

Nutrition information:

Calories: 404 Carbohydrates: 6g Proteins: 41g Fat: 24g Fiber: 2g

Scandinavian

Baked Tuna "Meatballs"

Serves: 4, Preparation: 10 minutes, Cooking Time: 20 minutes

Ingredients

1 can (11 oz.) tuna, canned and drained

1 green onion, finely chopped

2 cloves garlic, finely chopped

1 tbsp. grated ginger, about a 1 1/2" piece

A handful if fresh cilantro, chopped

2 green chilies, finely sliced

2 cardamom seeds

1/4 tsp. cinnamon

2 cloves

1 tsp. coriander, crushed seeds

3 tbsps. ground almonds

1 large egg

Grated hard cheese, like Parmesan, Pecorino Romano, Gorgonzola etc. (optional)

1 pinch of sea salt

2 to 3 tbsps. oil

Instructions
1. Drain and add tuna in a bowl.
2. Combine tuna fish with all remaining ingredients.
3. Knead the mixture until combine well.
4. Cover the bowl with foil and refrigerate for 1 hour.
5. Preheat the oven to 365^{0}F.
6. Remove tuna mixture from the fridge and make balls (10 - 12).
7. Place tuna balls in oiled baking dish.
8. Bake for 15 - 18 minutes. Serve hot.

Nutrition information:
Calories: 259 Carbohydrates: 7g Proteins: 15g Fat: 19g Fiber: 1.5g

Chilled Salmon Soup

Serves: 6, Preparation: 10 minutes, Cooking Time: 35 minutes

Ingredients
1 salmon fillet
5 cups of water
1/2 cup of white wine
1 small onion, cut in cubes
1 leek, only white part
2 tbsps. fresh butter
2 cups of cauliflower
3 tbsps. fresh celery, finely chopped
1 1/4 cups of cream
2 pinches of sea salt

Instructions
1. Cut the fish in pieces.
2. Add fish in a pot with boiling salted water and vine.
3. Reduce the heat and cook fish for about 10 minutes.
4. Remove fish on a plate, cover and set aside; reserve broth.
5. Heat the butter over Medium heat and sauté the leek and onion with a pinch of salt for 4 - 5 minutes; stir.
6. Add cauliflower and celery and stir for further 5 - 6 minutes.
7. Add the fish and reserved broth in a pot and cook for 10 minutes on Low heat.
8. Remove the pot from the heat and stir the cream.
9. Place the fish mixture in a large container, cover and refrigerate for 2 - 3 hours. Serve.

Nutrition information:
Calories: 276 Carbohydrates: 5g Proteins: 10g Fat: 24g Fiber: 1.5g

Creamy Cucumber and Egg Salad

Serves: 6, Preparation: 10 minutes, Cooking Time: 25 minutes

Ingredients
2 large eggs, hard boiled
3 cucumbers, sliced
2 tbsps. olive oil
1 cup of whipped cream
2 tbsps. mayonnaise
3 stalks of fresh fennel
Salt and ground pepper to taste

Instructions
1. Boil the eggs, clean and set aside.
2. Rinse and slice the cucumber into slices.
3. Boil the cucumber slices for 5 minutes and removed to drain.
4. Heat the oil in a pan, and combine cream, mayonnaise, fennel, and a pinch of salt and pepper.
5. Add the cucumber slices and gently stir.
6. Add sliced eggs and stir.
7. Cook all ingredients for 5 minutes over Moderate-low heat or until thick.
8. Combine the yolk, salt and black pepper, to make a sauce, place it in a water bath to thicken.
9. Add the cream a little, then add mayonnaise and sprinkle with sliced dill.
10. Taste and adjust salt and pepper to taste.
11. Serve immediately.

Nutrition information:
Calories: 170 Carbohydrates: 6g Proteins: 5g Fat: 14g Fiber: 2.5g

Grilled Tuna Fish with White Wine

Serves: 4, Preparation: 10 minutes; marinate for 4 hours, Cooking Time: 5 minutes

Ingredients

1 lemon juice, freshly squeezed
1 tbsp. dried parsley
1 tsp. minced garlic
1 cup dry white wine
Salt and pepper to taste
2 lbs. tuna fish
Olive oil for frying

Instructions

1. Pour lemon juice, parsley, garlic, wine, and salt and pepper in a large plastic bag.

2. Place tuna and close the bag; shake.
3. Marinate tuna for 4 hours.
4. Heat the oil in a large frying skillet over Medium-strong heat.
5. Remove tuna from marinade and dry on kitchen paper.
6. Fry tuna for 1 /2 - 2 minutes per side. Serve hot.

Nutrition information:

Calories: 316 Carbohydrates: 2.5g Proteins: 54g Fat: 10g Fiber: 0.1g

Marinated Salmon with Alfalfa Sprouts

Serves: 4, Preparation: 15 minutes

Ingredients

1 lb. salmon, cleaned
1/2 tbsp. fresh dill, chopped
2 pinches sea salt
1 tsp. granulated stevia
2 lemons
2 limes
2-3 tbsps. olive oil
Ground black pepper to taste
1/4 cup of alfalfa spouts
2 tbsps. fresh celery, chopped

Instructions

1. Cut the salmon in thin slices and season with the salt, sweetener and dill.

2. Wrap the fish slices in foil and refrigerate for about 6 hours or overnight.
3. Remove salmon from the fridge and rinse with cold water.
4. Place the salmon on a kitchen paper to drain, and then, transfer the fish in a bowl.
5. Pour lemon and lime juice, olive oil, black pepper and alfalfa sprouts over the salmon; gently stir.
6. Sprinkle with chopped celery and serve.

Nutrition information:

Calories: 261 Carbohydrates: 7g Proteins: 26g Fat: 15g Fiber: 4g

Smoked Salmon Omelet with Fresh Chives

Serves: 4, Preparation: 5 minutes, Cooking Time: 10 minutes

Ingredients

8 large eggs
Salt and pepper to taste
1/4 cup of olive oil
1 large onion, finely chopped
8 oz. of smoked salmon, chopped
3 tbsps. cream
Finely chopped chives, for serving

Instructions

1. Beat the eggs with a pinch of the salt and pepper.
2. Heat the oil in a skillet over Medium-high heat

and sauté onion for 3 - 4 minutes.
3. Add salmon and gently stir.
4. Pour the egg mixture and cook for 2 to 3 minutes.
5. Flip the omelet and cook for 1 minutes.
6. Transfer the omelet to the plate, generously sprinkle with chopped chives and serve.

Nutrition information:

Calories: 336 Carbohydrates: 3.5g Proteins: 22g Fat: 26g Fiber: 0.5g

Smoked Salmon Spread

Serves: 4, Preparation: 10 minutes

Ingredients

1 spring onion, finely chopped
1 cup of cream cheese
2 tbsps. sour cream
12 oz. smoked salmon
1 tsp. Worcester sauce
2 drops of Tabasco (optional)
1 tsp. fresh dill

Instructions

1. Combine all ingredients in a deep bowl.
2. Stir gently with wooden spoon until the mixture combine evenly.
3. Cover with foil and keep refrigerated.

Nutrition information:
Calories: 308 Carbohydrates: 3g Proteins: 20g Fat: 24g Fiber: 0.2g

Stewed Mackerel Fillets with Celery

Serves: 4, Preparation: 5 minutes, Cooking Time: 15 minutes

Ingredients

2 mackerel fillets, cut in small pieces
1 tbsp. wine vinegar
1 carrot, sliced
1 cup of fresh celery, chopped
1/2 cup of vegetable oil
6 - 7 stalks fresh parsley, finely chopped
1/4 tsp. sea salt
1/2 cup water
2 lemons for serving

Instructions

1. Pour oil in a large pot and add mackerel fish; sprinkle with a pinch of salt and pour vinegar.
2. Sauté for 2 minutes and combine all remaining ingredients from the list above and pour water.
3. Cook for 10 -12 minutes over Medium heat; stir 2 - 3 times.
4. Serve hot with lemon slices.

Nutrition information:
Calories: 397 Carbohydrates: 6.5g Proteins: 14g Fat: 35g Fiber: 1.5g

Stuffed Cucumbers with Tuna

Serves: 8, Preparation: 15 minutes

Ingredients

3 large cucumbers
3/4 cup of olive oil
1 can (11 oz.) tuna in oil, drained
1/2 cup of mayonnaise
2 tbsps. mustard
1 fresh lemon juice
2 tsps. fresh chopped dill
Salt to taste
Lemon slices for serving

Instructions

1. Rinse cucumbers and cut into thick slices.
2. With a teaspoon hollow out the inner part of cucumbers and add in a bowl.
3. Add all remaining ingredients in a bowl and combine well.
4. Place the cucumber slices on a large platter.
5. Fill cucumber with a little spread.
6. Decorate with lemon slices and refrigerate for 30 minutes. Serve.

Nutrition information:
Calories: 317 Carbohydrates: 7.5g Proteins: 11g Fat: 27g Fiber: 1.5g

Swedish Baked Creamy Meatballs

Serves: 4, Preparation: 25 minutes, Cooking Time: 3 minutes

Ingredients

3/4 lb. ground beef
1/4 lb. minced pork
1 onion red, finely chopped
1 tsp. natural sweetener, like stevia
Salt and pepper to taste
1/2 tsp. nutmeg

1 large egg
2 tbsps. fresh butter
3/4 cup of heavy cream
1/4 cup of bone broth

Instructions

1. Preheat the oven to 350⁰F.

1. Preheat the oven to 350^0F.

2. In bowl, combine ground beef, pork, onion, stevia, nutmeg, egg, and the salt and pepper.

3. Knead with your hands until the mixture is well combined.

4. From the mixture make meatballs; place them in oiled baking dish.

5. Heat the butter in a pan over Medium heat; add the heavy cream and bone broth.

6. Cook the mixture only for 2 - 3 minutes.

7. Pour the butter mixture over meatballs and place in oven.

8. Cover with foil and bake for 20 minutes.

9. Serve hot.

Nutrition information:
Calories: 492 Carbohydrates: 3.5g Proteins: 25g Fat: 42g Fiber: 0.5g

Janpanese

Baked Pork Loin with "Tonkatsu" Sauce

Serves: 4, Preparation: 15 minutes, Cooking Time: 20 minutes

Ingredients
1/2 cup almond flour
1 tbsp. extra virgin olive oil
4 pork loin chops, boneless
1 tsp. salt and freshly ground black pepper
1 large egg
3 tbsps. Worcester sauce
1 tbsp. roasted sesame seeds

Instructions
1. Preheat the oven to 400°F.
2. Preheat the olive oil in a skillet over Medium-low heat and stir the almond flour for 2 minutes.
3. Remove the almond flour on a plate and let it cool.
4. Remove any fat from the pork chops, and season with the salt and pepper.

5. Beat the egg in a bowl.

6. Dip each pork chop in egg, and then roll into almond flour.

7. Bake the pork in a baking sheet lined with parchment paper for about 15 - 20 minutes.

8. Remove the pork chops on a plate and cut in small pieces; place the meat on a platter.

9. In a bowl, combine the Worcester sauce with the roasted sesame, and with the pinch of ground pepper.

10. Serve the pork chops with the sauce.

Nutrition information:
Calories: 471 Carbohydrates: 6g Proteins: 57g Fat: 24g Fiber: 2.2g

Baked Turmeric Salmon Patties

Serves: 6, Preparation: 15 minutes, Cooking Time: 10 minutes

Ingredients
2 can (11 oz.) salmon drained, skin and bones removed
1 tsp. turmeric ground
1 cup sesame seeds, toasted
2 organic eggs
1 tbsp. olive oil for batter
1 cup scallions, chopped
1 tbsp. fresh lemon juice

Instructions
1. Preheat your oven to 380°F.
2. In a deep bowl, combine all ingredients from the list above. Stir the mixture until a combine well.

3. Form mixture into 6 equal patties.

4. Place patties in one oiled baking sheet, and bake for 10 minutes, turning once.

5. Transfer patties to a serving plate lined with absorbent paper and serve hot.

Nutrition information:
Calories: 289 Carbohydrates: 3g Proteins: 31g Fat: 17g Fiber: 1.5g

Delicious Keto Oyakodon - Japanese Rice Bowl

Serves: 4, Preparation: 15 minutes, Cooking Time: 15 minutes

Ingredients

6 chicken thighs, boneless and cut into strips
Pinch of salt and ground black pepper
1 green onion, finely sliced
4 large eggs, beaten
2/3 cup bone broth
1/4 cup of coconut aminos
1 tbsp. stevia granulated sweetener

Instructions

1. Season the chicken strips with the salt and ground pepper.
2. In a bowl, combine bone broth, coconut aminos and stevia; stir until sweetener dissolves well.
3. Heat a wok and stir finely sliced green onion with a pinch of salt.
4. Add the chicken strips and sauté for 4 - 5 minutes.
5. Pour the bone broth mixture, stir, cover and cook for 5 minutes over Low heat.
6. In a bowl, whisk the eggs and pour in wok; stir with the wooden spoon.
7. Cook for 4 - 5 further minutes or until eggs are set. Serve hot.

Nutrition information:

Calories: 347 Carbohydrates: 7g Proteins: 28g Fat: 23g Fiber: 1g

Eggs Stuffed with Creamy Salmon

Serves: 4, Preparation: 15 minutes, Cooking Time: 15 minutes

Ingredients

8 eggs, hard boiled
1 cup salmon, finely chopped
1 scallion, finely chopped (only green parts)
1 tbsp. mustard (Dijon, English, or whole grain)
2 tbsps. mayonnaise (without honey)
1 tsp. fresh lemon juice
Salt and ground pepper to taste
Fresh dill for garnish
Enough water

Instructions

1. Pour water in a saucepan, turn the heat to High, and bring the water to a boil.
2. Boil the eggs for 12-15 minutes; clean and cut the eggs in the middle. Remove the yolks.
3. Combine together the eggs, salmon, chopped scallions (only green parts), mayonnaise, lemon and mustard.
4. Stir well with the fork to achieve a puree mixture.
5. Season the salt and pepper to taste.
6. Fill the eggs with the salmon/mayo mixture and sprinkle with dill.
7. Refrigerate eggs until serving.

Nutrition information:

Calories: 224 Carbohydrates: 3g Proteins: 21.5g Fat: 14g Fiber: 0.2g

Grilled Gouda Topped Marinated Pork Roast

Serves: 4, Preparation: 15 minutes, Cooking Time: 8 -10 minutes

Ingredients

1 1/2 lbs. pork roast, sliced in pieces to 0.4-inch thickness
1/4 cup of coconut aminos
2 oz. Gouda cheese, cut in cubes

Instructions

1. Cut the pork meat in pieces and spread with coconut aminos.
2. Wrap in plastic membrane and refrigerate overnight.
3. Remove the pork from the fridge and place on kitchen paper.
4. Preheat your grill (any) on High temperature.
5. Place the pork on a grill and cook for about 4 minutes.
6. Flip the pork oven, and cover with the Gouda cheese.
7. Grill until cheese melt or about 3 - 4 minutes.
8. Serve immediately.

Nutrition information:

Calories: 428 Carbohydrates: 0.3g Proteins: 46g Fat: 27g Fiber: 0g

Grilled Salmon with Lemon Marinade

Serves: 3, Preparation: 10 minutes, Cooking Time: 15 minutes

Ingredients

1 lb. salmon fillets with skin
Juice of 3 lemons
Zest of 2 lemons
2 tbsps. extra-virgin olive oil
3 cloves garlic, minced
Salt and freshly ground black pepper, to taste

Instructions

1. In a bowl combine lemon juice, olive oil and minced garlic.
2. Place the salmon in a container, pour with lemon juice mixture, cover and refrigerate for 4 hours.
3. Preheat your grill (any) to High.
4. Take the fish out of the fridge and pour marinade in a saucepan.
5. Grill the fish for 5-7 minutes per side.
6. In a meantime, boil the marinade mixture and simmer over Low heat.
Serve grilled fish warm with the marinade sauce.

Nutrition information:
Calories: 346 Carbohydrates: 7.5g Proteins: 34g Fat: 20g Fiber: 2g

Hoikoro - Japanese Pork and Cabbage

Serves: 4, Preparation: 5 minutes, Cooking Time: 20 minutes

Ingredients

1 tbsp. olive oil
1 clove garlic, minced
1 1/2 lbs. pork belly, cut into long strips
2 cups of shredded cabbage
1 green bell pepper, sliced
1/2 cup water
2 tbsps. coconut aminos
1/2 tsp. chili pepper (optional)

Instructions

1. Heat the olive oil in a frying pan over Medium heat.
2. Add minced garlic and sauté for about 2 minutes.
3. Add the pork strips, water and coconut aminos.
4. Stir and fry for about 4-5 minutes.
5. Add shredded cabbage and chopped green pepper.
6. Stir and cook for 8 -10 minutes.
7. Add the chili pepper (optional) and stir well.
Serve immediately.

Nutrition information:
Calories: 616 Carbohydrates: 0.3g Proteins: 12g Fat: 63g Fiber: 2g

Keto Beef Gyudon

Serves: 4, Preparation: 10 minutes, Cooking Time: 15 minutes

Ingredients

1 tbsp. sesame oil
1 small red onion, finely chopped
2 green onions, finely chopped
1 1/2 lbs. beef, thinly sliced in strips
2 tsps. stevia granulated sweetener
2 tbsps. red wine
1 tbsp. coconut aminos
3 large eggs
Salt and ground black pepper

Instructions

1. Heat the oil in a large skillet over Medium heat.
2. Sauté the red onion and green onions with the pinch of salt.
3. Add the beef slices and sweetener and stir for 2 minutes.
4. Pour the red wine and coconut aminos; stir well.
5. Cook over Low heat for 3 - 4 minutes.
6. Whisk the eggs in a bowl with the pinch of salt and pepper and pour over meat and onions.
7. Cover and cook for 5 minutes or until the eggs are done. Serve immediately.

Nutrition information:
Calories: 413 Carbohydrates: 6.5g Proteins: 36g Fat: 27g Fiber: 0.5g

Ribeye Steak with Keto Adapted Teriyaki Sauce

Serves: 4, Preparation: 10 minutes, Cooking Time: 15 minutes

Ingredients

2 beef rib eye steaks
1 tsp. almond flour
1 tsp. water
1 tbsp. roasted sesame seeds
1 green onion/scallion
Teriyaki adapted sauce
1/4 cup of coconut aminos
1/2 cup of red wine
1 tbsp. ginger juice
2 tsps. granulated stevia sweetener

Instructions

1. In a bowl, whisk together the coconut aminos, red wine, ginger juice and sweetener.
2. Place the steaks in a plastic bag and add 4 tablespoon of coconut aminos sauce.
3. Refrigerate and marinate steaks for 1 hour.
4. Remove the meat from the fridge and let sit for 10 minutes on room temperature.
5. Pour adapted Teriyaki sauce in saucepan, add sliced onions and roasted sesame.
6. In a small bowl, whisk the almond flour and water, and pour in a saucepan; stir for 10 minutes.
7. In a wok heat the oil and cook steaks for 2 minutes per side.
8. Serve steaks with the hot sauce.

Nutrition information:

Calories: 528 Carbohydrates: 2.3g Proteins: 50g Fat: 35g Fiber: 0.6g

Shogayaki - Ginger Pork Loin

Serves: 4, Preparation: 5 minutes, Cooking Time: 20 minutes

Ingredients

2 lbs. thinly sliced pork loin
1/2 of onion, chopped
1 clove of garlic, grated
1 inch of ginger (about 1 tsp.)
Kosher salt and freshly ground black pepper
1 tbsp. olive
1 spring onion, finely chopped
2 tbsps. bone broth
2 tbsps. coconut aminos
Shredded cabbage for serving

Instructions

1. Season the pork meat with the salt and pepper.
2. In a bowl, combine the onion, garlic and ginger; set aside.
3. Heat the oil in a skillet and cook the pork for about 4 - 5 minutes, do not overcook.
4. Add the onion mixture and gently stir for 2 - 3 minutes.
5. Sprinkle spring onion and cook for further 2 - 3 minutes over Medium-low heat.
6. Pour the bone broth and coconut aminos; stir and cook for 2 minutes.
7. Serve immediately with freshly shredded cabbage.

Nutrition information:

Calories: 356 Carbohydrates: 3.4g Proteins: 52g Fat: 15g Fiber: 1g

Fareast

Arugula and Beef Salad with Sesame Dressing

Serves: 4, Preparation: 10 minutes

Ingredients

4 tbsps. sesame oil
2 tbsps. wine vinegar
2 tsps. granulated stevia (optional)
6 oz. fresh arugula, finely chopped
1 roasted beef fillet, cut into small strips
2 green onions, sliced
Salt and ground black pepper to taste
1 tbsp. sesame seeds

Instructions

1. In a small bowl, whisk the sesame oil, vinegar, the salt and pepper, and stevia if used.
2. In a separate large bowl combine arugula, green onions and the beef fillet; sprinkle little salt and pepper.
3. Pour the sesame oil dressing and toss to combine evenly.
4. Sprinkle with sesame seeds and serve immediately.

Nutrition information:

Calories: 414 Carbohydrates: 5g Proteins: 29g Fat: 31g Fiber: 4g

Bulgogi Beef (South Korea)

Serves: 4, Preparation: 10 minutes, Cooking Time: 12 minutes

Ingredients

1 1/2 lbs. beef steak, cut into small pieces
1/4 cup of coconut aminos
2 tbsps. granulated stevia
1 medium onion, finely chopped
2 garlic cloves, minced
2 tbsps. sesame seeds
4 tbsps. sesame oil

Instructions

1. Place the beef in a deep container.
2. In a bowl, stir coconut aminos, stevia, onion, garlic, sesame seeds, and sesame oil.
3. Pour the sweet sauce over the beef and toss to combine evenly.
4. Refrigerate the beef for 3 - 4 hours to marinate.
5. Remove the meat from the fridge and grill or bake it for 10 - 12 minutes in the oven on 350⁰F.
6. Serve hot.

Nutrition information:

Calories: 488 Carbohydrates: 4.5g Proteins: 41g Fat: 34g Fiber: 1.1g

Cantonese Lobster

Serves: 6, Preparation: 5 minutes, Cooking Time: 20 minutes

Ingredients

4 oz. butter
1 large onion, chopped
2 cups of chopped celery
2 1/2 lbs. lobster meat
8 oz. coconut water
1 inch ginger, sliced thinly
1/4 cup almond flour
1 quart water
Salt to taste

Instructions

1. Heat butter in a wok or frying skillet over Medium heat.
2. Sauté the onion and celery with a pinch of salt for about 3 - 4 minutes.
3. Add lobster meat and coconut water and cook for 2 - 3 minutes; toss the wok.
4. Add sliced ginger and gently stir.
5. Add slowly the almond flour and gently stir.
6. Pour water and toss the wok; cover and cook for about 5 - 6 minutes.
7. Taste and adjust seasonings. Serve.

Nutrition information:

Calories: 338 Carbohydrates: 5g Proteins: 34g Fat: 20g Fiber: 2g

Cantonese Roasted Char Siu (Pork)

Serves: 6, Preparation: 10 minutes, Cooking Time: 2 hours

Ingredients

3 pork baby back ribs
A pinch of salt and pepper
2 tsps. liquid stevia sweetener
3 tbsps. coconut aminos
2 tbsps. sesame oil
1 tsp. fresh ginger, minced
2 cloves of garlic, finely sliced
1 tsp. hot chili pepper sauce

Instructions

1. Preheat your oven to 350⁰F.
2. Line a baking dish with aluminum foil.
3. Season your ribs with the pinch of salt and pepper.
4. Place the ribs in a prepared baking dish, cover with foil and bake for 1 ½ - 2 hours.
5. Make a sauce; in a bowl, whisk all remaining ingredients.
6. Baste your ribs every 30 minutes with the sauce.
7. Remove from oven and let ribs rest for 10 minutes. Serve.

Nutrition information:

Calories: 638 Carbohydrates: 0.7g Proteins: 51g Fat: 48g Fiber: 0g

Chilo Raita Sauce (India)

Serves: 4, Preparation: 5 minutes

Ingredients

2 cups of full-fat yogurt
2 tbsps. onion, finely chopped
1/4 cup cucumber, grated
2 tsps. lemon juice
1/2 tsp. ginger powder
2 tsps. fresh mint, finely chopped

1 1/2 tsps. chili pepper powder
Salt to taste
Instructions
1. Place all ingredients in your blender.
2. Blend for 30 - 45 seconds or until smooth.
3. Taste and adjust seasonings.
4. Place in a glass bowl and refrigerate until serving.
Nutrition information:
Calories: 17 Carbohydrates: 1g Proteins: 1g Fat: 1g Fiber: 0.5g

Chinese Oriental Shrimp with Sauce (Hong Kong)

Serves: 4, Preparation: 5 minutes, Cooking Time: 15 minutes

Ingredients
1/2 cup of olive oil
4 plum tomatoes, cut into quarters
3 tsps. minced garlic
1/2 onion, chopped
2 green onions, chopped
1/4 cup red wine
1/2 cup of grated tomato
Salt and ground pepper to taste
1 tsp. garlic powder
1/4 cup stevia sweetener
24 oz. peeled and deveined white prawns
Instructions
1. Heat the oil in a frying skillet and cook tomato,
garlic, onion and green onion; sprinkle with the pinch of salt and pepper, and sauté for 5 minutes stirring occasionally.
2. Pour the wine, grated tomato, garlic powder, stevia, and the salt and pepper; stir.
3. Add shrimps and cook for 4 - 5 minutes over Medium heat.
4. Transfer shrimp to serving plate, pour with sauce and serve.
Nutrition information:
Calories: 287 Carbohydrates: 4g Proteins: 7g Fat: 27g Fiber: 1g

Egg Salad with Curry Dressing (Japan)

Serves: 6, Preparation: 20 minutes

Ingredients
3/4 cup of mayonnaise
1 tbsp. curry
1/2 tsp. turmeric powder
Salt and ground black pepper to taste
1/2 cup of extra virgin olive oil
A few leaves of green salad
1 cup of red cabbage, shredded
8 eggs, hard boiled, cut in half or quarter
1 lb. asparagus
Instructions
1. In the bowl, stir the mayonnaise, curry, turmeric powder, salt and pepper, and olive oil; set aside.
2. Cover the serving plate with green salad leaves, and shredded red cabbage.
3. Add boiled eggs and asparagus over salad.
4. Sprinkle eggs with a little salt, and drizzle with olive oil.
5. Pour the curry-mayo sauce and toss to combine well.
6. Refrigerate for 20 minutes and serve.
Nutrition information:
Calories: 221 Carbohydrates: 7g Proteins: 10g Fat: 17g Fiber: 2g

Fried Mongolian Chicken

Serves: 6, Preparation: 15 minutes, Cooking Time: 10 minutes

Ingredients
3 chicken fillets, boneless
1/2 cup of almond flour
1 cup of olive oil
2 cloves of garlic, minced
1 onion, finely chopped
2 spring onions, sliced
Salt and ground black pepper to taste

Marinade
1/2 cup of water
1 tbsp. ground almonds
3 tbsps. coconut aminos
1 tbsp. oyster sauce
2 tsps. stevia sweetener
2 tsps. ground cayenne pepper

2 tsps. apple cider vinegar

Instructions

1. In a bowl, whisk all ingredients for the marinade.
2. Cut the chicken fillets into strips and generously season with the salt and cayenne pepper.
3. Roll the chicken in almond flour, and then add into sauce; cover the chicken evenly, cover and refrigerate for 2 hours to marinate.

4. Heat the oil in a wok and sauté the garlic and onion with the pinch of salt.
5. Add spring onions and cook for 3 - 4 minutes; stir.
6. Add marinated chicken and cook for 3 - 5 minutes or until done.
7. Serve hot.

Nutrition information:

Calories: 541 Carbohydrates: 3.5g Proteins: 26g Fat: 47g Fiber: 1g

Mongolian Sour-Sweet Ukhriin makh (beef)

Serves: 2, Preparation: 15 minutes, Cooking Time: 10 minutes

Ingredients

1 cup of vegetable oil
1 tsp. fresh grated ginger
1 tbsp. finely chopped garlic
1/4 cup of coconut aminos
1/2 cup of water
2/3 cup of stevia granulated sweetener
1 lb. beef steak, finely sliced
1 cup almond meal
3 fresh onions (only the green part), finely sliced

Instructions

1. Heat the vegetable oil in a skillet over Moderate-low heat.
2. Add grated ginger and garlic and sauté about 2 minutes.
3. Pour the coconut aminos sauce, water and sweetener, and stir for 3 -4 minutes.

4. Remove the sauce from heat and set aside.
5. Combine the beef slices with almond flour; let them sit for 10 minutes.
6. Heat the oil in a wok or frying skillet over High heat.
7. Fry the beef slices for about 3 minutes until golden yellow but not overcooked.
8. Transfer beef on a parchment paper to drain.
9. Place the meat on a serving plate, pour with the ginger sauce and sprinkle with sliced green parts of fresh onions.
10. Serve immediately.

Nutrition information:

Calories: 430 Carbohydrates: 3g Proteins: 19g Fat: 38g Fiber: 0.3g

Bok Choy and Chicken Stir-fry

Serves: 4, Preparation: 5 minutes, Cooking Time: 25 minutes

Ingredients

1/4 cup olive oil
2 green onions, finely chopped
2 chicken breasts, cut into cubes
1 lb. bok choy, finely chopped
2 tsps. fresh dill, chopped
2 tsps. fresh parsley, chopped
1 tbsp. ginger powder
1/2 tsp. chili powder
2 tbsps. apple cider vinegar or fresh lemon juice
Salt and pepper to taste

Instructions

1. Heat the oil in the wok or in a frying skillet and

sauté the onions with a pinch of salt.
2. Add the chicken pieces and cook for 3-4 minutes, stirring occasionally.
3. Add bok choy along with all remaining ingredients; gently stir, cover and cook for 10 minutes.
4. Remove from the heat and let it rest for 10 minutes.
5. Taste and adjust seasonings. Serve.

Nutrition information:

Calories: 280 Carbohydrates: 4g Proteins: 28g Fat: 17g Fiber: 2g

Spiralized Zucchini with Lap Ceung (Chinese Sausage)

Serves: 2, Preparation: 5 minutes, Cooking Time: 50 minutes

Ingredients

4 cups of water
1 chicken breast boneless, cut in strips
2 tbsps. sesame oil
2 tbsps. minced garlic
1/2 cup chopped onion
Salt and ground pepper to taste
1/2 lb. shrimp, deveined, and cut lengthwise
1/2 cup lap ceung - Chinese sausage, sliced
2 small spiralized zucchini or low carb noodles like Shirataki
1 cup cauliflower, divided into flowerets
1 cups of shredded cabbage
1 carrot, diced
1 cup celery, finely chopped
1/4 cup fresh onions, sliced
2 tbsps. coconut aminos

Instructions

1. In large pot, boil chicken until tender, about 15 - 20 minutes over Medium-low heat.
2. Remove chicken from the pot and place on a plate; reserve 3 cups of broth.
3. Heat the oil in wok or frying skillet and sauté the garlic and onion until translucent, season with the pinch of salt.
4. Add chicken and shrimp, and cook for 15 minutes over Low heat.
5. Pour reserved broth and add all remaining ingredients; gently stir.
6. Cover and cook for further 10 - 12 minutes over Low-medium heat.
7. Serve in bowls, and sprinkle with fresh onion slices.

Nutrition information:
Calories: 296 Carbohydrates: 5g Proteins: 17g Fat: 23g Fiber: 2g

Seolleongtang (Korea)

Serves: 8, Preparation: 15 minutes, Cooking Time: 6 hours

Ingredients

3 lbs. beef leg (marrow and knuckle) bones, cut up
2 lbs. beef shank
Salt and pepper to taste
Water
4 chopped scallions for serving

Instructions

1. Soak the bones in cold water for about 2 - 3 hours.
2. In a separate bowl soak the beef meat for several hours; keep refrigerated.
3. Remove bones from the bowl and put in large and deep pot; cover with water completely.
4. Cook on High heat; bring to boil, and then reduce the heat to Medium-low, and cook for 10 minutes.
5. Drain and rinse the bones.
6. Rinse and clean the pot and return the bones.
7. Pour the water enough to cover the bones and cook on Medium heat for 4 - 6 hours.
8. Add the soaked meat, and cook until meat is tender, for 2 hours about.
9. Remove the bones and the meat; pour the broth through the colander and place in another pot.
10. Slice the meat and add to the soup; season with the salt and pepper to taste.
11. Serve with chopped scallions.

Nutrition information:
Calories: 451 Carbohydrates: 0.3g Proteins: 27g Fat: 38g Fiber: 0.2g

Shurinpu Stew (Japan)

Serves: 6, Preparation: 5 minutes, Cooking Time: 15 minutes

Ingredients

1/4 cup sesame oil
2 fresh onions, finely chopped
2 cups fresh celery, sliced
1 green peppers, sliced
1 1/2 lbs. frozen shrimp, peeled and deveined
3/4 lb. fresh mushrooms, sliced
1/2 cup coconut aminos (from coconut sap)
2 tbsps. natural sweetener, such as stevia, erythritol
1/2 cup water

Instructions

1. Heat the oil in a frying skillet over Medium-high heat.
2. Sauté onions, celery, green pepper with a pinch

of salt until softened.

3. Add shrimp and mushrooms and sauté for 1 - 2 minutes.

4. Pour coconut aminos sauce, stevia sweetener and water; stir.

5. Reduce heat and simmer for about 10 - 12 minutes or until shrimp turn pink.

6. Serve.

Nutrition information:

Calories: 203 Carbohydrates: 4g Proteins: 22g Fat: 11g Fiber: 2g

Spicy Mongolian Lamb

Serves: 6, Preparation: 15 minutes, Cooking Time: 25 minutes

Ingredients

2 lbs. frozen lamb, boneless

Chinese cabbage leaves

1 tbsp. of fresh spinach leaves

Olive oil for baking

Sauces Ingredients

4 green onions, finely chopped

2 tbsps. fresh ginger

1/2 cup of sesame paste

3 tbsps. sesame oil

3 tbsps. coconut aminos

2 tbsps. chili sauce

1/4 cup of fresh chopped coriander

Instructions

1. Let the lamb to thaw; cut into very thin slices, and season with the salt and pepper.

2. Preheat oven to 400⁰F.

3. Grease the baking dish with the olive oil and place the lamb slices.

4. Bake for 25 minutes or until done.

5. Remove the lamb from the oven and let it sit for 5 - 10 minutes.

6. Cover the large plate with the cabbage and spinach leaves.

7. Place the lamb slices over the salad.

8. Combine the green onions and ginger in one small bowl.

9. In a separate bowl, whisk the sesame paste and sesame oil.

10. In a third small bowl, combine the coconut aminos with colander; stir well.

11. Serve the lamb with sauces and enjoy!

Nutrition information:

Calories: 408 Carbohydrates: 6g Proteins: 32g Fat: 28.5g Fiber: 2.5g

Yangnyeom-tongdak Chicken (Korea)

Serves: 8, Preparation: 5 minutes, Cooking Time: 15 minutes

Ingredients

24 chicken wings

Salt and ground black pepper to taste

1/4 cup of almond flour

1 egg

1/2 tsp. baking soda

3/4 cup of olive oil

2-3 cloves of garlic, minced

2 tbsps. hot pepper paste

4 tbsps. cider vinegar; more to taste

Instructions

1. In a deep container, combine the salt and pepper, almond flour, baking soda and one egg.

2. With your hand cover the chicken wings with this mixture.

3. Heat the oil in a large frying skillet over high heat until bubbles.

4. Fry the chicken wings for 15 minutes or until golden brown.

5. In the case that your skillet is not large enough, divide the chicken into batches.

6. Remove the chicken wings on a platter lined with parchment paper to drain.

7. In a meantime prepare the sauce: in a bowl stir the oil, garlic, hot pepper sauce and vinegar.

8. Transfer the chicken wings on a serving plate and cover with the sauce evenly.

9. Serve.

Nutrition information:

Calories: 354 Carbohydrates: 0.3g Proteins: 14.5g Fat: 33g Fiber: 0.1g

Appendix recipe index

Made in the USA
Columbia, SC
27 June 2020